KOREAN STUDIES OF THE HENRY M. JACKSON
SCHOOL OF INTERNATIONAL STUDIES

Clark W. Sorensen, Editor

KOREAN STUDIES OF THE HENRY M. JACKSON
SCHOOL OF INTERNATIONAL STUDIES

Over the Mountains Are Mountains: Korean Peasant Households and Their Adaptations to Rapid Industrialization, by Clark W. Sorensen

Cultural Nationalism in Colonial Korea, 1920–1925, by Michael Edson Robinson, with a new preface by the author

Offspring of Empire: The Koch'ang Kims and the Colonial Origins of Korean Capitalism, 1876–1945, by Carter J. Eckert, with a new preface by the author

Confucian Statecraft and Korean Institutions: Yu Hyŏngwŏn and the Late Chosŏn Dynasty, by James B. Palais

Peasant Protest and Social Change in Colonial Korea, by Gi-Wook Shin

The Origins of the Chosŏn Dynasty, by John B. Duncan

Protestantism and Politics in Korea, by Chung-shin Park

Marginality and Subversion in Korea: The Hong Kyŏngnae Rebellion of 1812, by Sun Joo Kim

Building Ships, Building a Nation: Korea's Democratic Unionism under Park Chung Hee, by Hwasook Nam

Japanese Assimilation Policies in Colonial Korea, 1910–1945, by Mark E. Caprio

Fighting for the Enemy: Koreans in Japan's War, 1937–1945, by Brandon Palmer

Heritage Management in Korea and Japan: The Politics of Antiquity and Identity, by Hyung Il Pai

Wrongful Deaths: Selected Inquest Records from Nineteenth-Century Korea, compiled and translated by Sun Joo Kim and Jungwon Kim

The Emotions of Justice: Gender, Status, and Legal Performance in Chosŏn Korea, by Jisoo M. Kim

Buddhas and Ancestors: Religion and Wealth in Fourteenth-Century Korea, by Juhn Ahn

Flowering Plums and Curio Cabinets: The Culture of Objects in Late Chosŏn Korean Art, by Sunglim Kim

Top-Down Democracy in South Korea, by Erik Mobrand

The Shaman's Wages: Trading in Ritual on Cheju Island, by Kyoim Yun

Korean Skilled Workers: Toward a Labor Aristocracy, by Hyung-A Kim

KOREAN SKILLED WORKERS

Toward a Labor Aristocracy

HYUNG-A KIM

UNIVERSITY OF WASHINGTON PRESS
Seattle

Korean Skilled Workers was supported in part by the Korea Studies Program of the University of Washington in cooperation with the Henry M. Jackson School of International Studies.

Copyright © 2020 by the University of Washington Press

Composed in Minion Pro, typeface designed by Robert Slimbach

24 23 22 21 20   5 4 3 2 1

Printed and bound in the United States of America

All rights reserved. No part of this publication may be reproduced or transmitted in any form or by any means, electronic or mechanical, including photocopy, recording, or any information storage or retrieval system, without permission in writing from the publisher.

UNIVERSITY OF WASHINGTON PRESS
uwapress.uw.edu

LIBRARY OF CONGRESS CATALOGING-IN-PUBLICATION DATA
Names: Kim, Hyung-A, 1948– author.
Title: Korean skilled workers : toward a labor aristocracy / Kim Hyung-A.
Description: Seattle : University of Washington Press, [2020] | Series: Korean studies of the Henry M. Jackson School of International Studies | Includes bibliographical references and index.
Identifiers: LCCN 2019041013 (print) | LCCN 2019041014 (ebook) | ISBN 9780295747200 (hardcover) | ISBN 9780295747217 (paperback) | ISBN 9780295747224 (ebook)
Subjects: LCSH: Skilled labor—Korea (South)—History—20th century. | Labor movement—Korea (South)—History—20th century. | Labor policy—Korea (South)—History—20th century. | Economic development—Korea (South)—History—20th century.
Classification: LCC HD5828.A6 K5154 2020 (print) | LCC HD5828.A6 (ebook) | DDC 331.11/42209519509045—dc23
LC record available at https://lccn.loc.gov/2019041013
LC ebook record available at https://lccn.loc.gov/2019041014

Cover design: Katrina Noble
Cover illustration: Container cargo terminal, Port of Busan, South Korea (nitimongkolchai/iStock)

The paper used in this publication is acid free and meets the minimum requirements of American National Standard for Information Sciences—Permanence of Paper for Printed Library Materials, ANSI Z39.48–1984.∞

To Adrian and Eugene

Contents

List of Figures and Tables . . . . *ix*
Acknowledgments . . . . *xi*
List of Abbreviations . . . . *xv*
Note on Korean Romanization . . . . *xvii*

INTRODUCTION: Unveiling Korean Skilled Workers 3

1. The Creation of Industrial Warriors: Mass Training of the
First Generation of Skilled Workers 20

2. From Industrial Warriors to Goliat Warriors:
A New Labor Militancy 41

3. Counterrevolution: The Corporate Culture Movement
and HCI Workers' Response 67

4. The Asian Financial Crisis: HCI Workers' Social Closure
and the Rise of *Chaebŏl* Dominance 91

5. The Rise of HCI Workers: A Labor Aristocracy vis-à-vis
Nonregular Workers 115

CONCLUSION 142

Appendix 1. Characteristics of Hyundai WIA Corporation Respondents *155*
Appendix 2. Characteristics of Doosan Heavy Industries Respondents *156*
Appendix 3. Characteristics of Hyundai Heavy Industries Respondents *157*

*Appendix 4. Korean Educational Institutions by Type, Age at Entry,
  and School Year* 159

Appendix 5. Training and Ranks of Engineers and Craftsmen 160

Notes. 161

Bibliography. 177

Index. 195

Figures and Tables

FIGURE

5.1 Union density and membership in South Korea, 1986–2016 139

TABLES

1.1 Supply of and demand for craftsmen by occupational sector, 1972–1981 27
1.2 Number of graduates, technical high schools, 1969–1987 35
1.3 Skilled labor (craftsmen) training through vocational training institutes 38
2.1 Labor disputes in Korea, 1985–1993 54
3.1 Four main program areas of the Corporate Culture Movement 73
3.2 Formation of the Korean labor force in the shipbuilding industry, 1990–1993 76
3.3 Kia Machine Tools employees' benefits and privileges, March 1993 84
4.1 Fluctuations in employment by occupational category, before and after the 1997 crisis 93
5.1 Average monthly salary and fixed bonus at main industrial parks in the Ulsan area, 1990 and 1993 117
5.2 Living conditions of members of Korean Metalworkers' Union, Ulsan, January 2000 121
5.3 Results of Hyundai Motor's wage negotiations, 2001–2010 123
5.4 Characteristics of the thirty-nine respondents from three corporations, 2014 and 2015 130
5.5 Survey results: On the need for labor unions, 1978 136

5.6 Survey results: Workers' views on labor unions, 1978............137
5.7 Survey results: On the necessity of labor unions at the
     workplace, 1987...138
5.8 Survey results: On the militancy of Korean labor union
     activities, 2005 140

Acknowledgments

The idea of writing a book on the first generation of Korean skilled workers was initially sown in my mind after visiting the Ch'angwŏn Heavy Industry Park in January 2004. This totally unexpected opportunity fell into my lap due mainly to Mr. O Wŏn-ch'ŏl, former senior economic secretary under President Park Chung Hee, who invited me on his two-day trip to the complex together with his two former staff members, Kim Kwang-mo and Kang Young-t'aek. In this specially arranged visit supported by the Ministry of Commerce, Industry, and Energy, not only did we visit half a dozen large firms, including Doosan Heavy Industries, Hyundai WIA, and Hyosung Heavy Industries, but we also met many noteworthy people, both managers and skilled workers, in each firm. The compelling question that played on my mind throughout the trip and many years later was "How and when did Korea train that army of soldier-like industrial workers?" During the many years of my earlier research for *Korea's Development under Park Chung Hee*, I must confess that I did not even think of this question, as if the issue of workers, especially the newly emerged skilled workers, was unrelated to Korea's rapid industrialization during the Park era.

It took seven years for me to finally begin the new journey of writing a book in 2011 based on this yet to be answered question, which of course developed and became more complex as my research deepened, far more than I had initially expected. In the course of this fascinating and yet equally grueling research, I received much support and a wide range of suggestions and advice from many people. I am particularly grateful to the late O Wŏn-ch'ŏl (who passed away in May 2019) and to Kim Kwang-mo, who, by providing me with the wealth of their personal experience and various rare documents related to the development of the first generation of Korean skilled workers as a vital part of Korea's heavy and chemical industrialization, empowered me to apply a holistic approach to this research.

I am equally grateful to Yu Han-sik, former CEO of EM Korea, who helped me in so many ways from the beginning of this research, from providing me access to his private collection of internal documents from his former company, to making the arrangements for my in-depth surveys and interviews with the first generation of Korean skilled workers, union leaders of various firms, both large and medium, as well as with other individuals, including irregular skilled workers, related to this research. His selfless and unreserved support enabled me to write this book with rich insight and with the direct voice of the first generation of Korean skilled workers. I am very fortunate to have known Yun Sŏk-man, former CEO of POSCO Engineering and Construction, who supported not only my research on Korean skilled workers in various ways, but also more broadly Korean studies at the Australian National University, where the establishment of the Korea Institute in 2008 was due largely to his support. Indeed, I am indebted to the Australian National University, more specifically, the School of Culture, History and Language in the College of Asia and the Pacific, which has supported my various research projects, including this book. In particular, a valuable and timely small grant that I had received from the college in 2011 enabled me to obtain two larger grants for a pilot project for this ground-breaking book.

I owe special thanks to Lew Seok-choon and other scholars in the Department of Sociology at Yonsei University, where I was invited to teach during the 2014 academic year. There I had the rare opportunity not only to learn many invaluable lessons of university life at Yonsei and to explore its unique culture, but also to closely observe Korean society and its people, especially the first generation of skilled workers, the main subject of this book. My 2014 living experience in Korea indeed helped me to articulate this important story about the Korean skilled workers.

In gathering data and arranging the interviews of Hyundai Heavy Industries workers and union leaders in Ulsan, as well as in Seoul, I owe a vast thanks to Shin Seung-bae, whose generous support and expertise in survey data analysis helped me to shape and then polish the text of this book. Many thanks also go to Young-mi Kim, who invited me to deliver a special lecture at the Korea Foundation Global E-School in Eurasia Project in September 2013 and again in June 2014, which helped me to develop my ideas further. And I benefited greatly from the critical comments and suggestions by Clark Sorensen, who read my manuscript with much dedication and vigor.

I owe to special thanks to Hahm Chaibong, former president of the Asan Institute for Policy Studies, Seoul, who supported this research from the very beginning. I also thank my dearest students, especially Shin Seung-hugh, who helped me as my research assistant to collect many digital data and other material in the early stages of this book. Peter Ban-seok Kwon was another very helpful research and teaching assistant during 2014, when we both were at Yonsei University, where he was a visiting PhD candidate from Harvard University. In Canberra, Australia, Paik Yŏn-jae, a PhD candidate at the Australian National University, helped me most generously whenever I needed to obtain or locate documents in the latter stages of writing this book.

I thank those skilled workers, union movement activists, labor movement experts and scholars, as well as journalists, whom I either interviewed or who interviewed me, in the course of my research for this book. The article on the first generation of Korea's skilled workers published by Chong Chang-yŏl of the *Weekly Chosun* as its cover story in November 2013, based on his interview with me, aroused much public interest in Korea, and I benefited greatly from comments and suggestions from the readers who subsequently contacted me directly.

I also thank my editor, Lorri Hagman, and associate acquisitions editor Mike Baccam for their generous help throughout the process of preparing the final version of my manuscript for this book.

Two substantial grants in 2011, one from AMCI Australia and the other from the Asan Institute for Policy Studies, Seoul, Republic of Korea, provided the financial support for my research related trips and fieldwork, not only to Korea but also to many countries in Europe and the United States. I am particularly grateful to Hans Jurgen Mende, cofounder, president, and CEO of AMCI Worldwide Limited, who supported this research-based book project while also sharing his own personal experience with Pak T'ae-jun, founding chairman of POSCO, a South Korean steel-making company, especially concerning Park's business approach, particularly in the early stages of founding POSCO during the 1970s and 1980s.

Finally, I am grateful to my family, both in Korea and Canberra. My only remaining brother, Ik-sang, two sisters, and sister-in-law, plus several nieces and nephews have been a major source of my strength and self-confidence. Most of all, Adrian, my husband, and Eugene, my only son, have been the guiding stars of my long journey with this book. I salute them with gratitude.

Abbreviations

CCM	Corporate Culture Movement
CIP	Ch'angwŏn Industrial Park
CMCU	Council of Masan and Ch'angwŏn Unions
DJ	Kim Dae-jung
DS	developmental state
FKTU	Federation of Korean Trade Unions
GWS	Great Workers' Struggle
HCI	heavy and chemical industrialization; heavy and chemical industries
HHI	Hyundai Heavy Industries
HHIU	Hyundai Heavy Industries Union
HMU	Hyundai Motor Union
HSEP	High School Equalization Policy
IMF	International Monetary Fund
KCTU	Korean Confederation of Trade Unions
KMT	Kia Machine Tools (Kia Kigong)
KMTU	Kia Machine Tools Union
KOSSDA	Korean Social Science Data Archive
KSEC	Korea Shipbuilding and Engineering Corporation
KTHS	Kŭmo Technical High School
MFEZ	Masan Free Export Zone
MSEP	Middle School Equalization Policy
MST	Ministry of Science and Technology
NCTU	National Council of Trade Unions
NTQS	National Technical Qualification System
OECD	Organization for Economic Cooperation and Development
SMEs	small and medium-size enterprises
USAID	US Agency for International Development

Note on Korean Romanization

This book uses the McCune-Reischauer system of Korean romanization, except for those Korean names and places that are widely known in English with alternate spelling, such as Park Chung Hee, Syngman Rhee, Seoul, and the names of individuals who have personally chosen another spelling. The transcription of Korean names in the book abides by the Korean practice of romanizing surnames and given names.

KOREAN SKILLED WORKERS

Introduction

Unveiling Korean Skilled Workers

SOUTH Korea (hereafter Korea) initially built its position as a global powerhouse in manufacturing sectors such as shipbuilding, automobiles, semiconductors, and telecommunications, all of which became key foundations of the country's triumphant development, based on heavy and chemical industrialization (HCI) in the 1970s. By as early as 2005, Korea had become the tenth-largest economy in the world, with a literacy rate of over 95 percent. According to *Trading Economics*, Korea's GDP per capita from 1960 to 2015 averaged US$9,632, reaching US$25,023 in 2015.[1] Although Korea went through the traumatic Asian financial crisis in 1997 and the 2008 global financial crisis, the country was in 2015 again ranked the eleventh-largest economy in the world. By then some of Korea's large family-owned conglomerates, or *chaebŏl*s, had become the world's preeminent manufacturing brands. Samsung Electronics' smartphones, Hyundai Heavy Industries' shipbuilding, Hyundai Motor's automobiles, LG's electronic appliances, and various Korean telecommunication brands are only a few examples of these, each with a global reputation and associated market power. Unlike the prominent *chaebŏl*s, Korea's highly disciplined and technologically competent skilled workers are little known, other than for the union militancy that has branded them a "labor aristocracy" (*nodong kwijok*) and an object of social criticism for their perceived collective "selfishness" in Korean society today.[2] How has this happened?

This book tells the story of Korea's first generation of skilled workers in the HCI sector, covering more than forty years since the early 1970s. This story involves their sociopolitical trajectory of dramatic transformation, tracing how they initially became patriotic and obedient "industrial warriors" (sanŏp chŏnsa) of the Korean state's HCI program during the 1970s, then morphed into self-proclaimed "Goliat warriors"[3] during the democratic transition from 1987 to the early 1990s, representing the democratic (minju) labor union movement and the solidarity movement of the Korean working class in their partnership with radical minjung (the people) intellectuals, and finally became a "labor aristocracy" by consolidating their collective status in the Korean labor market as regular workers at large HCI firms. In fact, their guaranteed job security, superior wages—and most of all, the privilege of so-called job inheritance (chigŏp sesŭp) for their offspring under the protection of their powerful unions—has made them a distinct class in Korean society today. In contrast, millions of Korea's nonregular workers struggle, as in many countries throughout the world, with the problem of precarious employment, as job security becomes "a thing of the past" (Standing 2013).

Korea's regular workers in large HCI firms, especially the first generation of skilled workers—the HCI workers who are the main subject of this book—became incipient labor aristocrats in the 1990s, up to the 1997 financial crisis. An extraordinary change in the HCI workers' collective attitude resulted from the Corporate Culture Movement (Kiŏp Munhwa Undong) led by the Korean state and capitalist chaebŏls, who aimed to restore their control over labor, especially by breaking down militant unionism at the workplace, where HCI workers had become the leading force against authoritarian management practices. In this regard, HCI workers' collective role in leading the revolutionary nationwide industrial strikes known as the Great Workers' Struggle, which began soon after Korea democratized in 1987 and continued until May 1991, cannot be overemphasized. The HCI workers' sociopolitical trajectory represents the path of their collective identity, which was created by the state under President Park Chung Hee (1963–79). By inculcating a collective identity as industrial warriors, the state trained the HCI workers to become conscious of their distinctive responsibility and position in the labor hierarchy, starting with their technical high school or vocational training days. As Korea's newly trained first generation of skilled workers, they became a class of their own through militant union activism, especially after the Asian financial crisis of 1997 and the subsequent restructuring that consolidated their class position.

To understand this complex and controversial development, it is necessary to investigate how HCI workers initially conformed to the Park state's nation-building HCI project during the 1970s and until 1987, and then instigated a seismic nationwide industrial strike, known as the Great Workers' Struggle (see chapter 2), before realigning into the state/*chaebŏls*-led neoliberal transformation under the slogan Corporate Culture Movement starting in the 1990s.[4] This book has two goals. The first is to examine the formation and transformation of the HCI workers and their collective character in the course of state-led industrialization and to consider why they, as hitherto relatively conservative industrial warriors, suddenly rose up as radical Goliat warriors protesting not just their own military-style work environment and related deprivation, but also the workplace despotism inflicted on the Korean working class as a whole. The other goal is to illuminate how the collective trajectory of the HCI workers was shaped and reshaped over time in response to Korea's rapidly changing political and economic conditions since the 1980s, especially following the Asian financial crisis and during the subsequent neoliberal restructuring in a highly globalized and competitive environment.

This book argues, by connecting to the labor and "class politics" of East Asian development studies, that the dramatic change in the collective character or identity of Korea's first generation of skilled workers, HCI workers, from conservative industrial warriors to radical Goliat warriors and finally to a labor aristocracy, over some forty years or more was the consequence of multiple factors in Korea's rapid development.[5] The most notable factors were the shift from state-led accumulation to *chaebŏl*-led accumulation and the limits of broad-based labor solidarity in the context of capital's counteroffensive against militant unionism since the 1980s, especially in postrestructuring Korea following the Asian financial crisis. The study of Korea's HCI workers is important because it alerts us to the need to rethink the conventional understanding of the East Asian model of development espoused by elite development theory traditions, which have focused heavily on dichotomous categories of either "weak labor, strong state" as in the statist political economy model, or "oppression" versus "resistance," as assumed in the Marxist modernization model.[6] In the Korean success story, it is true that the interventionist role of the state was crucial in planning and managing markets under the state's policies to accelerate growth, just as large and diversified business groups, namely capitalist *chaebŏls*, have been the most active engines of state-led economic growth.

The capitalist *chaebŏls*, however, were able to become active not only because the Korean strategy of industrialization effectively expedited the rapid education of a class of salaried engineers and white-collar workers (Amsden 1989, 159–73; Vartiainen 1999, 226), but also because Korea under Park's HCI Policy (officially unveiled in January 1973) radically strengthened the tie between the state and the then newly emergent HCI workers. They readily committed to the state's HCI project, initially by committing to their technical education and skills training mainly at the high school and other state-approved levels, and then by becoming skilled workers in the HCI sector from the 1970s onward, except those who were dismissed or have left for various reasons, including retirement. Overall, the collective role of HCI workers, with their technical competence and ideological commitment to Korea's rapid industrialization, not only helped Park Chung Hee achieve his nation-building aims but also enabled the HCI workers themselves to rise as a dominant labor force, or labor aristocracy, behind Korea's spectacular transformation into what we see today, warts and all.

The Korean experience illuminates why we have to pay more attention to workplace bargaining power, to borrow sociologist Beverly J. Silver's phrase relating to the power of labor unions.[7] In the Korean case, this bargaining power became almost a lethal weapon for militant unions, especially for male workers in the HCI sector, who are now famous not only for "taking radical political stands against authoritarian regimes, free trade agendas, and neoliberal economic policies" (Chun 2009, 6), but also for shaping and reshaping their relationship with both the state and corporate management over time, especially through their umbrella organization, the Korean Confederation of Trade Unions (KCTU), in the course of democratization, which has paralleled neoliberal globalization, especially in postrestructuring Korea.

Consideration of skilled labor is essential for expanding our historical understanding of Korea's development. As many scholars have argued, the study of that development needs to include a broader range of nonstate political, economic, social, and military actors and agencies, while also looking at the gendered aspect of technical education, which has strategically favored young males over females. In this respect, this study affords a deeper understanding of the Korean developmental state-led mass production of a skilled labor force, which, in spite or perhaps because of its military-style technical education, skills training, and ideological inculcation, played a key role in Korea's rapid development. The critical role of HCI workers in shaping today's intriguing labor politics in Korea is also of regional relevance. Korea's rapid development, even after more than four decades, draws much interest among scholars, policymakers, and various general practitioners in a range of fields at the global level.

A NEW GENERATION OF KOREAN SKILLED WORKERS AND THE PARK STATE'S EDUCATION POLICIES

Too often, the existence of Korea's skilled and educated workforce is attributed to historical and cultural legacies. Yet most Korean workers were unskilled and had low levels of technical understanding and education in the early 1970s. In fact, the low standard of technical understanding and education among the country's industrial workers was one of the main reasons for the Park Chung Hee state's introduction of what was called the National Technical Qualification System in December 1973, which in effect radically standardized the level of skills and craftsmanship in Korean industry through a state-approved grade based on the provisions of the National Technical Qualification Act (which took effect in July 1973). Another, even more revolutionary change, made by the Park state and persisting until the 1980s, was the implementation of egalitarian education policies, most notably the High School Equalization Policy in 1974. As one of the core strategies of HCI policy, the implementation of the High School Equalization Policy, despite its draconian measures in education reform, in line with the Middle School Equalization Policy (introduced in 1968), in fact normalized education by dramatically narrowing the gaps among schools and ending some serious "school ills," such as excessive educational competition caused by the public's obsession with elite schools, while also broadening educational opportunities (Kang Yŏung-hae et al. 2005).

The broadening of educational opportunities, in particular, went well beyond the norm established in other societies, which provided the basis of the egalitarian social contract in Korea's educational policymaking for decades as empirically shown in one PhD study (Sang-young Park 1999). This "basis of the egalitarian social contract" included subsidies for technical education and vocational training under the Korean developmental state's "subsidies as contracts," to borrow Vivek Chibber's term, or what I have characterized as the reciprocal social contract. Under this reciprocal social contract, the Korean developmental state in the 1970s and 1980s drafted a massive number of young people into technical high school education and vocational training by providing financial subsidies and other social opportunities, including future promotion. In return, these young people were committed to serving state-led industrialization by supplying skilled labor as what the state characterized as industrial warriors, in many cases replacing mandatory military duty as so-called special soldiers (*t'ŭngnyebyŏng*).

The aim of the Korean development state's reciprocal social contract was geared mainly toward promoting national unity and discipline through educational expansion and social mobility, almost identical to the aim of the egalitarian social contract in Korea's educational policymaking.[8] Accordingly, some two million young people, predominantly males from economically deprived family backgrounds in rural areas, received a technical high school education or vocational training subsidized by the state in various forms, including in-plant training and military-run training between 1972, when the Park state commenced its HCI project, and 1987, when Korea began its democratic transition after almost twenty-six years of military authoritarian rule since 1961 under Park and Chun Doo-hwan (1980–87).

Subsequently, the annual number of technical high school graduates more than trebled, from 20,195 males in 1972 to 62,685 in 1987, producing a total of nearly 800,000 graduates over that time. The majority of these graduates obtained a class II skills license by passing the National Technical Qualification Test before graduation (Mun'gyobu 1977, 171). In addition, over one million young people completed their skills training through the various vocational institutes, which were radically expanded from 59 in 1971 to 695 in 1980, training about 100,000 annually by that year. Many of these well-disciplined young people, like most graduates of technical high schools at that time, were subsequently employed in large *chaebŏl* firms in the then burgeoning HCI sector. Those who had been categorized as special soldiers (*t'ŭngnyebyŏng*) working in firms classified by the state as in the defense goods industry (*pangwi sanŏp*), according to the Military Service Special Cases Law (introduced in 1973), however, were required to serve a five-year probation in their firms in lieu of mandatory military duty.

This special-soldiers system strategically removed the "distinction between soldiers . . . and workers, engineers, and researchers" (Moon 2005, 55) under the newly promulgated authoritarian Yusin (Restoration) system. The Park state's policy of a "self-reliant national defense" (*chaju kukpang*), in particular, provided the basis for Korea's industrial revolution by creating an HCI sector focused on the construction of a defense industry. The top priority of Korea's HCI project under Park's despotic Yusin system was in fact to build Korea's "self-reliant" defense capacity after the rivalry between North and South Korea turned into a crisis following North Korean commandos' attempt to assassinate President Park in January 1968 (Hyung-A Kim 2004, 110–30; Hyung-A Kim 2011; Peter-Banseok Kwon 2016).

The special-soldiers system in many ways typified the Park state's mass mobilization strategy to create an anticommunist industrial corps together with a modern national identity based on the can-do discipline of the Korean people inculcated through the state-led New Community Movement (Saemaŭl Undong) during the 1970s.[9] The special-soldiers system also typified Park's militarist use of mandatory conscription as a way of mobilizing young men to become disciplined industrial workers, serving as the pillars of export in Korea's key industries in the HCI sector. In this regard, historian Carter Eckert's (2016, 2) definition of the term "militarist," specifically linked to what he described as "the Park modernization regime," is illuminating as "a belief that in a national crisis of sufficient gravity, the army had not only a right but also a duty to intervene in the political system." These quasi-soldier skilled workers of the 1970s, with a work record of some thirty years or more today with or without a special-soldier record, are still at work, except those who have left for reasons such as retirement.[10]

RETHINKING SKILLED LABOR IN EAST ASIAN DEVELOPMENT LITERATURE

Until recently, Korea's industrial skilled workers, known broadly in today's Korea as *kinŭngsa* (craftsmen or technicians), were rarely discussed among prominent contemporary advocates of statist political economy in East Asian development literature.[11] The main reason for this was that they were not regarded independently as historical actors having agency, but seen as passive labor in general with organizational weakness and exclusion from politics. This widely held view, based on the colonial legacy of "strong state, weak labor" within the dichotomous framework of a "strong state, weak society" (Migdal 1988), was most apparent in development literature of East Asian newly industrializing countries. Dissatisfied with the dominant statist political economy perspective depicted in East Asian development literature, as well as the reductionist or essentialist approach in most writings of Korean analysts, who have assumed that "classes emerge, more or less automatically, from the structure of the capitalist relations of production," Hagen Koo (2001, 15) challenged these approaches by scholars in both the East

Asian development literature and the writings of "Korean analysts"[12] nearly two decades ago, analyzing the formation of a Korean working-class identity in his award-winning book, *Korean Workers: The Culture and Politics of Class Formation.*

Koo's masterly use of personal narratives, especially focused on the distinctive pattern of Korean workers' struggles from the 1960s until the late 1990s, brought to life the voice of workers, while also depicting young Korean female workers as a symbol of the labor struggle against political, cultural, and historical oppression in Korean society. Curiously, Koo offered little explanation of what male skilled workers in the HCI sector were up to between the 1970s and the Great Workers' Struggle of 1987. The only notable exception was his discussion of the six-day Daewoo Auto Strike of April 16–22, 1985, at the Daewoo Auto Company's Pup'yŏng Plant (Koo 2001, 109–11). However, the lived experience of young male skilled workers in the HCI sector and young female workers in the light industry sector up to 1987 and thereafter was vastly different, in terms not only of their levels of formal education and technology and skills training but also of their immensely different work environments. The difference in the size of their workplaces together with the vastly larger number of soldier-like skilled workers, with their quasi-military workplace, in the HCI sector distinguished the male HCI workers' trajectory from that of female workers and other labor forces in general, including workers at small and medium manufacturing firms in Korea's light industries.

Koo's analysis, especially in regard to the level of skill of Korean workers, echoed the thinking of radical intellectuals when he characterized them as semiskilled until the mid-1980s. Koo affirmed that the great majority of Korean workers were semiskilled, concluding, "Not only was there little differentiation in terms of skills (as well as age and family background), there were also few differences in terms of wages, job security, and welfare benefits" (2001, 205). Koo explained, "By the early 1980s, the core of the Korean industrial structure was represented by the heavy and chemical industries, and by predominantly semi-skilled and skilled male workers employed in this sector" (2001, 180). Was there, then, little difference in the skill levels of Korean workers? Where did those semiskilled and skilled male workers in the HCI sector of the early 1980s come from? Koo's depiction of the Korean workers' levels of skill largely reflects the standard portrayal of Korean workers, including that depicted in comparative studies of organized labor movements in the East Asian development literature focused on the dichotomous model of struggle versus oppression.

Historian Namhee Lee's study of Korean workers in the 1970s is a good example, especially in depicting "modernization Marxism," to borrow Benjamin Selwyn's term. It echoes Koo's line of thinking, with neo-Marxist views of class warfare assumed on a false dichotomy of state versus civil society in pursuit of modernization by reducing the role of agency, especially that of skilled labor, to an "object of the state's totalizing drive for [economic] development" (2007, 5). It is true that the Park state imposed its authoritarian rule in the name of what Park called "Koreanized democracy," while also inculcating a new "modern citizenship" that characterized the Park state's politics of identity as focused on anticommunism and economic nationalism during the 1970s and thereafter. In spite of these obvious factors behind the Park state's totalizing drive for development, the dichotomous approach of struggle versus oppression, based on development theory, has failed to appreciate or account for the unique roles of social groups in various sectors in the course of Korea's development under Park.

This complex story of the Korean case of industrial skilled workers essentially shows that there was a "gray zone" (An Pyŏng-jik 2002) between the state, especially under Park, and its "oppressed society" and the workers. It also shows that the widely accepted analysis focused on the "strong state, weak society" dichotomy in modes of "strong state, weak labor" or oppression and resistance (Im Chihyŏn and Kim Yongwu 2005, 402–3) ironically increased a compelling need for reinterpretative literature on this particular force of industrial skilled workers. In this regard, Hwasook Nam's case study, *Building Ships, Building a Nation: Korea's Democratic Unionism under Park Chung Hee* (2009), challenged the dichotomous framework of "weak labor, strong state" by arguing that "subscribing to the notion of 'weak labor, strong state' hides workers' agency, ignoring what workers were able to achieve on their own at certain junctures" (8). Nam's challenge to the standard view, through her meticulous study of the union and its members of the Korea Shipbuilding and Engineering Corporation (KSEC, the first and largest shipyard during the 1960s in Korea, now Hanjin Heavy Industries), is persuasive and adds a new dimension to understanding the vitality of Korean workers as a whole and their democratic and militant union activism, especially in the shipbuilding industry during the 1960s. What Nam's study inadequately explained, however, is why KSEC workers, like most other young male workers in heavy industries, willingly maintained their decade-long collective acquiescence during the 1970s.[13]

The Park state's totalitarian labor suppression, especially under the infamous Yusin Constitution and the military dictatorship led by another general-turned-president, Chun Doo-hwan, would not be a sufficient answer, because under the same suppression, young female workers in export-dependent light industries, as Nam noted, were "waging bloody battles to organize unions or democratize their existing pro-company unions" (Hwa-Sook Nam 2009, 9). Was there a more compelling reason for the KSEC workers to maintain their docility until they exploded in the Great Workers' Struggle? In her efforts to explain this puzzle, Nam recounted two key factors. One was the spectacular real-wage increases of "more than 250 percent" provided to Korean manufacturing workers from 1969 to 1979, while many workers experienced "fast promotion from temporary to regular status and then swiftly went up the occupational ladder during the 1970s" (195, 197–98). The other factor Nam recounted was ideological inculcation of development-first ideology and the mobilization of national consensus through the state-led Factory New Community Movement of the 1970s (see chapter 1).

These factors were important but in themselves not enough to keep the majority of young male rank-and-file workers in heavy industries voluntarily docile, even after Park's demise in 1979. The majority of male rank-and-file workers in the heavy and chemical industries, including the KSEC workers, remained compliant during this period mainly because they were legally bound to complete their individual obligation, which they had accepted as a precondition to receiving technical high school education or skills training under the state's subsidies and other societal benefits, including promotion opportunities. Their collective acquiescence up to the Great Workers' Struggle of 1987, in other words, was not merely the result of the dirigiste labor policy of the Park state and the succeeding Chun Doo-hwan regime, but more the result of their individual interest in procuring employment security by fulfilling their legal obligation, especially if their employment conditions were subject to the special-soldier category in a defense industry.

Just as any *chaebŏl* that had failed to fulfill its set of tasks set by the Park state, especially those in line with its HCI policy, was barred from receiving the state's guarantee of survival through various subsidies and low-interest loans, among many other privileges, any newly employed skilled worker who failed to meet the company's requirements was dismissed and, in the case of the *t'ŭngnyebyŏng,* immediately conscripted into military service. Constrained by this legal requirement and other workplace despotism, the majority of new HCI workers were eager to perform well even during their education and skills training. In this sense, the answer to the question that Nam raised as to how labor later became so strong must be found not only outside the labor movement, as Nam argued, but also beyond the dichotomous model of "weak labor, strong state" or the struggle-versus-oppression framework.

Similarly, if one subscribes to the standard view that there was little differentiation in terms of skills among the great majority of Korean workers, as they were mostly semiskilled, the question of where those semiskilled and skilled male workers in Korea's HCI sector came from in the early 1980s cannot be adequately answered. A recent PhD dissertation on the history of Korea's defense industry development during the Park era, however, shows that as early as 1976 Korea had become an independent weapons manufacturer and arms exporter (Peter-Banseok Kwon 2016, 144). This means that the skill levels of Korean workers by the mid-1970s were competitive enough for Korea to manufacture and export military goods. Recognizing these unresolved questions and issues, this book aims to contribute to broadening the general understanding of development in Asia, especially with reference to the HCI workforce. The HCI workforce in the Korean case has become a class of its own through political union activism, enabling it to consolidate its classification as a labor aristocracy, a long way from its original objective role as conservative industrial warriors committed to serving Korea's industrial revolution by building an HCI sector in the 1970s and up to the eruption of the Great Workers' Struggle of 1987.

RETHINKING THE ROLE OF SKILLED WORKERS IN EAST ASIAN DEVELOPMENT

Korea, as a quintessential model of a developmental state, along with Japan, Taiwan, Singapore, and more recently Vietnam, has been widely researched and debated, especially regarding the distinctive nature of the market-conforming policies of developmental states, or more broadly the role of the state as the key mechanism for the East Asian economic miracle (World Bank 1993; Woo-Cumings 1999; Leftwich 2008).[14] Developmental state theory is an explanation of economic life in capitalist Northeast Asia that, according to Ha-Joon Chang (1999, 183), "can create and regulate the economic and political relationships that can support sustained industrialization, or in short, a developmental state (DS)." This does not mean that the definition of the key DS concept is clear and consensual, largely because of the "swirl of various competing trends in social science analyses," as Richard Stubbs (2009, 5) pointed out. Thus the DS concept is used by many scholars according to what they see as its main characteristic, to the extent of it having become "a generic term to describe governments that try to actively 'intervene' in economic processes and direct the course of development rather than relying on market forces" (Beeson 2007, 141).

Another notable point is that the changed focus in recent decades of literature on East Asian DSs has taken a drastic turn in characterizing the nature of and causes underlying the Korean debt crisis and other social ills, prior to and following the Asian financial crisis of 1997 (Pempel 1999; David Kang 2002; Kyung-sup Chang 2007; Myung-Koo Kang 2011). Terms like "crony capitalism," "developmentalist mentalité," and "*chaebŏl*-centered developmentalism" reflect not only perspectives critical of the laudatory narratives of the "East Asian Miracle," but also the ongoing debate about a variety of developmental-neoliberal mixes in the East Asian developmental states, including a Chinese model of DS focused on terms like "Beijing consensus" or "China model" and "Chinese authoritarian capitalism."[15] Overall, most scholars tend to allude to "three key ingredients" (Stubbs 2009, 5–6), such as institutional, relational, and ideational aspects of the DS concept, with the understanding that the term "developmental state" has been used in connection with the political economies of East Asia. Given that some key components are conducive to the DS developing its institutional capacity, however, it is necessary to rethink these widely accepted key components, outlined in a recent study by Vivek Chibber (2014, 33–34):

- *Extractive capacity* for the DS to increase domestic savings and to hold a quotient of these savings taken as state revenue;
- *Bureaucratic integrity* to secure a baseline level of bureaucratic cohesiveness to ensure bureaucrats follow the duties attached to their station;
- *Internal cohesiveness* able to coordinate the bureaucracy around developmental tasks;
- A *nodal agency* to secure the needed institutional coordination; and
- *Dense and secure ties to firms* in order to allow a regular flow of information between state economic agencies and local firms.

This summary of the key components, which reflect the standard view prevalent in institutionalist literature on East Asia, emphasizes the DS's political motivation from the perspective of developmental, export-oriented, growth-promoting policies. Conspicuously missing in these key components, however, is technical competence, especially skilled manpower. Strong states, as Charles Tilly's analysis (1990) demonstrated, cannot be developed unless sufficient resources, such as money, skilled manpower, and organizational and technical knowledge, are available. Chalmers Johnson (1989, 4) also noted four key elements that need to exist in the following order for the rise of what he termed a "capitalist developmental state (CDS)": (1) a receptive social environment; (2) determined leadership; (3) technical competence; and (4) money (i.e., capital). Rapid capital accumulation and equally rapid accumulation of physical and human capital, especially through investment and technical progress in manufacturing, according to Jong-il Kim and J. Lawrence (1994) and Young (1994), have explained Asia's growth, and this remarkable growth has been mostly credited to two key actors: a well-disciplined, strong bureaucracy and equally well-committed capitalists, as in the case of Korea.

Amazingly, far too little is known about the role of technical competence, especially regarding skilled blue-collar workers, in Asia's rapid growth. It would be absurd to think that technical competence played a significant role in Asia's rapid growth unless workers with a high level of appropriate skills and technical knowledge, not to mention collective discipline in the workplace, efficiently operated and maintained a vast range of technologically sophisticated machinery in manufacturing to generate productivity growth. Most of the East Asian miracles, as is widely known, were led by authoritarian systems that were famous for tyrannical labor repression. If so, how did Asian governments motivate their country's labor, or more specifically potentially skilled labor, to increase their skill levels within a short time frame, thus enabling the mass production of export goods and achieving a quantum leap in the level of national productivity, as in Korea in the 1980s and 1990s and beyond? A highly skilled work force should be credited for its role in the rapid economic development in Asia, alongside the two key actors: a strong bureaucracy and committed capitalists. No machine, no matter how technologically advanced in terms of production capacity, can produce goods by itself, without technologically competent skilled labor, while no strategic state intervention in the market can induce both economic growth and industrial transformation without a force of committed capitalists, as well as an equally committed skilled workforce with strong and secure ties to the state's nation-building and modernization project, such as Korea had.

But then, what happens if a developmental state has neither a committed skilled workforce capable of carrying out industrial transformation as planned nor a sufficiently strong and secure relationship with those skilled workers for them to commit themselves to the state's project? In either case, no industrial transformation or rapid growth would be possible regardless of how a developmental state pushed industrial transformation and sustained economic growth based on its embeddedness either with the bureaucracy or with the capitalists, or both, because no bureaucracy or capitalists could take over the role of skilled workers. Assuming that technical competence of skilled workers is not something any government or authoritarian leaders can produce by force or repression, or by any other cohesive means apart from the motivation and commitment of the workers to skills training and upgrading, then a question that needs to be asked is, how did the governments of newly industrialized countries in Asia motivate their countries' labor forces to upgrade their skills and technical understanding, or did they each train an entirely new generation of skilled workers, as Korea did?

In Korea's case, some two million young males who received technical high school education or vocational training between 1972 and 1987 consistently proved their efficiency, loyalty and, above all, productivity, in order to retain their financial and other entitlements while studying or receiving skills training or upgrading. In return, they also reciprocated the state's favor by actively providing their skilled labor, especially for the state-led HCI project during the 1970s and thereafter, even in recent years, despite their widely known union militancy behind their negative image as a labor aristocracy. The vast majority of these skilled workers have since been working in the main for large HCI firms, which played the key role in Korea's rapid economic ascent from a low-wage, light-industry base to a world leader in electronics, automobiles, and other advanced industries. In this respect, the collective role of these HCI workers has been no less essential to Korea's rapid development than the roles of the Korean bureaucracy and the committed capitalist *chaebŏls*, while also helping to reshape East Asia and the capitalist global economy (Kyong-ho Shin and Paul Ciccantell 2009). The study of the East Asian developmental state therefore needs to rethink its approach to pay attention to the historical transformation in relations among the state, capitalists, and skilled workers in order to build and promote both industrial capacity and technical competence in the process of development, with a broadened view beyond the current focus in developmental state theories.

SOURCES AND DATA COLLECTION

This book is based on the lived experiences and testimonies of HCI workers, as well as on analysis of newly declassified sources from Korea's presidential and national archives; internal documents of Kia Machine Tools (currently Hyundai WIA Machine Tools, hereafter Hyundai WIA), an engine and transmission manufacturer since the merger in 1999; and data on Korean workers' views on the role of unions taken from surveys conducted in 1978, 1987, and 2005. I also conducted my own in-depth interviews in 2014 and 2015 to obtain up-to-date information on the situation and perspectives of HCI workers.

I was extremely blessed in meeting and interviewing HCI workers, union leaders, former and current CEOs, and middle managers of large and medium manufacturing firms in heavy industries, as well as former high-ranking policymakers of the Park state, including O Wŏn-ch'ŏl and Kim Kwang-mo, two key HCI policymakers who—as the respective head and deputy head of the Second Economic Secretariat (Kyŏngje Che-2 Pisŏsil) in President Park's office, Ch'ŏngwadae, known as the Blue House—were in charge of Park's heavy and chemical industrialization plan, including the development of skilled workers. In fact, the documents I received from them, especially a copy of the Park state's master plan for HCI, *On the Restructuring of Industry in Accordance with the Declaration on Heavy and Chemical Industry Policy* (Chunghwahak kongŏp chŏngch'eak sŏnŏn e ttarŭn kongŏp kujo kaep'yŏnnon),[16] and *Improvement Scheme for Skills Education System, 1973* (Kisul kyoyuk chedo kaesŏnan, 1973),[17] convinced me to trace a new narrative that would transcend the dualism of both the developmental state view and the Marxist view of class warfare in the Park Chung Hee state's pursuit of modernization.

I interviewed nearly fifty HCI workers, including many union leaders at national, regional, and company levels, as well as company executives, other policymakers, labor union experts, and academics during this study, which took almost eight years. I was very fortunate to meet Mr. Yu Han-sik, CEO of the machine industry company EM Korea, who provided two volumes of internal documents from Kia Machine Tools (KMT), titled *Status Report, 1993* (Hyŏnhwang pogo, 1993), which detailed the company's management strategy from 1987 to 1992. Mr. Yu, a former director of KMT's Department of Human Resources Support in the early 1990s, also provided me his personal handwritten notes regarding KMT's union management strategy at that time, as well as many other important materials, including some rare documents regarding KMT's merger with Hyundai Motor Group in 1998 (discussed in chapters 3 and 4). The *Status Report, 1993* entailed a thorough analysis of the KMT Union and the KMT management's counterstrategy, which ultimately brought the KMT workers' union, with its widely known record of militancy, to "voluntarily" withdraw from both the National Council of Trade Unions (Chŏnnohyŏp) and the Council of Masan and Ch'angwŏn Unions (Mach'ang Noryŏn) in February 1993. These were the first such withdrawals from major union councils and sparked the withdrawal in rapid succession of many other democratic militant unions, which I discuss in chapter 3.

I have also included data from three surveys on Korean workers' views on the role of unions, conducted in 1978, 1987, and 2005. The significance of these surveys lies in what each of those years represented. The year 1978, for example, saw the peak of the Park Chung Hee state's technical education and skills training at the high school level, producing 49,807 graduates, before Park was assassinated in October 1979. This number subsequently increased to an annual average of 60,609 graduates from 1979 to 1987. The year 1987 is significant because Korea then began its democratic transition, which encouraged rank-and-file HCI workers to generate a nationwide industrial strike from July to September that came to be known as the Great Workers' Struggle, creating a turning point for the Korean workers' democratic militant unionization movement. The year 2005 is significant because the emergence of a labor aristocracy became a full-blown social issue at that time, as the leftwing progressive President Roh Moo-hyun (2003–7) publicly criticized regular workers and their "aristocratic" unions in large HCI *chaebŏl* firms, accusing them of being the main cause of the rising social polarization driven by income inequality.

Terms like "militant union" (*kangsŏng nojo*), "iron rice bowls" (*ch'ŏlbapt'ong*), and "theory of labor aristocracy" (*nodong kwijongnon*) were frequently used by both the liberal progressive Roh administration and the media to bring attention to the rapidly growing problems of nonregular workers' job insecurity and income inequality, as well as youth unemployment.

The issue of social polarization, in particular, became a key agenda of Roh's national management in 2006.[18] For this reason, I have included data in the 2005 survey regarding the term "labor aristocracy." To supplement these three surveys, I conducted two sets of in-depth interviews in 2014 and 2015 on the living conditions and personal views of thirty-nine HCI workers from three leading firms, Hyundai Heavy Industries (twenty), Hyundai WIA (formerly Kia Machine Tools; ten), and Doosan Heavy Industries (formerly Daewoo Heavy Industries; nine).[19] I also obtained five volumes of autobiographies written by sixty "skilled Koreans" (kinŭng Han'gugin), chosen monthly by the Korean government from 2007 to 2011. All were HCI workers.[20] One notable fact about HCI workers is that they do not write or talk freely about their lives as blue-collar factory workers, unlike many former female factory workers of the pre-1987 era, whose autobiographies are relatively easy to find in bookshops or online in today's Korea.[21]

In fact, the HCI workers who have written autobiographies make little or no mention of their personal views on or experience of the working-class movement, nor of the widely known patriarchal ideologies embedded in the Korean labor movement. Instead, they often describe in detail how they pursued their goals as skilled workers, focusing on their own personal development, whether of their skills or more broadly, over time. Lastly, this book engages heavily with Korean-language news reports, government documents, several large HCI companies' internal printed materials, and academic studies, as well as the large volume of literature on East Asian developmental states and newly industrialized countries, especially related to Korea's industrial skilled workers. All translations of Korean materials cited in this book are mine unless otherwise specified.

CHAPTER 1

The Creation of Industrial Warriors

Mass Training of the First Generation of Skilled Workers

THE mass production of well-disciplined industrial skilled workers was one of the most defining characteristics of Korea's heavy and chemical industrialization during the 1970s and into the 1980s. The impact of these newly emerged HCI workers on Korea's rapid development was distinctive in terms of not only their key role in the country's spectacular economic development but also their collective relationship with the Korean developmental state. Under President Park Chung Hee, in particular, they were molded into what the Park state called industrial warriors to be "the flag bearer of the modernization of the fatherland" (*choguk kŭndaehwa ŭi kisu*), essentially reflecting the Korean developmental state's HCI policy aimed at state-led heavy and chemical industrialization in the 1970s and 1980s.[1]

THE PARK STATE'S CONCEPT OF INDUSTRIAL WARRIORS

Indeed, the Park state's concept of industrial warriors was inseparable from the mass production of an industrial skilled workforce, especially craftsmen/technicians known commonly in Korea as *kinŭngsa*, who were initially trained through technological education and vocational training under a subsidy system as a top priority of the state's HCI policy (PS 1975). In

January 1973, Park Chung Hee declared what he called the National Scientization Movement as a precondition for Korea's heavy and chemical industrialization. Accordingly, that movement became an official instrument in the upgrading of Korea's technological infrastructure and the technical education of all industrial workers, especially in the HCI sector, which at that time barely existed, except for the shipbuilding industry.[2] Park urged that "every Korean should learn technological skills and master them" by participating in the National Scientization Movement, because, he declared, "if we wish to achieve our export goal of US$10 billion by early 1980, heavy and chemical products must exceed well over 50 percent of total export goods," to be reached mainly by accomplishing Korea's heavy and chemical industrialisation by 1980 (PCHTY 1973, 58–59).

Equally instrumental in the technological upgrading of Korea and its people was the New Community Movement (Saemaŭl Undong), which from 1973 expanded into a pan-national campaign to inculcate national discipline in the Korean people, especially in terms of national unity (*kung'min ch'onghwa*) and cooperation through self-renewal as "modern citizens" under Park's Restoration (Yusin) system, declared under martial law on October 17, 1972. Under this centralized political system, postulated by the newly adopted Yusin Constitution, which guaranteed Park's presidency for life with almost monolithic power, Park imposed training in national values and discipline through New Community Movement programs as a way of inculcating support for his planned HCI program.[3] Park in fact defined the civic values of diligence, self-help, and cooperation as "the root of patriotism" and "the spirit of the New Community Movement" (Chung Hee Park 1979, 209), and he officially designated these core civic values as fundamental to each worker's code of conduct.

Similarly, the Park state's term "industrial warriors" explicitly referenced soldiers, prepared for building what Park envisioned as a "self-reliant national defense" (*chaju kukpang*) capability through the HCI program, focused on a massive expansion of technological education and vocational training. The concept of industrial warriors, according to the Park state's master plan, *On the Restructuring of Industry in Accordance with the Declaration on Heavy and Chemical Industry Policy* (Chunghwahak kongŏp e ttarŭn kongŏp kujo kaep'yŏnnon 1970, 4 and 22), thus incorporated a ten-year plan for human resource development of not only industrial craftsmen but also engineers, scientists, and researchers in various areas and institutes, both government and private, in order to upgrade the Korean workforce from predominantly unskilled simple labor to skilled and educated manpower.

For this ambitious nation-building project, Park utilized a military conscription system by introducing a new Military Service Special Cases Law (T'ŭngnyebyŏng pŏp), under which the state encouraged and mobilized a massive number of educated young men, predominantly graduates of what the state categorized as specialized technical high schools, as "special soldiers" (t'ŭngnyebyŏng) for the construction of core industries, especially the defense industry, within the HCI plan. Under the law, the state removed the distinction between soldiers and skilled workers, engineers, and researchers, among other technologically relevant groups. This was a similar approach to Park Chung Hee's February 1968 call for all-out national mobilization, which established a civilian force of 2.5 million Homeland Guards (Hyangt'o Yebigun) across the country under the slogan "Construction on the one hand, national defense on the other" (Ilmyŏn kŏnsŏl, ilmyŏn kukpang), by asking every citizen to take up his/her dual duty as a citizen and as a soldier.

Remarkably, though, the Park state did not publicly articulate what "industrial warrior" or "industrial warrior spirit," or other similar phrases, meant other than equating them to the spirit of the New Community Movement. In this regard, elite technocrats of the Park state, most notably Park Chung Hee's senior economic secretary, O Wŏn-ch'ŏl, and the staff members of his office in the Blue House, as well as other active civil servants, readily identified themselves as the "Industrial Corps" (Sanŏp Kundan) behind Korea's HCI project.[4] They thus alluded to their highly odd collective status in an industrial war under Park as their commander-in-chief, especially facing the security threat from North Korea. In this respect, the Office of Military Manpower, in a 1986 publication, explained the role of the Military Service Special Cases Law in the Park state's pursuit of national development: "[The state] faced the urgent problem of obtaining skilled labor in its pursuit of national development through building core industries, namely, defence industries and heavy and chemical industries. This law was founded as a countermeasure to deal with this problem by making effective use of a surplus of conscripts" (quoted in Moon 2005, 56).

The concept of the industrial warrior, or what can be characterized as industrial warrior consciousness, however, makes little sense without considering the indoctrination of the Korean people through the New Community Movement. In fact, Park promoted the movement as a "spiritual revolution" (chŏngsin hyŏngmyŏng), which in effect became the basic ideology (*kibon inyŏm*) of the bureaucracy, the army, all schools and universities, factories, cities, and rural areas. Every Korean individual, except underage children and citizens over sixty-five, for example, attended mandatory New Community Movement education courses and monthly neighborhood meetings called *pansanghoe*, mainly to learn and practice the Park state's concept of "modern citizenship," which was focused on anticommunism, economic nationalism, and national unity and discipline.[5] The structure of the Factory New Community Movement (Kongjang Saemaŭl Undong), in particular, mirrored the military-style organization of the national community networks, especially after 1973, to inculcate a new family culture of so-called family-like labor-management ties assumed on the ideational nexus of "my cooperation = my family = my fatherland" or "transforming workplaces into a second home" (Hyung-A Kim 2004, 142). Similarly, nationalistic slogans such as "We can do it" (*Hamyŏn toenda*), "We, too, can do it" (*Uri to halsu itta*), and "Nation-building through export" (*Such'ul ipkuk*) became mottos of daily practice in every Korean factory, government ministry, and public and nonpublic institution, including the military and every educational institute.

To make this state-led industrial modernization project more systemic and comprehensive, the Park state grafted the National Scientization Movement onto the New Community Movement by mobilizing an army of university professors, engineers, and other science/technology-related experts in every sector as state agents, officially named the New Community Technology Service Group (Saemaŭl Kisul Pongsadan). This group, together with the Korean Federation of Science and Technology (Kwahak Kisul Tanch'e Ch'ongyŏnhaphoe), ran a comprehensive National Scientization Movement program (Yi Yŏng-mi 2009), overseeing a wide range of activities from publishing science and technology guidebooks and audio materials, to consulting and supervising rural communities, including the provision of science and technology information and culture classes to prepare housewives to become technologically more adepted modern citizens. University professors in particular, including retired academics, played a wide range of roles as the state's key emissaries, from assessing newly constructed New Community Movement factories in regional areas, to advising various communities on the state's polity of science and technology, to delivering practical skills training in agricultural machinery, and to public lecturing, as well as observing the whole process of both the New Community Movement and New Scientization Movement at the grassroots level (PS 1973a; PS 1977a).

The term "modern citizenship," according to Park, meant that all Koreans, through active participation in the New Community Movement, would become "good citizens" armed with a self-reliant posture, a strong spirit of anticommunism, and most of all, "the necessary attributes and characteristics to preserve the national sovereignty and independence of the Republic of Korea" (Chung Hee Park 1979, 138). In this respect, the state's interrelated concepts of "industrial warrior" and "industrial warrior consciousness" were inseparable from Park's idea of "modern citizenship," which, in practice, was strictly gendered and stratified, especially in the course of HCI implementation. Men, especially the newly emerged young HCI workers, for example, were required to actively serve state-led industrialization through their Factory New Community Movement, especially in the case of those designated as "special soldiers" (*t'ŭngnyebyŏng*) in lieu of military duty. The primary obligation of female workers, in contrast, lay in their traditional obligations under the paternalistic familial culture both in the home and the workplace.

This structurally gendered stratification of industrial workers not only shaped the central character of the Korean labor market in the 1970s and 1980s, and even in today's Korean labor market (Joonmo Cho and Jaeseong Lee, 2015), but also promoted the masculinity of the Korean labor movement. In fact, the masculinity of the Korean labor/union movement became a dominant characteristic of the rise of HCI workers as the leading force of the Korean workers' democratic union movement, with their labor militancy together with their elitist consciousness of what came to be socially perceived as a labor aristocracy vis-à-vis other ordinary workers. The masculinity of the Korean labor union movement, especially in terms of HCI workers' elitist consciousness, however, was initially unnoticed under their newly articulated collective identity as Goliat warriors in the course of the Great Workers' Struggle, which continued for almost four years, from July 1987 to May 1991. Ironically, Park's top-down Factory New Community Movement of the 1970s, in which all workers were required to participate in small-group discussions and quality control activities in order to improve efficiency, productivity, and cooperation, would reemerge in the Korean industrial community in the early 1990s. By then, the original "community circle-activity" of the Factory New Community Movement, based on a the activities of small units of participants, was promoted as a core strategy of the so-called Corporate Culture Movement (Kiŏp Munhwa Undong) led by the leading *chaebŏl* firms in the HCI sector as a means of their own company's neoliberal restructuring drive under the then newly inaugurated Kim Young-sam administration in 1993 (see chapter 3).

SCIENCE AND TECHNOLOGY MANPOWER TRAINING, 1970S

Under the inherently nationalistic concept of industrial warriors, the state strategically recruited young people, especially the brightest boys of poor families from rural and fishing areas, by offering them financial subsidies and other support for technological education and training. The driving factor behind this highly strategic recruitment was Korea's spectacular economic growth, achieving US$1 billion in export earnings in 1970, which ultimately confirmed President Park's political will to shift Korea's low-cost export-oriented industrialization to higher value-added heavy and chemical industrialization. Park also promulgated the development of industrial technology through the third Five-Year Technology Advancement Plan (1972–76), focused on research and development and the importation of new technology. This ambitious project was also embedded in the Park state's Five-Year Military Modernization Plan (1971–76) under the "self-reliant defense" (*chaju kukpang*) policy, which enabled Park to initiate a top-secret military light-weapons development program under the code name "Lightning Operation" (Pŏn'gae Saŏp) in November 1971.[6]

For this top-secret program, which became a pilot project for Korean defense industry development, Korea desperately needed not just any skilled workers but precision machinists with machining accuracy of at least 1/100th millimeter, which had tightened to 7/1000th millimeter by 1979. This was made the official required standard for every technical high school student or equivalent to obtain a class II license as a technician/craftsman, or *kinŭngsa* (Mun'gyobu 1980, 185–86). Given that Korea at that time had manufacturing technology that was only capable of precision to 1/10th millimeter (O 1995, 3), it is not difficult to imagine just how rigidly skills training programs were structured to obtain the class II license as a *kinŭngsa*. Moreover, as a consequence of the requirements of the tightened standard, the Park state ran into a critical shortage of skilled workers to meet the changed labor market demand, particularly from the then newly established and expanded manufacturing companies in the HCI sector.

Even earlier, during the second Five-Year Economic Development Plan (1967–71), the labor market had demanded an estimated 493,500 skilled workers, especially licensed technicians/craftsmen, or *kinŭngsa*. An additional 165,000 skilled workers were urgently required for that period, but technical high schools were only able to supply 68,700 additional skilled workers over that time; the remaining 96,300 had to come from other modes of vocational training (Kim Chin-gyun 1978, 413, 422, 433). In February 1970, the Economy and Science Council of the Ministry of Science and Technology (MST) reported that 62 percent of Korea's demand for new labor in 1969 was for primary school graduates, while 52 percent of job seekers were middle school graduates, but only 44 percent of middle-school-graduate job seekers were employed in that year (KKS 1970, 10).[7] The MST also reported that over 80 percent of new employees were nonskilled workers with less than a middle school education, and the major reasons for the critical shortage of skilled workers were the lack of an active education policy for skills training, poor vocational training, and the low wages for manufacturing workers compared to clerical workers, in addition to the deeply rooted "societal trend of looking down on industrial craftsmen/technicians [*kinŭng ch'ŏnsi p'ungjo*]" (KKS 1970, 1, 10, 16).

The number of higher-grade engineers (*sanggŭp kisa*) in Korea at the end of 1968, according to the MST, was a "mere 75," and thus their minimum wages needed to be guaranteed while they also needed to be provided with compensation through various funds and conditions (KKS 1970, 41). Accordingly, the MST recommended comprehensive education reform, including radical revision of the secondary school curriculum to include practical subjects, as well as revision of the curriculum of every level of schooling and all other educational institutions in order to resolve "the fundamental shortage of craftsmen amid abundant labor" (KKS 1970,1). The MST, in fact, issued projections for Korea's overall supply and demand for skilled workers, or what was officially termed "science and technology manpower," including scientists/engineers (*kwahak kisulcha*), field technicians (*hyŏnchang kisulcha*), and craftsmen/technicians (*kinŭngsa*), from 1972 to 1981.[8]

Table 1.1 shows the Korean developmental state's ten-year comprehensive projections for skilled labor supply and demand, reflecting the extent of its detailed manpower planning. In 1972, the first year of the third Five-Year Economic Development Plan (1972–76), Korea estimated a capacity to supply just 448,700 *kinŭnggsa* over the years 1973–81, but demand was projected to rapidly increase from an estimated total of 451,500 in 1972 to 1,991,800 *kinŭngsa* in 1981. This almost impossible gap between the supply-demand capacity called for an estimated supply of 1,789,900 new *kinŭngsa* over

TABLE 1.1. Supply of and demand for craftsmen by occupational sector, 1972–1981

	Heavy and chemical industry	Light industry	Agriculture and fisheries	Total
Demand 1972 → 1981	177,100 → 905,900	245,500 → 806,800	28,800 → 279,000	451,500 → 1,991,800
Required new supply	836,000	678,100	275,800	1,789,900
Current supply capacity[a]	187,900	102,300	158,500	448,700
Supply shortage	Δ648,100	Δ575,800	Δ117,300	Δ1,341,200[b]

Source: Based on Kim Chin-gyun (1978, 433).
[a] Current supply capacity is based on the standard student quotas of technical high schools and vocational high schools.
[b] Δ means "at least."

1973–81 (taking natural attrition into account), leaving an estimated shortfall of 1,341,200. In terms of occupational fields in the heavy and chemical industry, in 1972 Korea had the current capacity to supply just 187,900 new *kinŭngsa* over 1973–81, but the state projected that the demand for additional *kinŭngsa* in the HCI sector would increase from 177,100 in 1972 to 905,900 by 1981. This was without counting the shortage of *kinŭngsa* for light industry, for which the state estimated demand to increase from 245,500 in 1972 to 806,800 by 1981.

The expected shortage of industrial *kinŭngsa* was therefore potentially disastrous, with the state predicting that the number of employed in the heavy and chemical industries alone would increase by over a million by 1981 with the completion of HCI, which was the top priority of the fourth Five-Year Economic Development Plan (1977–81). Based on this estimate, the Korean developmental state aimed to supply 47 percent of the total required new *kinŭngsa* through the technical high school system, and the remaining 53 percent through the vocational training system (Kim Chin-gyun 1978, 433). Here *kinŭngsa*, according to the Ministry of Science and Technology, was defined as "craftsmen [who], through their formal school education, vocational training, and other practical experience for a certain period of time, could work in the specialized areas of production" (KKS 1970, 1). In order to increase the number of *kinŭngsa* on a large scale, especially for the construction and expansion of heavy and chemical industries focused on the new building of defense industries, the Park state implemented a radical education reform, the High School Equalization Policy (HSEP), officially unveiled in 1974.

The HSEP was designed to promote national unity, social cohesion, and discipline by abolishing high school entrance examinations, similar to the abolition of middle school entrance examinations under the Middle School Equalization Policy (MSEP, introduced in 1968). Instead of the compulsory entrance examination, in other words, all students, regardless of their individual academic record or ability or any other consideration, were allocated places through a district-wide lottery system (Sang-young Park 2010, 584–86), which in effect opened a new opportunity for all students to go to a local school in their own residential area—even, for the lucky few, to various highly prestigious middle and high schools. As a result, this seemingly draconian equalization policy effectively altered the traditionally elitist middle and high school tier system to the extent that the percentage of middle school students who received private tutoring plummeted to 18.6 percent in five major cities where the policy was implemented (Kim Yun-t'ae et al. 1978, 42). A national ban on illegal private tutoring, in particular, was given a legal basis in 1981 under the Chun Doo-hwan regime's draconian education reform and became even more rigid in 1984 under revised legislation (Sahoe Ch'onghwa Wiwŏnhoe 1986, 161). Although the decline of tutoring did not necessarily bring on the decline in the elitist school system, especially in the post-developmental state's neoliberal education reforms under the Kim Young-sam regime (1993–97), this education reform, focused on both the MSEP and HSEP, not only normalized education by ending excessive competition caused by "education fever" (*kyoyungyŏl*), especially among the affluent Korean middle class, but more notably broadened educational opportunities to the extent of creating the new social phenomenon of the "dragon from a stream" (*kaech'ŏne yong*). This typically Korean phrase commonly refers to a person who often succeeds in passing an entrance examination to a prestigious school, university, or company in spite of his/her modest background.

In this regard, the most visible phenomenon was the mass production of some two million skilled HCI workers. To implement this revolutionary change in Korean society, especially by increasing the number of technical high schools, students, teachers, skills instructors, and many other related technical facilities, among other resources throughout the country, the Park state swiftly introduced what it called the Improvement Plan for Korea's Technological Education System (1973) and later the Plan for the Priority

Promotion of Technical High Schools (1975), under the direct guidance of the President's Office (PS 1975). Park in fact introduced a new scholarship system for training in precision manufacturing skills as early as April 1972 (PS 1972). These comprehensive plans for a technology education system, along with the state's education subsidies and various practical benefits and welfare measures to expand the number of technical high schools and vocational institutes throughout the country, ultimately led to the establishment of elite technical high schools within the framework of what Andy Green characterized as a "developmental skills formation system," which he related to "citizen formation" rather than to "skills formation" (Andy Green 1999, 264).[9]

Concerning the development and maintenance of skills, especially to meet the international standard of what the Korean state defined as a science and technological labor force relevant to heavy and chemical industries, such as precision manufacture and some eighty-one other categories of industrial skills, the Park state introduced what was officially called the National Technical Qualification System (NTQS) in December 1973.[10] The state claimed that the introduction of the NTQS was aimed at improving the standard of technical high schools and the social standing of skilled workers in general. Based on this rationale, the existing qualification systems were radically "rearranged and integrated" into the newly introduced system, under which the qualifications for the *kinŭngsa* group were divided into four categories: (1) assistant craftsman; (2) class II; (3) class I; and (4) master craftsman. Within this structure, an assistant craftsman (*kinŭngsabo*) qualification, according to the heavy and chemical industrialization plan of 1973, "can be given to anyone who passes a skills test, regardless of his educational or vocational background," whereas the class II craftsman qualification was presented to "assistant craftsmen who have completed more than 2 years of vocational high school education, and to those with more than 1,800 hours of vocational training, providing that they pass a written test and a skills test" (Planning Office 1976, 136).[11]

In order to implement the National Technical Qualification Act, which took effect in July 1973, however, the Ministry of Science and Technology had to rely on the top-down push from O Wŏn-ch'ŏl, President Park's senior economic secretary, for dismantling, altering, or even suspending some twenty-six existing laws and enforcement ordinances spread across nine key government ministries. O's intervention was necessary because this radical restructuring generated some strong objections, even within the nine core ministries, including the Ministry of Education.[12] Yet the state made the

National Technical Qualification Test a compulsory requirement for all technical high school students proceeding beyond their second year, as well as for other trainees in vocational programs to obtain their class II skills license as a *kinŭngsa*.

MASS TRAINING VIA TECHNICAL HIGH SCHOOLS AND VOCATIONAL INSTRUCTION

The Park state relied on two main channels to train Korea's first generation of industrial skilled workers, the nation's industrial warriors: technical high schools and public or in-plant vocational training institutes (*chigŏp hullyŏnso* or *chikhun*). Although Korea's technical education system in the 1970s was complex and sometimes confusing,[13] the Park state, through the radical education reform known as the Technical High School Characterization Policy (Kongŏp Kodŭnghakyo T'ŭksŏnghwa Chŏngch'aek), restructured technical high schools into four specialized categories: (1) machinery; (2) experimental; (3) specialized; and (4) general.[14] This strategic development was also guided directly by Park's senior economic secretary, O Wŏn-ch'ŏl. To promote this plan for elite technical skills training within the high school education system, the state provided financial subsidies and technological support with a variety of scholarships and other incentives, including opportunities to continue study at university or undertake skills training abroad.[15] The recipient schools and students in turn were strictly bound to produce the outcomes that the state had assigned to them, and if any student failed to achieve their required tasks, whether academically or in their assigned skills training, among other nonacademic requirements, their financial subsidies and other privileges were withdrawn.

The machinery technical high schools (*kigye konggo*), for example, were assigned to produce craftsmen with the skills to achieve the machinery precision desperately needed in military weapons factories and other defense-related precision manufacturing firms of heavy machinery industries. In 1973, machinery-technical students were required to master detailed machining skills to at least 1/100th millimeter precision, which was increased to 7/1000th millimeter by 1979 as a requirement to pass the National Technical Qualification Test for a class II license. To bring students to the required level, the state provided modern equipment using loans from the Agency for International Development, initially provided to six selected technical high schools (Sŏngdong [Seoul], Pusan, Ch'ungnam, Chŏnbuk, Chŏnnam, and

Kŭmo-Kyŏngbuk) in 1973–74,[16] and gradually increased to nineteen machine technology high schools by 1979, with a total annual admission capacity of 13,920 new students.[17] The curriculum was focused on specialized subjects instead of the general theory-oriented study of the past, allocating a time ratio of 3:7 split between general subjects and specialized subjects. Students were required to undertake at least 2,400 hours of major skills training over the three-year course, at twenty hours per week, which comprised 800 hours of elementary skills training and 1,600 hours of precision-machinist skills practice and theory.

Experimental technical high schools (*sibŏm konggo*) were designated as such in March 1976, when Korea had run into a critical shortage of skilled workers to meet the demand from Korean companies operating in the Middle East.[18] Eleven technical high schools in Seoul as well as in cities in every province were selected by the state to train and dispatch skilled workers in machine assembly, metal plating, welding, electrical works, and pipe laying. An initial 1,500 students were selected for training mainly to fill the pressing demand from two large export firms, Hyundai Construction and Daelim Industrial Co., Ltd (O 2006, 402). For this extremely urgent task, the state selected those 1,500 students from third-year students with an outstanding level of learned theory and fundamental skills, not to mention mental and physical fitness, especially equipping them to obtain a class II *kinŭngsa* qualification by passing the National Technical Qualification Test before graduation. These students were put through eight hundred hours of skills training after school for six months, and the cost of this extra training, ₩241.66 million, was approved by the president (FEPS 1976a).

The Park state also introduced an industry-education co-op system (*san-hak hyŏptong*) under which any company that sought technicians had to provide a grant of ₩200,000 per student, while also providing the costs of various instruments and materials for their practical skills training.[19] In 1977, for example, Daelim Industrial Co., Ltd., and Hyundai Construction sponsored eleven experimental technical high schools with a total of ₩300 million, while also providing meals and accommodation, as well as ₩20,000 extra pay per month for the student-trainee's two months of work experience. With this industry sponsorship, a total of 2,140 students passed the National Technical Qualification Test in 1977, exceeding by 640, or 43 percent, the initial target of 1,500 students set by the state.[20] About 2,000 of them (93 percent) were sent to the Middle East, and in some cases students seem to have left for the Middle East even before graduation.

Specialized technical high schools (*t'uksŏnghwa konggo*), established in 1977, trained students in areas such as electronics, construction, steelmaking, chemical tools, and military machinery (PS 1975). The primary task of this category of schools was to produce craftsmen able to build and repair in-plant equipment. Regular technical high schools (*ilban konggo*), distinct from the above three categories, trained a wide range of craftsmen to meet general demand from shop floors, and about 25,000 students seem to have graduated in 1979 alone, given that about 25,000 students out of a total of 50,645 were graduates of the three above-mentioned categories of specialized technical high schools.[21] The elite machinery technical high schools received the most financial and technical support, receiving a total of ₩12.6 billion between 1973 and 1978, with a further ₩6.5 billion and ₩1 billion in 1979 and 1980, respectively (Mun'gyobu 1980, 202). The specialized technical high schools also received ₩4.8 billion, while the experimental technical high schools were allocated ₩3.6 billion in 1979. The state also provided a variety of scholarships to the students of these three categories of elite technical high schools. More than half the students in the machinery technical high schools, for example, received tuition waivers along with other privileges and financial incentives, including loans for living costs. Students at the specialized technical high schools received similar benefits, because they were managed in the same way as the machinery technical high schools.

The students of Kŭmo Technical High School (KTHS), which Park Chung Hee founded in 1973, received almost everything, from school fees to skills training costs, textbooks, uniforms, and other study-related materials, as well as meals and accommodation, and a guarantee of employment after graduation.[22] Candidates at KTHS were not required to sit for an academic entrance examination but were selected according to the guidelines set by the President's Office, which limited recommendations for selection only to students in the top 10 percent of their school. Candidates were initially recommended by their school principal, then by the education committee of the county or city, and finally by the governor of the relevant province (PS 1973b; PS 1977b). According to a report to the president dated June 9, 1973, 360 students were selected for the second class of 1974. Of these, 146 had graduated as the top student of their class, 209 were within the top 5 percent, and just 5 had been ranked in the top 5 to 10 percent range.[23]

The training system of Kŭmo Technical High School, particularly in relation to Park's strategy to produce an elite level of skilled manpower, is noteworthy because it was used as a template for the restructuring of Korea's technical high school model from 1977 onward, as well as for training what the Park state categorized as middle-grade technicians/craftsmen. Under the school's "three-*chŏng*" principles—*chŏngsŏng* (sincerity), *chŏngmil* (precision), and *chŏngjik* (honesty)—KTHS represented Park's vision of technical high school education and skills training, especially for Korea's industrial warriors armed with anticommunism, economic nationalism, solidarity, and above all, a sense of mission as the essence of the industrial warrior spirit or consciousness. As such, students and teachers at KTHS lived in a military-style dormitory, getting up at 6:00 a.m. and going to sleep at 11:00 p.m., and carrying out various tasks within and outside the school in addition to their schoolwork, such as military science (taught by active-duty soldiers), military drills, self-training in leadership skills, compulsory anticommunism education, and of course, hours of daily skills training.[24] To build and lead this perfectly militarized elite technological institute, Yi Tong-ho, a former two-star general in the marine corps, was hand-picked by Park Chung Hee as the school's principal in 1973,[25] and students were assigned to the Reserve Noncommissioned Officers' Training Corps a month before graduation.[26] Recalling his own experience of Kŭmo Technical High School and his views on the KTHS curriculum and other rules, one former student wrote:

> The reason I chose Kŭmo Technical High School, like many other students, was because it was regarded as the most prestigious school in Korea at that time. The second reason was that I could not even dream of going to university, although some students I knew had chosen KTHS mainly because President Park, our "sun" [*uri ŭi t'aeyang*] had built it. It was an extremely rigid life with roll call every morning and evening like the military ... and then we were automatically recruited into the army RNOTC a month before graduation.[27]

Classified as reserve noncommissioned officers in the military, KTHS graduates had a mandatory duty to complete a five-year term instead of the normal three-year term of military service, just as graduates of other technical high schools had to serve for five years as special soldiers when employed in a defense company. In spite of this rigid requirement, the vast majority of KTHS students, like those of other elite technical high schools, were eager to excel in their studies and skills training, among other mental and physical tasks. One obvious reason was the state's subsidies for their education, which were then exceptional, especially when Korea's per capita GNP was just US$556 in 1974. Hence entry to those elite technical high schools was extremely competitive, especially among the high-performing boys from poor rural areas.[28] The successful students often became the heroes of their families and their villages, often referred to as the "dragons from streams." One former student from the remote farming village of T'aebaek, in Kangwŏn Province, proudly told the author in his interview: "As the eldest son of a family with six children, I was the pride and hero of my family and village because I was the only "dragon from a stream" who succeeded in being admitted to a prestigious technical high school at that time. I never missed scoring the top or second of the entire school because I was happy just studying, although my nostrils were charred under a kerosene lamp."[29]

Another interviewee wrote that the Park state's epithets "flag-bearers of the modernization of the fatherland" (*choguk kŭndaehwa ŭi kisu*) and "industrial warriors" (*sanŏp chŏnsa*, also *sanŏp yŏkkun*) provided his own aspirational "bursting dream." He wrote: "I became a skilled worker with my bursting dream to become a 'flag-bearer of the modernization of the fatherland' and an 'industrial warrior,' but my dream turned into a bubble [*mulgŏp'um*] after President Park's death" (author interview, Ch'angwŏn, April 27, 2012).

By 1979, there were 19 machinery technical high schools, 12 specialized technical high schools, 11 experimental technical high schools, and 55 regular technical high schools (Kim Yun-t'ae 2002, 109), while the total number of technical high schools increased from 72 in 1975 to 197 in 1980 (Pak Hyŏn-jung 2003, 43). A total of 391,870 technical high school graduates were produced during the ten years of Korea's third and fourth Five-Year Economic Development Plans (1972–81). As table 1.2 shows, this number nearly doubled to 772,256 over the next six years, from 1982 to 1987, with an average of over 60,000 technical high school graduates produced annually over that period. Amazingly, about 85 percent of them, in the case of 1979, obtained a class II licence as *kinŭngsa* by passing the state-authorized National Technical Qualification Test.[30]

Female students, however, were strategically discouraged or even excluded from entering the aforementioned specialized technical high schools according to the state's HCI policy, except for training in skills related to electronics and other light industries. Table 1.2 shows that the number of female graduates from 1972 to 1987 amounted to just 9,069, or 1.2 percent of the

TABLE 1.2. Number of graduates, technical high schools, 1969–1987

Year	Number of graduates	Number of female graduates
1969	13,672	221
1970	14,035	204
1971	18,138	141
1972	20,195	198
1973	24,608	95
1974	27,349	136
1975	29,414	221
1976	33,152	233
1977	42,245	452
1978	49,807	1,820
1979	50,645	403
1980	55,308	1,928
1981	59,147	390
1982	62,645	239
1983	63,957	863
1984	63,880	277
1985	63,613	279
1986	63,606	1,124
1987	62,685	411

Source: Data from Mun'gyobu (1999).

total graduates. Hence, they were effectively excluded from the HCI sector.[31] As has been common in many East Asian countries, including Japan, the gendered division of labor was most notable in Korea's HCI program, except for electronics (Kim Ch'un-su 2003).

Vocational Training

Just as all technical high schools were radically restructured to specialize, each in its own category of skills training and technical education, the state's reform of the vocational training system for the upgrading of workers' skills was equally comprehensive and radical. Historically, at the end of the first Five-Year Economic Development Plan in 1966, Korea had faced the simultaneous problems of a shortage of industrial skilled workers on the one hand and an excess supply of unskilled youth on the other. The introduction of the Vocational Training Act in January 1967 had been designed to deal with Korea's skilled labor supply problem by establishing scores of vocational training institutes in a short period of time, while also providing subsidies to existing vocational institutes in three modes: public training, including government agencies and military-provided skills training; programs at recognized nonprofit organizations and vocational institutes; and in-plant training involving mostly large companies.

These modes of training initially concentrated on unemployed youth who held either a general high school or middle school graduate certificate—or even less education—turning them into the skilled labor required for export industries such as construction and shipbuilding, both abroad, especially in the Middle East, and in Korea. In addition, military facilities had been mobilized to train young people in skills, especially those who were scheduled to be discharged from military service (FEPS 1976a), while local government agencies had focused on short-term training courses with an emphasis on handicrafts or indigenous products in order to increase exports, as well as raise the incomes of farming families. The Vocational Training Act, in effect, thus generated a threefold increase in the number of trainees in public training institutes within four years, from 10,738 in 1967 to 30,558 in 1970. The subsequent full-scale expansion of public training in the early 1970s was supported initially by international grants, credit, and loans from the Asian Development Bank and the International Bank for Reconstruction and Development, as well as from several advanced countries, including Japan and Germany.[32]

The state's subsidy policy of the 1960s for the various modes of vocational training, however, was replaced with a regulatory policy in 1972, the year Park Chung Hee declared his authoritarian Yusin Reform. Without the subsidy, the number of in-plant trainees plummeted to 10,800, which drove the state to promulgate the Vocational Training Special Measure Act in 1974. Under this law, private companies with over five hundred employees in key industries, such as manufacturing, mining, construction, and electronics, among others, were required to train new workers up to at least 15 percent of their total workforce. Any firm that failed to conduct an in-plant training program was punishable under the Yusin Emergency Act. In spite of significant success in some areas, however, the law was replaced in 1976 by the

Vocational Training Basic Act, in response mainly to stiff opposition from large *chaebŏl* firms in the heavy and chemical sector, especially in the wake of the first oil shock (1973–74). The new law lowered the threshold for private companies required to provide in-plant training from those with five hundred or more employees to those with three hundred or more employees.

These companies now had to provide in-plant training for new workers to at least 10 percent of their total employees, down from the earlier 15 percent. Firms that failed to comply were fined by way of a levy scheme. Under this policy, the number of trainees in in-plant training programs grew from 177,350 during the third Five-Year Economic Development Plan (1972–76) to 337,388 during the fourth Five-Year Economic Development Plan (1977–81). The effectiveness of the policy, however, drastically weakened under the new general-turned-president, Chun Doo-hwan (1980–87).

As table 1.3 shows, more than half a million newly employed industrial workers received in-plant training between 1972 and 1981, and over 800,000 persons undertook vocational training during the same period. Between 1972 and 1987, the year Korea began to democratize, nearly two million young people received skills training either by graduating from technical high schools (a total of 772,256 persons) or by completing vocational training or in-plant training (1,081,626 persons by 1986). In combination, they supplied a massive young skilled workforce, mostly with a class II license, either as craftsman/technician (*kinŭngsa*) or as assistant craftsman/ technician (*kinŭngsabo*).[33] This new skilled workforce was mostly mobilized en masse as HCI workers to the centers of Korea's heavy and defense manufacturing industry, the southern coastal cities of Ulsan, Masan, and Ch'angwŏn, which constituted the newly constructed or expanded industrial belt that ultimately led Korea's economic miracle of the 1970s.

For this spectacular all-out march toward Korea's economic miracle, tens of thousands of newly emerged HCI workers—the Korean state's industrial warriors—were deployed to the Middle East, where the majority of them thrived in their work, not just in achieving their collective mission for Korea's export-led Middle East boom, but more importantly for securing and consolidating their own future in Korea's then-burgeoning HCI sector. The following extract from a letter sent from Saudi Arabia on January 3, 1977, may shed some light on the collective consciousness of the industrial warriors, who, as newly employed skilled laborers in private companies, were determined to uphold their country's "honor . . . with a sense of mission

TABLE 1.3. Skilled labor (craftsmen) training through vocational training institutes

Institution type	2nd FYEDP* (1967–71)	3rd FYEDP (1972–76)	4th FYEDP (1977–81)	5th FYEDP (1982–86)	6th FYEDP (1987–91)	Total
Public	36,317	81,294	120,117	121,044	113,802	472,574
In-plant	48,225	177,350	337,388	114,773	116,389	794,125
Authorized training institutes	14,321	54,092	38,234	37,334	83,084	227,065
Total	98,863	312,736	495,739	273,151	313,275	1,493,764

Source: Yi Sŏng-Ch'ŏl (1994), 165; data from Nodongbu (1992).
*FYEDP = Five-Year Economic Development Plan

and pride," just as they had a burning desire to "take charge of our homeland's modernization as skilled workers." The letter states:

> Today we began work for the first time in our lives as a first step in society.... We understand well that there must be plenty of difference from the level of knowledge or personality of the skilled workers who are already here.... Even so, we will consistently discipline ourselves with strong will and belief no matter what difficulties and sufferings we might encounter ... till we return to our country....
>
> Shouldering our country's honor and with a sense of mission and pride..., we will end this letter by pledging to become competent skilled workers as quickly as possible so that we become the pillar to take charge of our homeland's modernization as skilled workers.... The first advance party, all thirteen members.[34] (Mun'gyobu 1977, 125)

These young men, like many other graduates of experimental technical high schools who were sent to the Middle East, were mostly eighteen or nineteen at that time, born in either 1958 or 1959. Considering that the above letter was signed on January 3, 1977, they would have had to leave for Saudi Arabia before their graduation ceremony, which was normally held in February. In praising these budding HCI workers' pioneering spirit and their collective contribution, Chŏng Chu-yŏng (Chung Ju-yung), founding chairman of the Hyundai Group, openly expressed that these young industrial warriors "remedied ... some shortcomings of every entrepreneur in our country, as well as those of the mainstay technicians and managers" (cited in Mun'gyobu 1977, 127). Chŏng attributed his firm's spectacular success in winning the major contract to build the harbor in the Persian Gulf in 1976 — worth $930 million, equivalent to ₩460 billion, or about 50 percent of Korea's national budget that year — to the HCI workers' collective contribution (Chŏng Chu-yŏng 1998, 208). Nearly ninety thousand Korean workers with various levels of skill and other technical know-how formed an overseas-based industrial army at the peak of the Middle East boom in the late 1970s (Kirk 1994, 86).

CONCLUSION

Ultimately, the mass production of HCI workers, primarily led by the Park state as the state's industrial warriors with their collective consciousness was spectacularly successful for Korea's heavy and chemical industrialization. Korea's manufacturing and mining sectors alone averaged more than 30 percent annual growth in exports throughout the 1970s, while many newly developed and expanded industrial cities emerged, including Ulsan, Masan, and Ch'angwŏn, among other neighboring cities in the southeastern coastal area. What made the Korean developmental state's mass production of skilled HCI workers so effective was that this highly centralized nation-building project was carried out strictly under subsidies-as-contracts, or a reciprocal social contract. The reciprocal social contract worked well, especially for the highly self-motivated and conservative prospective HCI workers, who were eager to seize this unprecedented educational opportunity not only for their country's modernization but also for their own goal of a better life with a secure job and better upward social mobility. Hence, these strategically selected young people not only willingly committed themselves to becoming the "flag-bearers of modernization of the fatherland" as their own "bursting dream," but also dutifully complied with their collective tasks to the extent of generating Korea's economic miracle during the 1970s and even until 1986, when Korea recorded a trade surplus for the first time, totaling US$4.2 billion.

The paradox of Park's creation of industrial warriors, however, was that as much as Korea under Park benefited from the cumulative service of these young skilled workers in their country's top-down economic modernization, their shared goals, especially for their own survival and well-being, were a far greater priority to them than their reciprocal social contract with the state. For this reason, the industrial warriors' collective discontent with the draconian new labor laws under the Chun Doo-hwan regime ultimately exploded, resulting in the seismic eruption of the Great Workers' Struggle.

CHAPTER 2

From Industrial Warriors to Goliat Warriors

A New Labor Militancy

THE Chun Doo-hwan regime's new labor policies, initially issued even before Chun's rise to the presidency in August 1980, were "the most restrictive and oppressive in South Korean history" (Hart-Landsberg 1993, 219).[1] After seizing power illegitimately through two military coups—on December 12, 1979, shortly after Park Chung Hee's assassination on October 26, and again on May 17, 1980, which led to what became known as the Kwangju Uprising in the southwestern city of Kwangju on May 18—the Chun regime brutally suppressed any further nationwide protests and was especially harsh on the industrial workers' democratic union movement. Chun worried about the eruption of further massive protests, led in particular by industrial workers, akin to the so-called Pu-Ma democratic protests in the southeastern industrial cities of Pusan and Masan, which had brought down Park Chung Hee. As a result, hundreds of union leaders and activists were sent to prison or military "purification camps" to undertake forced labor, while unionization itself became illegal at workplaces with fewer than thirty employees. The new laws introduced a string of new draconian measures, including a measure to restrict so-called third-party involvement in labor activity. This new labor law was designed to destroy the effectiveness of unions as well as to sever union ties to radical university students and intellectuals, and to progressive church groups behind the popular *minjung* (people's) democracy movement.²

Under Chun's draconian new labor laws, however, HCI manufacturing firms in the southeast, especially the newly developed industrial cities, including Ulsan, Masan, and Ch'angwŏn, grew rapidly, with a massive increase in the number of HCI workers, mostly employed for the first time. Employment in the manufacturing firms in Ulsan, Masan, and Ch'angwŏn, in particular, grew extensively during the 1980s, jumping by 61 percent from 1981 to 1986, "almost double the national rate of 34 percent and faster than any other large or medium-sized city" (Markusen and Park 1993, 160). The remarkable growth in employment in these three major industrial cities inevitably influenced the increase in wages in the manufacturing area, which boasted a stable average annual increase of 8.9 percent during the four years from 1983 to 1986. From 1987 to 1990, the average annual wage increase jumped to 16.4 percent, recording annual increases of 10.1 percent, 15.5 percent, 21.1 percent, and 18.8 percent during this four-year period.³ The extraordinary increases in wages during this period, however, were not entirely due to the rise in productivity. Equally or perhaps more significantly, the newly elected president, Roh Tae-woo, another army general turned politician as Chun's confidant, following his declaration of Korea's democratization on June 29, 1987, could not suppress the then newly established democratic union movement as the core of the nationwide Great Workers' Struggle. Hence, the astonishing increase in both employment and workers' wages, especially in the three major industrial cities, directly reflected the massive increase in the then newly emerged democratic union movement with its newly adopted labor militancy, while the equally massive growth in HCI firms' profits from exports resulted in Korea's economic boom, which generated unprecedented national account surpluses of $46.1 billion in 1986, $98.6 billion in 1987, 141.7 billion in 1988, and $50.6 billion in 1989 (Dae-Oup Chang 2002, 19).

The overwhelming rebirth of labor activism, especially around mid-1985, became inseparable from the labor union movements promoted by radical students-turned-workers and other activist intellectuals to inculcate a *minjung* consciousness in the workers. The nationwide *minjung* movement in fact convinced even the hitherto conservative rank-and-file HCI workers, or industrial warriors, to give vent to their collective discontent with workplace despotism. This discontent essentially led to the rise of a new labor militancy among HCI workers less than a week after the declaration of political democratization on June 29, 1987. In the process, the HCI workers completely ignored their hitherto unbroken social contract with the state by instigating the Great Workers' Struggle, which, with their newly formed partnership with radical students and *minjung* intellectuals, turned into a solidarity movement of the Korean working class for almost four years, until May 1991.

This chapter explores the factors behind the sudden rise of the HCI workers' new labor militancy, especially by tracing the formation of HCI workers' communities in newly developed industrial cities in Korea's southeastern coastal area. It focuses on the rise of the HCI workers' democratic labor union movement in the pre-1987 period prior to the Great Workers' Struggle, while also answering several key questions: What was distinctive about the three industrial cities of Ulsan, Masan, and Ch'angwŏn, especially in terms of shaping the collective attitude and consciousness of HCI workers in their own residential communities? How were the HCI workers different from other workers, differentiating themselves later as militant Goliat warriors but representing the Korean workers as a whole? What motivated them to form a partnership with radical intellectuals, especially in the solidarity movement of the Korean working class in the second phase of the Great Workers' Struggle? And how did the difference in their ideology and goals, among other factors, affect the outcome of this partnership?

THE RISE OF INDUSTRIAL CITIES AND HCI WORKERS' COMMUNITIES

The new industrial cities were distinctive in that they generated what a Korean sociologist has described as "the blind formation of workers' residential communities" (Kim Chun 2005, 81–93) around specific *chaebŏl* firms, drawing tens of thousands of industrial skilled and semiskilled workers from all over the country, mostly newly emerged industrial warriors in the HCI sector. As new migrant workers, whether single or married with young families, they initially settled into densely populated bachelors' dormitories or in rented rooms for months or even years. And then they sought company housing (*sat'aek*), mostly in large apartment complexes with little or no guarantee of privacy but with frequent interaction with other worker-occupants, which facilitated the formation of an HCI workers' community.

Through frequent interaction, both at the workplace and their residential community, they developed typically Korean-style social ties and labor solidarity, especially by building a blue-collar workers' collective attitude or consciousness, as well as their own working-class community culture. This new blue-collar workers' collective attitude and community culture made what became the most distinctive characteristic of Ulsan as the largest industrial city of Korea's heavy industry. The Hyundai workers' two apartment complexes, Ojwabul (for bachelors) and Man Sedae (Ten Thousand Households), in particular, morphed into what became known as the "freedom community" (*haebang kongdongch'e*), especially during the Great Workers' Struggle, symbolizing the solidarity of not only Hyundai workers but also the Korean workers as a whole in their collective struggle for a democratic unionization movement free from their authoritarian company's interference.

Ulsan and Hyundai Workers

Ulsan was originally elevated to a city from a small town (*ŭp*) in 1962, as a representational investment included in the Park state's first Five-Year Economic Development Plan (1962–66). From the establishment of a petrochemical industry, Ulsan grew rapidly after the construction of Hyundai Motor Company in 1967, followed by Hyundai Heavy Industries in 1975, which quickly became the biggest car manufacturer and shipbuilder in Korea. The Hyundai Group, with thirteen other firms and thirty-seven subsidiaries by the end of 1988, became the largest conglomerate in Korea (Yi Sang-ch'ŏl 1991, 100). Understandably, a large proportion of the newly arriving industrial warriors found employment in Ulsan, where the number of workers in secondary industries, including manufacturing, grew by a multiple of 77.5, from 1,300 in 1962 to 100,800 in 1989, while Ulsan's population increased by a massive 618 percent, from 85,000 to 610,000. Of the 100,800 manufacturing workers in Ulsan in 1989, about 70,000 were employed by Hyundai firms, mostly by Hyundai Motor and Hyundai Heavy Industries (HHI; about 30,000 and 22,000 workers respectively), which together provided one-third of the government's tax revenue raised in Ulsan (Han'guk Kidokkyo Sahoe Munje Yŏn'guwŏn 1989, 407–22).

The heavy manufacturing district in Ulsan was divided into Hyundai Motor's automobile industrial park in the central district, and HHI's shipbuilding industrial park in the eastern district, which was often called Hyundai Dynasty or Hyundai City Shipbuilding District, where HHI constructed not only company housing complexes but also many public facilities, such as schools, hospitals, department stores, and shopping centers, as well as various recreational amenities. From the end of 1972 to 1986, for example, 9,991 company housing units were either rented out (4,433) or sold to Hyundai workers (5,558), predominantly HHI shipbuilding workers (Kim Chun 2005, 82). HHI's Ilsan apartment complex, Man Sedae, accommodated about four thousand households in more than one hundred apartment blocks by 1986. Similarly, HHI's three dormitories, Ojwabul, Samjŏngwan, and Kwakchŏngwan, accommodated some 7,436 Hyundai workers in the mid-1980s (Kim Chun 2005, 82).

As a result of this systematic and massive construction of workers' housing complexes, which were managed under the company management's strict control in a method somewhat similar to the factory floors, the Hyundai Group was known for its military-style labor control. Of all the Hyundai companies, Hyundai Heavy Industries was the harshest, so much so that the former president of the HHI Union, Yi Kab-yong, recalled that they worked like "dogs" and were treated like "animals" or "prisoners," censured even for the length of their hair by their security guard (author interview, April 27, 2012). Yet there was no labor struggle in Ulsan during the 1970s, except for the Hyundai shipbuilding workers' strike in 1974, until the eruption of the Great Workers' Struggle in July 1987. This may well explain just how conservative the HCI workers were—to the extent of gaining a reputation as a docile group during Korea's heavy and chemical industrialization.

Their conservatism or docility, especially in the case of the shipbuilding workers (95 percent of them male), seems to have led HHI workers to amass a longer average continuous work record of 8.4 years from 1983 to 1990, according to one PhD dissertation (Yi Sang-ch'ŏl 1991, 118–19), compared to Hyundai Motor workers, who averaged 4.5 years during the same period. The HHI shipbuilding workers were also significantly older and had less formal education than the workers at Hyundai Motor. In 1989, for example, over three-quarters of Hyundai Motor workers were under thirty, with one-quarter under twenty-five, and 78 percent of this entire workforce had graduated from high school. In contrast, HHI shipbuilding workers averaged thirty-four years of age in 1989, many with less than a high school education (42 percent). In some cases, especially factory-floor areas, according to Ch'oe Kil-sŏn, CEO of HHI, they barely had a primary school education or even less, and some were unable to write their own names. One reason for this was that workers at the shipyard did not need a high school education as much as physical strength and the required skills to work under harsh conditions (author interview, November 19, 2012). In contrast, the heavy industry workers of the steel-making company POSCO (formerly Pohang Iron and Steel), according to Yun Sŏk-man, former CEO of POSCO Engineering and Construction, were all high school graduates, as required by the company's rules (author interview, November 19, 2012).[4]

Masan, Ch'angwŏn, and HCI Workers of the Ch'angwŏn Industrial Park

In stark contrast to Ulsan, the twin cities of Masan and Ch'angwŏn grew into a newly expanded (in the case of Masan) or constructed industrial city from a traditional rural district, each with its own distinctive industrial character and features. Masan, a medium-size port city since 1949, for example, was dramatically developed when, in 1973, the Masan Free Export Zone (MFEZ) began to operate, with a 90,000 or 43.8 percent increase in the city's population that year (Yi Sang-ch'ŏl 1991, 143). The inhabitants of Masan consisted of residents who had lived there since the pre-1970s and migrants who had come as a result of Korea's industrialization. Many local entrepreneurs ran their firms as subcontractors to large firms in the Masan area, especially in the MFEZ, where a total of 115 foreign-invested firms, mainly from Japan, operated in 1973, reaching a peak under the radically eased regulations and restrictions of the Foreign Capital Inducement Law (initially promulgated on August 3, 1966, and amended twice, in March 1973 and December 1983). Most of the firms in the MFEZ, other than several large firms, were small and medium-size subcontractors of foreign firms, with an average of 330 workers. Unlike Ulsan, Masan had no large-scale workers' housing complexes, even though some 23,000 industrial workers were employed in seventy manufacturing firms within the MFEZ by the end of 1989.

Historically, Masan was famous for its democratic protests of March 15, 1960, which led to the April 19 Revolution led by university students, and the Pusan-Masan or Pu-Ma democratic protests in October 1979, which ultimately brought on Park Chung Hee's demise. Some researchers argue that the Pu-Ma democratic protests exploded mainly because of an economic slump in the MFEZ and the Ch'angwŏn Industrial Park (CIP) in 1979, which hit those industrial workers much harder than workers in any other area in Korea (Yu Chong-yŏng 1983). This argument is convincing largely because in Masan, eleven firms in the MFEZ shut down in August 1979, while a further forty-six firms had plans to shift to Southeast Asia. The average operating capacity of established firms in Masan's twin city, Ch'angwŏn, also fell to less than 30 percent in the CIP alone, and thus the economic downturn severely affected HCI workers in the Masan-Ch'angwŏn area.

Ch'angwŏn was a small farming town with a population of about 10,000 until September 1973, when Park Chung Hee ordered its development based on his ambition to build the largest defense industrial park in the world. Consequently, from 1973 to 1989, a total of 270 manufacturing firms, including 19 defense firms, moved to the CIP, employing 81,000 workers. About 34,000 of these were employed in defense firms, of whom a large number were special soldiers. Naturally, they were most vulnerable to the tyranny of their authoritarian management. The core difference between workers in the CIP, MFEZ, and many other light industrial cities in Korea, however, was that the majority of male HCI workers in the CIP had a relatively high formal education, whereas Masan's 74 percent female workers, who were predominantly employed in small and medium-size enterprises in the MFEZ similar to other light industry workers, had limited skills and relatively low levels of formal education (Yi Sang-ch'ŏl 1991, 199 and 200).

In today's Korea it is hard to imagine that anyone would think Park Chung Hee genuinely feared another war to the extent of requiring the city plan for Ch'angwŏn to be configured as a military fortress. In particular, the plan required the main street to be able to be converted into an emergency landing strip if war should erupt (author interview with O Wŏn-ch'ŏl, June 18, 2010). Ironically, twenty-eight trade unions operated in various firms within the CIP during the pre-1987 period. Furthermore, the HCI workers in Ch'angwŏn-Masan and neighboring areas, who were predominantly employees of small and medium-size enterprises (SMEs), turned into extremely militant unionists, who had developed their political consciousness, especially in regard to their own labor rights, through so-called small club (*somoim*) activities from late 1986. In developing their political awareness related to labor rights, they benefited particularly from the Catholic Women's Association with its affiliated labor counsel center led by religious leaders and intellectuals who were predominantly former university student activists.[5]

In this regard, the consciousness-strengthening activities of HCI workers in Ch'angwŏn, with the support of the Catholic Women's Association's labor counsel center, were similar to those of Hyundai workers in Ulsan, supported by the Ulsan Council of Social Missionary Action (Ulsan Sahoe Sŏn'gyo Silch'ŏn Hyŏbŭihoe) and its labor counsel center. According to

Kwŏn Yong-mok, a charismatic leader of the Great Workers' Struggle, that outside support marked a turning point in the Korean labor union movement in July 1987, as the council helped in various ways in shaping public opinion, holding talks and providing many different labor services during the Great Workers' Struggle, when numerous democratic trade unions were being formed throughout the country (Kwon Yong-mok 1988, 308). To account for the radically changed collective attitude of the HCI workers, from conservative industrial warriors to a radical force of what became known as Goliat warriors, in the course of the Great Workers' Struggle, let us consider a brief overview of the contemporary history of the Korean union movement.

LABOR UNION MOVEMENTS, 1945–1987

The history of Korean labor union movements has been overshadowed by their suppression by the state since the leftist union, Chŏnp'yŏng (Chosŏn Nodong Chohap Chŏn'guk P'yŏngŭihoe; National Council of Korean Labor Unions), was outlawed by the American Military Government in Korea (1945–48). Any remnants of Chŏnp'yŏng were eliminated during the Korean War, as the Syngman Rhee regime (1948–60) transformed the rightist union, the Federation of Korean Trade Unions (FKTU; Taehan Noch'ŏng), into a political device for consolidating Rhee's power base, especially after 1955 when the FKTU was officially assimilated into the ruling Liberal Party as its auxiliary arm under the pretext of anticommunism and national security.[6] A new union, Han'guk Noch'ong (Han'guk Nodong Chohap Ch'ong Yŏnmaeng, with the same acronym, FKTU), was created in 1961 by the military junta led by then Major General Park Chung Hee, but its role as a pro-state and pro-company union, or *ŏyongnojo*, was dramatically strengthened under the Yusin Reform, which Park declared in October 1972. Park's draconian labor reform of 1973–74, in particular, was tailor-made to suit the Park state's implementation of the HCI program (unveiled on January 12, 1973).

In 1980, the labor laws were changed again by Chun Doo-hwan, becoming the most repressive in South Korean history in four major respects: 1) they changed union structures from industry-level to enterprise-based; 2) they made it vastly more difficult to set up a union by increasing the required number of endorsements from two to thirty or more persons or one-fifth of the total number of workers in a firm; 3) they empowered the relevant government authorities to dissolve any union, or to order it to reelect its board members, among other changes; and 4) they banned all industrial strikes in government and public organizations and defense industries (Yi Wŏn-bo 2005). Yet the democratic labor union movement of the 1970s continued under the leadership of young female workers in light manufacturing industries, in alliance with university students following the self-immolation of Chŏn T'ae-il, a garment worker at the P'yŏnghwa market, on November 13, 1970 (Cho Yŏng-rae 2001), whose death triggered the rise of what became known as the "worker-student alliance" (*no-hak yŏndae*).

The worker-student alliance of the 1970s and 1980s involved two key groups in addition to workers and university students: intellectuals and church organizations, especially the Urban Industrial Mission, the Young Catholic Workers' Organization (Jeunesse Ouvrière Chrétienne), and the Christian Academy. These groups were crucial in popularizing union activities, mainly through student-led small-group activities (*sogurup*) in light industries, which aimed to cultivate and strengthen political consciousness, especially as a working class, through various forms of informal "study, discussions and recreational activities" (Koo 2001, 106). Following the Kwangju Uprising of May 18, 1980, during which about two hundred workers, students, and civilians were massacred,[7] the democratic labor union movement of the 1970s dramatically changed into a radical working-class struggle as part of the *minjung* democracy movement of the 1980s. In fact, the worker-student alliance became instrumental not only in raising political and class consciousness among the Korean workers, but also in developing their *minjung* solidarity with radical student activists, or *undongkwŏn*,[8] migrating into factories as "disguised workers" (*wijang ch'wiŏpcha*) or students-turned-workers (*hakch'ul*), especially in the mid-1980s.

This phenomenal development, however, was mainly limited to female-dominated light industries in the Seoul-Kyŏngin area.[9] The male skilled workers in the southeastern region, who were predominantly HCI industrial warriors, in contrast, were not on the radar of the Seoul-Kyŏngin-based *hakch'ul* and other radical intellectual activists. In this regard, the three major industrial strikes that erupted between April and June 1985 show most concretely how labor activism led by the *hakch'ul* in the female-dominated light industries in the Seoul-Kyŏngin area, has been placed at the center of Korea's pre-1987 labor history, whereas the industrial strikes in male-dominated heavy industries in the southeast region have been overlooked. The three major industrial strikes of 1985 included the Daewoo autoworkers' strike at Pup'yŏng plant near Seoul on April 22–23; the T'ongil Corporation workers' strike at the Ch'angwŏn Industrial Park (CIP), Ch'angwŏn, on April 22–25; and the solidarity strike at the Kuro Industrial Park, also near Seoul, on June 22. Of these, the Daewoo autoworkers' strike and the Kuro Industrial Park solidarity strike were widely publicized, whereas the T'ongil workers' strike in Ch'angwŏn was overlooked until the 2000s.[10]

An Emerging New Labor Militancy

In spite of this oddity, the T'ongil workers' strike of April 1985 foreshadowed an emerging new militancy in the Korean labor movement on two main grounds. The first was the significance of the T'ongil workers' strike at the CIP, where a total of 81,000 predominantly male HCI industrial warriors were employed. Of these, about 34,000 were employees of defense firms, including a large number of special soldiers, who were particularly vulnerable to their company's authoritarian management and labor exploitation. Their collective sense of relative deprivation, therefore, ultimately brought them to detonate the powder keg of their long-suppressed grievances, especially through their all-out militant industrial protest.

The industrial strike at T'ongil Corporation in April 1985, the third-largest firm in the CIP, with 2,800 production workers in four separate factories had an explosive effect, not only by stirring up many other discontented HCI industrial warriors in the CIP but also by generating region-based solidarity struggles in other neighbouring industrial cities, especially Ulsan, Kŏje, and Kyungju. The T'ongil workers' strike, like the Daewoo Auto strike on the same day, was strategically planned by Mun Sŏng-hyŏn, one of the first generation of students-turned-workers (*hakch'ul*) in the 1970s, and his team of hard-core members of the T'ongil Corporation Union. As founding members of Mun's "small-club," Ch'adolhoe (White Pebble), Mun and his team members had voluntarily transferred to Ch'angwŏn from Seoul in 1983 with the specific aim of "saving" their union, which was embroiled in their initial company's merger with T'ongil Corporation.

Mun and his team, now members of the T'ongil union, initially demanded wage increases, then quickly turned their focus to protesting the military-style working conditions, especially "unjustified disciplinary action" against Mun, who was under threat of being dismissed as a "resident spy" (interview with Mun, November 12, 2012). Through their militant strike, the T'ongil workers not only won their battle with management, which accepted the workers' demands entirely, including the withdrawal of disciplinary action against Mun and other union executives, but also formed their own democratic union, replacing the old pro-state, company-controlled ŏyong union. Not surprisingly, Mun was elected as the new leader of the revamped union. This was the first case of a union victory achieved through the systematic application of a new labor militancy in the Masan-Ch'angwŏn area since Korea was liberated from Japanese colonization in 1945.

The T'ongil workers' strike of April 1985 foreshadowed an emerging new labor militancy in the Korean labor movement, as it was the first industrial strike to take place in Korea's highly centralized defense industry (*pangsan ŏp*). In fact, unions had been banned in the defense industry. As one study noted (Yi Sang-ch'ŏl 1991, 184), the effect of the T'ongil workers' strike, especially on worker solidarity with an uncompromising new labor militancy under democratically elected leadership, was immediate in popularizing the T'ongil workers' model of new labor militancy in the southeastern industrial region as the preferred union strategy of "strike first, negotiate later." Given that this new labor militancy became the norm among Korean workers' newly founded democratic unions across the country after 1987, the T'ongil workers' strike of April 1985 was nothing less than a prelude to the Great Workers' Struggle, which was similar but far more effective in terms of mobilizing a massive force of HCI industrial warriors led by the legendary Hyundai industrial warriors in Ulsan, compared to the Daewoo Auto strike and the Kuro solidarity strike, far from Ulsan, the hub of the Great Workers' Struggle. The T'ongil workers' sit-down strike for twenty-two days, from August 7 to 28, 1987, in fact, epitomized the new mode of labor militancy, especially of HCI industrial warriors of SMEs in the Masan-Ch'angwŏn area, even though this renowned solidarity struggle was overshadowed by the massive scale of the Hyundai industrial warriors' labor militancy, armed with various heavy machine tools and other powerful equipment, not to mention their unparalleled mobilization. This was how the Hyundai industrial warriors dramatically emerged as the leading force of the Korean workers' solidarity struggle in the summer of 1987, the beginning of the Great Workers' Struggle.

GREAT WORKERS' STRUGGLE, 1987–1991

The seismic Great Workers' Struggle (GWS) was initially set off on July 5, 1987, by 101 workers of Hyundai Engine, a relatively small division of the Hyundai Group in Ulsan, who secretly formed a union while meeting downtown. Kwŏn Yong-mok, a thirty-year-old licensed welder, was their leader.[11] Encouraged by Korea's political democratization, which came rather unexpectedly, Kwŏn established the Hyundai Engine Union within a week of the declaration of political democratization on June 29, 1987.[12] The surprise announcement of democratization also convinced the Korean industrial workers throughout the country, including the hitherto conservative rank-and-file HCI industrial warriors to rise up, expressing their long-suppressed grievance, known in Korea as *han*, against the deeply rooted workplace despotism in Korean society, especially in the course of rapid industrialization. The Korean workers, popularly portrayed as historically oppressed *minjung*, were particularly angry at the military Chun regime, which had become extremely tough on labor, as already noted, especially against the industrial workers' democratic union movement.

Their demands for labor rights—including the right to establish democratic unions instead of the old pro-state and pro-company unions, compensation for their relative deprivation through more substantial bonuses, shorter working hours, and the ending of the status distinction between white-collar and blue-collar workers, among other discriminatory practices—were virtually identical across the various enterprise unions. Hyundai industrial warriors, for example, demanded 25–30 percent wage increases in addition to the legal right to form union organizations, as well as ending the discriminatory system of wage competition among workers, elimination of the restriction on hair length, improvement in the quality of workplace lunches, and an end to compulsory morning exercises.

In this regard, the Hyundai workers' famous four-kilometer march from the Hyundai Heavy Industries plant to downtown Ulsan on August 18, 1987, escalated into the tsunami-like nationwide labor unrest with a newly adopted labor militancy. This march followed a clash between Kwŏn Yong-mok, the newly elected president of the Council of Hyundai Group Unions (Hyŏndae Kurup Nodongjohap Hyŏbŭihoe), founded on August 8, 1987, and management over the council's demand for group-level wage negotiations and recognition of the newly formed Hyundai Heavy Industries Union. Outraged that management refused to recognize the council as a lawful organization, the Hyundai industrial warriors were determined to show their new militancy by mobilizing forklifts, dump trucks, and sanding machines at the head of their march. They became even more militant and tenacious when the Ojwabul, one of the Hyundai workers' bachelor apartments, regarded by them as a "freedom community," was shut down, leaving its several thousand residents with no place to sleep or eat, let alone to gather together without management intervention.

Some sixty thousand angry workers, including about two thousand family members, marched from the grounds of Hyundai Heavy Industries toward city hall, shouting "Down with Chŏng Chu-yŏng [Chung Ju-young]," referring to the founding chairman of the Hyundai Group. As a result, the deputy minister of labor hurried down from Seoul late at night and accepted all of the workers' demands, including a significant wage increase and recognition of the independent democratic (*minju*) union at Hyundai Heavy Industries (An Sŭng-ch'ŏn 2002, 95–96). This historic march quickly led to the rise of the Hyundai workers as the leading force behind what became the Great Workers' Struggle, drawing in about 1.2 million workers within less than two months, while Ulsan became "the shrine of the labor movement." The march ultimately led to the mushrooming of new democratic unions in more than 3,300 firms, with a new doctrine of militant unionism that peaked in 1989 with a national union density of 19.8 percent (see figure 5.1). It also led to a rapid shift in the leadership of the Korean workers' labor movement, from female workers in labor-intensive light industry, who had laid the groundwork for the democratic union movement of the 1970s and early 1980s, to skilled and semiskilled male HCI workers at large heavy manufacturing firms.

The impact of this surge in militant unionism was game changing. The total number of labor disputes, which had initially exploded from 276 in 1986 to 3,749 in 1987, as table 2.1 shows, remained at 1,873 and 1,616 in 1988 and 1989, respectively. Behind this massive number of labor disputes lay the militant strike by Hyundai shipbuilding workers that lasted 128 days, from December 12, 1988, to April 18, 1989, the longest strike recorded in Korean contemporary history, drawing in 20,000 riot police, who occupied the Hyundai Heavy Industries shipyard from land, sea, and air. This epoch-making period of labor militancy saw not only a dramatic surge in the number of independent democratic labor unions but also an increase in militant *minjung* solidarity among Korean workers as a whole.

Between January 1988 and November 1989, for example, a total of seventeen regional union federations (Chiyŏk Nojo Hyŏbŭihoe) were formed with 263,540 union members, mainly from manufacturing blue-collar HCI firms, as well as thirteen occupational union federations (under the National Council of Occupational Trade Unions [Chŏn'guk Ŏpchong Nodongjohap Hyŏbŭihoe]) with 173,800 union members, mostly white-collar office

TABLE 2.1. Labor disputes in Korea, 1985–1993

Year	Number of disputes	Number of participants (1,000s)	Loss of days (1,000s)	Labor militancy (1,000s/day)	No. of strike days
1986	276	47	72	8.5	—
1987	3,749	1,262	6,947	755.8	—
1988	1,873	293	5,401	562.0	—
1989	1,616	409	6,351	611.3	19.2
1990	322	134	4,487	409.8	19.1
1991	234	175	3,271	279.6	18.2
1992	235	105	1,528	128.3	20.1

Source: Reconstructed based on data from the Labor White Paper published annually by the Ministry of Labor.

workers (Kim Chin-gyun 2008, 27–28). Riding on this extraordinary wave of labor solidarity, the National Council of Trade Unions (NCTU; Chŏn'guk Nodong Chohap Hyŏbŭihoe or Chŏnnohyŏp) was established in January 1990, based mainly in small and medium-scale firms in light industries with a substantial proportion of female workers. This organization served as an independent alternative to the conservative Federation of Korean Trade Unions, which workers had rejected as pro-state and pro-company, or *ŏyongnojo*. The NCTU was illegal, but its illegal status ironically helped popularize the Korean workers' democratic unionization movement, which quickly converged into a solidarity movement of the Korean working class under the slogan "Goliat Struggle."

Goliat Struggle: A Solidarity Movement of the Korean Working Class

On April 27, 1990, Yi Kab-yong, the director–general secretary of the Hyundai Heavy Industries Union (HHIU), and sixty hard-core rank-and-file unionists initiated their all-out strike from the top of a mammoth crane named Goliat, which stood eighty-two meters above the ground. To stop this radical protest before it turned into a united labor struggle, some 12,000 riot police occupied the HHI grounds while the army, navy, and air force, among others, such as the specially trained martial arts police unit Paekkoltan, staged a military-style operation by mobilizing bulldozers, helicopters, and even coast guard vessels, among other armored vehicles. Under the code name Lonely Wolf (*Oeroun Nŭkttae*), this conspicuously political protest boldly declared the Korean workers' newly articulated collective identity as Goliat warriors by denouncing their "stigmatizing identities of industrial warriors" (Koo 2001, 210). This extremely hostile class warfare was triggered by two major incidents. One was the preemptive arrest on February 9, 1990, of Yi Yŏng-hyŏn, the newly elected president of the Hyundai Heavy Industries Union, and three of its executives, which effectively paralyzed the union.[13]

The other major incident was the imposition of excessive jail sentences on the blue-collar union leaders, mostly of the Hyundai Heavy Industries Union, in comparison to the light sentences handed out for an ongoing strike at the Korean Broadcasting Service to 117 white-collar workers, who had all been released in April 1990. The culturally deep-seated societal prejudice against blue-collar workers quickly convinced the then newly formed NCTU to call a general strike in support of the HHI workers' Goliat Struggle.

On May 1, 1990, Labor Day, about 120,000 workers from almost 150 enterprises across the country, including many large *chaebŏl* HCI unions, began a sympathy strike, which confirmed the collective status of not just Hyundai workers but more broadly militant HCI workers as the leading force of the solidarity movement of the Korean working class. In so doing, the HCI workers directly challenged patriarchal labor control by both Korean capitalist *chaebŏls* and the military regime of Roh Tae-woo's ostensibly democratic transition (1988–92). The Goliat Struggle, however, lasted only briefly. On May 4, Yi Sang-bŏm, president of the Hyundai Motor Union, unilaterally ordered his member-workers to resume work, thus ending their sympathy strike, which drastically undermined the militancy of Yi Kab-yong and his team on the Goliat crane, who climbed down on May 10, signaling the end of the Goliat Struggle.[14]

This failed drama of the general strike concretely showed that the Goliat Struggle, despite the NCTU's noble plan highlighting the fraternity of the Korean working class, essentially represented mainly the HHI workers' struggle for their own collective interests, including the release of jailed HHIU leaders and other hard-core rank-and-file unionists, as well as annual wage increases and various other welfare conditions. This is not to overlook or reduce the significance of the HHI workers' collective role in the Great Workers' Struggle as its leading force, involving all workers and their newly established democratic unions within the Hyundai Group, even though there emerged growing division between the militant democracy faction (*minjup'a*) dominated by the HHIU and the more moderate or pragmatist faction (*sillip'a*) of the Hyundai Motor Union.[15]

Moreover, the failure of the Goliat Struggle did not mean that the new labor union militancy adopted by HCI workers at other large *chaebŏl* firms, such as Daewoo, Kia, and Ssangyong, as well as numerous small and medium-size HCI firms, also ended. On the contrary, efforts continued with yet another general strike on May 18, 1991. On this day, over 500,000 NCTU members protested the brutal death of a student, Kang Kyŏng-dae, who had been beaten by police riot squads on April 26, and also the suspicious death of a worker, Pak Ch'ang-su, president of the Hanjin Heavy Industries Union, on May 6, 1991. Pak's death, in particular, brought a new twist to a political situation that was already tense over Kang's death and a string of self-immolations in protest, as leaders of ninety-eight unions called a stop-work strike nine days before the general strike on May 9. Amid this massive mobilization of highly organized labor protests, later known as the May Struggle of 1991, the leaders of the HHIU had become severely divided by their company's divide-and-rule management policy.

The Hyundai management's divide-and-rule policy resulted in betrayals by both the HHIU's acting president, U Ki-ha, and the secretary-general, U Chin-bŏm. These two union officials had assisted in election campaigns for both their company owner, Chŏng Chu-yŏng, and his son, Chŏng Mong-jun, who had won a seat to represent the eastern district (*tonggu*), Ulsan, in the general elections of March 1992. Later, in December 1992, Chŏng Chu-yŏng had competed in the presidential election, for which the entire "100,000 Hyundai family-employees" had been mobilized to support their chairman, and some workers had become actively involved, either resigning or taking a leave of absence to work on the campaign (Yi Kab-yong 2009, 115–20).

Overall, the effect of union collaboration in these elections seems to have been a dramatic decrease in the number of labor disputes at the national level for three consecutive years, from 1,599 in 1989 to 322 in 1990, 234 in 1991, and 235 in 1992. This decrease in labor disputes at the national level meant that the HHI workers' 128-day strike (from December 12, 1988, to April 18, 1989), followed by the Goliat Struggle of May 1990, had made little difference, especially to the rapidly declining labor solidarity across the country. Against this background, the May Struggle of 1991 effectively ended the Great Workers' Struggle by exposing the collapse of inter- and extra-industry worker solidarity, including the collapse of the HCI worker-intellectual partnership that had epitomized the militant *minjung* solidarity movement of the Korean working class, the Goliat Struggle.

THE COLLAPSE OF HCI WORKER-INTELLECTUAL PARTNERSHIP AND CONFLICT

According to Kim Wŏn (2011, 257), the May Struggle of 1991 exposed the radical *undongkwŏn* (student) activists' negative view of Korean *minjung* workers as narrow-minded "violent protesters" or "*papp'ulttegi*" (a piece of rice-paste), a derogatory term mocking the blue-collar workers' "passive obedience or disorganized character" (Kim Wŏn 2011, 260) in the course of Korea's democratization movement. In this regard, two major effects are noteworthy, especially in terms of what was seen as the labor movement crisis in the early 1990s. One is that a large number of workers, including HCI workers, canceled their union membership altogether, turning their backs on militant unionism for fear of losing their employment during an economic recession amid the Great Workers' Struggle, which had threatened South Korea's export economy. One example of this crisis was the collapse in July 1992 of the POSCO Union, which had a membership of some 16,000.[16]

The other and perhaps more fundamental effect was the departure of a massive number of radical *undongkwŏn* activists from the factory-based labor movement by changing their ideological priority from the revolutionary *minjung* democracy movement to the newly burgeoning civil society movement (Kim Sun-Hyuk 2000). This sea change had begun long before 1993, when the newly inaugurated president Kim Young-sam (1993–97) systematically sponsored these "born-again" *undongkwŏn* activists and progressive liberal academics as the principal agents of his neoliberal reform campaign for a "New Korea" in parallel with his equally driven globalization (*segyehwa*) campaign, officially unveiled in November 1994. Some observers suggested that the "third wave" of democratization and the collapse in Europe of "actually-existing socialism" brought about a substantial demobilization of the radical labor movement in Korea to the extent of a crisis (Gray 2008, 76).

Others argued that the collapse of the Soviet Union led to the departure of many *undongkwŏn* activists from organizational and labor movements, mainly because they had lost hope in the Marxist model of revolution, which they came to comprehend as a dream that would not be realized in their lifetime (An Sŭng-ch'ŏn 2002, 149–50). Others argued that the change in workers' consciousness, which had become less class-conscious and more individualistic as a result of three major wage increases between 1987 and the mid-1990s, provided the background to the labor crisis theory. They also argued that the change in workers' consciousness deepened the polarization of the labor union movement, especially between unionized regular workers and nonregular subcontracted workers with no union membership. These explanations are insightful, but they did not consider the HCI worker-intellectual partnership and conflict during this revolutionary period in its own right, and they ignored the obvious collapse of the partnership, which became public especially after the May Struggle of 1991.

In this regard, three key factors need to be considered. First, HCI workers at large outside the Seoul-Kyŏngin area had little or no contact with the radical *undongkwŏn* activists until they migrated to the southern industrial area after 1987. Unlike the light industries, where thousands of students-turned-workers (*hakch'ul*) and other "disguised workers" (*wijang ch'wiŏpcha*), could find jobs with relatively simple skills and without going through serious security checks and skill requirements, the majority of HCI *chaebŏl* firms required workers with formal skills training or often a class II skills license, except in the shipbuilding area, and several proven references for security purposes. In defense manufacturing firms, in particular, military-style security checks were a daily routine. For this reason, plus the geographical distance from Seoul, even committed *hakch'ul* activists were prevented from making contact with HCI workers until they had formed a partnership with HCI workers, mainly after 1987 by helping dismissed workers. There were, of course, some exceptions, such as the *hakch'ul* unionist Mun Sŏng-hyŏn, of the T'ongil Corporation Union, who introduced the new mode of labor militancy as a strategy of the militant union movement in the Ch'angwŏn-Masan area as early as 1985. Not surprisingly, the HCI worker-intellectual partnership during this period was far more cautious, if not more strategic, than the earlier worker-student alliance of the 1970s and early 1980s, which had flourished in the labor-intensive light manufacturing factories in the Seoul-Kyŏngin area.[17]

Second, HCI workers relied only selectively on their partnership with radical *undongkwŏn* activists and intellectuals, unlike female workers in light industries with little or no formal education, who were dependent on the worker-student alliance of the 1970s and early 1980s. With their fierce pride as elite HCI workers with higher levels of formal education, they engaged in this partnership mainly to promote their collective struggle to change repressive labor policies in a more socially acceptable way, aligning themselves with the student-led popular *minjung* democracy movement. In so doing, HCI workers took over leadership of the Korean workers' democratic unionization movement from female workers without any opposition, although the female workers had maintained their leadership since the early 1970s. Here the Korean developmental state's patriarchal gender ideology since the mid-1960s unquestionably benefited HCI workers' rise to the top of the Korean working class, unlike the female workers' collective status in the workplace, which has remained at the bottom of that hierarchy ever since.

The third and perhaps most notable key factor about the HCI worker-intellectual partnership during this period was that the two groups were utterly incompatible, especially in terms of their own motivations linked to why they had become factory workers. Whereas the HCI workers, despite their newly elevated status as a blue-collar elite, needed to earn a living for their basic survival, the student activists had become "disguised" factory workers with a specific political and ideological goal to "cultivate class identity and consciousness among workers" (Koo 2001, 106). In their view, becoming a disguised factory worker was crucial to achieve their collective aim of a proletarian revolution. This ideological incompatibility between the HCI workers and the radical students/intellectuals was no less problematic than that of the worker-student alliance during the 1970s and 1980s. In this regard, anthropologist Seung-Kyung Kim's observation on the young female factory workers in the Masan Free Export Zone is illuminating: "Student activists aimed at leading workers to a higher level of understanding of their social location, and sometimes regarded the improvements in workers' lives as hindering their progress toward achieving class consciousness" (1997, 142).

Korean intellectuals, especially the radical *undongkwŏn* activists, not only objectified workers with their own presumed idea of "workers' identity, culture, attitude and value system that orders the workers' daily life differently to that of intellectuals," but also thought of "workers as objects of their agitation and mobilization, rather than as agents of their own movement" (Nam-Hee Lee 2005, 926 and 929).[18] Not surprisingly, HCI workers openly rejected the dissident intellectuals' interference in their industrial strikes. At the height of the Hyundai Heavy Industries Union's 128-day strike, for example, Sŏ T'ae-su, president of the HHIU, openly demanded that the intellectual "dissident activist force" (*chaeya seryŏk*)[19] leave the strike immediately because of their politically motivated interference.[20] Sŏ argued: "What is the identity of the intellectual *chaeya* activist forces that control union movements?... They have no purpose other than taking hold of power by confusing the political situation and denouncing the government through instigation of the workers who have little political interest.... Don't ridicule poor workers... and stop immediately the interference... which helps nothing" (HPPC 2007, 125).

Sŏ's criticism of Roh Moo-hyun (No Mu-hyŏn), who was then a human rights lawyer and later became president of South Korea, in particular, was brisk, accusing him of the politically motivated instigation of workers: "By twice visiting our company's sporting arena, Mr. Roh incited the [HHI] workers with the exhortation that the victory is the workers' as long as they fight to the end.... Although his readiness to fight from *chaeya* with his false justification that he disliked institutionalized politics seems plausible, what responsibility could he... take for some eighteen thousand [HHI] workers?" (HPPC 2007, 125).

This open message, on reflection, demonstrated the irreversible breakup of the HCI worker-intellectual partnership at the peak of the Great Workers' Struggle. The rupture became even more apparent when a large number of *undongkwŏn* activists emerged as the leading force in civic movements as early as 1989, arguing that a "change of direction" for the labor movement was needed to win back public support, especially from the middle class. While many militant union leaders from the "on-site" shop floor had little or no opportunity to improve their own careers other than on the shop floor as factory workers, many *undongkwŏn* and other intellectual labor union movement activists either returned to university or entered management positions in various areas or even joined the then conservative ruling party as born-again politicians by using their democratic labor movement record as credentials. Since then, many militant union leaders and rank-and-file HCI workers developed a strong distrust of, if not resentment against, white-collar workers and intellectual activists. One of the most frequently repeated comments among the HCI workers and union leaders whom I interviewed during this study was that the changed stance of the *undongkwŏn* and other intellectual activists, especially in the early 1990s, taught them an important lesson: "They are different from us, and we must look after our own interests."[21]

THREE TYPES OF GOLIAT WARRIORS

Just as there were fundamental differences in the collective aims of HCI workers and *undongkwŏn*/intellectuals, HCI workers' transformation from their initial state-imposed industrial warrior identity to a newly self-articulated identity as Goliat warriors was profound. Their approach to work, background, ideology, goals, lifestyles, age, and education, among other factors all affected how their transition to Goliat warriors took place. Their initial identity as industrial warriors with a conservative attitude under a reciprocal social contract with the state complied fundamentally with anti-communist state ideology in their collective aim of pursuing the nation-building heavy and chemical industrialization project. HCI workers' changed identity as radical Goliat warriors, however, comprised three main types, each showing huge differences at the workplace, especially regarding their changed attitude toward militant unionism, their ideological commitment, and their personal goals.

The first type of Goliat warriors included rank-and-file workers who had become militant labor union leaders in HCI manufacturing firms, predominantly large *chaebŏl* corporations. These newly emergent democratic labor movement leaders showed a strong sense of what can be described as a Goliat warrior consciousness in adopting a new labor militancy as a weapon in both the democratic unionization movement and the solidarity movement of the Korean working class. These new union movement leaders were mostly young and single, between their mid-twenties and mid-thirties when the Great Workers' Struggle erupted in 1987. They had less than a high school education and had often undertaken vocational training after dropping out of high school or middle school. In some cases they had just a primary education, especially those who found employment in shipbuilding firms. They seem to have been more frustrated and angry than others at the top-down military-style management, toward which they had a long-suppressed resentment well before 1987.

Well-known leaders of the militant democratic union movement, such as Yi Kab-yong, O Chong-soe, Yi Sang-bŏm, Yi Hŏn-gu, and Chŏng Kap-tŭk, found employment in Hyundai shipbuilding or automobile firms after completing their vocational training with either a high school or middle school diploma. They participated in the Great Workers' Struggle from its beginning. Kim Chin-suk, a well-known female trade union movement activist who protested for 309 days on top of a thirty-five-meter crane in Yŏngdo shipyard against mass layoffs by Hanjin Heavy Industries and Construction in 2011, is another HCI worker who fits this type.[22] Some of these militant union leaders attended classes on labor history, law, and union operation, among other relevant topics, mainly through small group activities, with outside help from labor union movement activists (*hwaltongga*), who were mostly dismissed workers. And they became leading agents of the democratic union movement following the eruption of the Great Workers' Struggle. One of some fifty HCI workers whom I interviewed during this research project said that he initially learned about workers' rights at a meeting organized by the Young Men's Christian Association in Masan in 1986. This worker, like many of my interviewees, never even thought that factory workers had labor rights as such before 1986. Yet he played an active role in the Kia Machine Tools Union, especially during the Great Workers' Struggle.

The second type of Goliat warriors consisted of students-turned-workers or *hakch'ul*, with their long-held ideological and political objectives. The collective aim of these intellectual democratic labor movement activists was a Marxist-Leninist revolution. As a radical prodemocracy group, they were often known as "disguised workers" (*wijang ch'wiŏpcha*) or *undongkwŏn*, renowned for their collective role in the consciousness-raising of factory workers in major light-industrial centers around the Seoul-Kyŏngin area. In contrast to these light-industrial centers, where up to 10,000 university students were known to have worked as *hakch'ul* or *wijang ch'wiŏpcha* by the mid-1980s (Im Yŏng-il 1998, 81), *hakch'ul*s were extremely rare in the heavy and chemical industries in the southeastern industrial belt, except for Mun Sŏng-hyŏn and a few others.

The third and most utilitarian type of Goliat warriors consisted of mainstream rank-and-file HCI workers. In contrast to the politically and ideologically motivated *hakch'ul*s-turned-unionists, this third type of workers were primarily interested in developing their own livelihoods as skilled workers by cautiously supporting their union's new militancy, even during the Great Workers' Struggle. This type of Goliat warriors tended to regard the new militancy as a preferred protest strategy for obtaining wage increases, greater benefits, and improvement of working conditions, among other remunerative benefits, mainly through company-based collective bargaining. For this purpose, they supported their union leader's often unrealistic demands for annual pay raises and other welfare benefits.

As graduates of specialized technical high schools or cadets/workers having completed vocational training or similar in-plant training between

1972 and 1987, these first-generation HCI workers had either completed or were still serving the five-year reciprocal social contract as special soldiers when the Great Workers' Struggle erupted. Although some turned into militant unionists, this pragmatic type of Goliat warriors tended to show the least enthusiasm for their newly invented collective identity as Goliat warriors or as a labor aristocracy, a term that had first appeared in the Korean media in 1993 (see chapter 3). Expressing their uneasiness or even frustration with their new identity, these HCI workers tended to see themselves as professional craftsmen. The vastly different trajectories of the three individuals discussed below may shed light on these three types.

Yi Kab-yong, the leader of the HHI workers' Goliat Struggle of May 1990, symbolizes the first type. Yi was born in Pusan in 1958 as the eldest son of a middle-class family. He found employment at Hyundai Heavy Industries in 1984 with a vocational training background, after finishing middle school in Pusan. He recalled working "like an animal," going to work each day at 7:00 a.m. and leaving work at 10:00 p.m., as well as working overtime on weekends. He was paid at the rate of ₩630 per hour (approximately US$0.71 at that time), plus a basic monthly wage of ₩150,000 (approximately US$168 in 1985–86). With overtime, Yi received over ₩400,000 (US$448) monthly, which, Yi claimed, made him one of the lowest wage earners at HHI (author interview, April 26–27, 2012). As one of the first representatives of the HHI Union founded in July 1987, Yi went to prison three times. When he was released from prison in October 1996 for the third time, he had been laid off from work and his marriage had broken up. Yi was elected president of the Korean Confederation of Trade Unions for a fixed one-year term in March 1998 amid the Asian financial crisis. His subsequent term as mayor at the Tonggu Municipal Office in Ulsan was cut short when a court found him guilty of refusing to reprimand public servants who had participated in the general strike led by the Public Service Union in November 2004.[23] In 2013, Yi failed in his election bid for the seventh presidency of the KCTU.

Mun Sŏng-hyŏn, in stark contrast, was arguably the most representative of *hakch'ul* activists, the second type of Goliat warrior. Born in February 1952 as the eldest son of a schoolteacher in the southeastern region, Mun joined the labor union movement in his second year at Seoul National University in 1974 after having been inspired by the "spirit of Chŏn T'ae-il," the icon of the Korean workers' labor movement since his self-immolation in 1970. Mun moved to Ch'angwŏn in 1983 with three other members of his social club, White Pebble (Ch'adolhoe), primarily to save their union when his firm, Tongyang Machinery Industry (Tongyang Kigye) merged with a weapons manufacturer, T'ongil Corporation (T'ongil Sanŏp), which had moved into the newly established Ch'angwŏn Industrial Park. In April 1985, Mun led the T'ongil Corporation workers' strike, which became a template for the regional solidarity strikes prior to the Great Workers' Struggle.[24]

Mun played a key role in establishing the Council of Masan and Ch'angwŏn Unions (Ma-Ch'ang Noryŏn, founded on December 14, 1987), which became the matrix of the Korea Confederation of Trade Unions. Throughout the 1990s, Mun, like many *hakch'ul* and radical *undongkwŏn* and other radical intellectual activists, enjoyed positions of leadership in democratic labor union organizations, including joint chair of the Council of National Labor Movement Organizations (Chŏn'guk Nodong Undong Tanch'e Hyŏbŭihoe, or Nounhyŏp), before he was elected president of the Democratic Labor Party in 2006. In 2017, Mun was appointed head of the Economic and Social Development Commission after his long campaign for the then opposition Democratic Party candidate Moon Jae-in in both the 2012 and 2017 presidential elections.

Kim Ki-ha, a master craftsman whose life story typifies the third type, was born in March 1956 into a poor farming family with six children in one of the remotest villages in Kangwŏn Province. He explained that, having been a child who often missed meals during middle school, he became "the pride and hero of my village . . . because I was the 'dragon from a stream' as the only child in the village who had succeeded in being admitted to the state-sponsored technical high school." His highest ambition during high school had been to become a "salaried worker as a top technician." In June 1976, when his company moved to Ch'angwŏn Industrial Park from Seoul, Kim voluntarily moved there because he wanted to learn a new heat treatment skill that had never been available or required until the specialized equipment was installed. Kim recalled his earlier life as a blue-collar factory worker during the 1970s up until 1987: "In those days, those white-collar office workers with a university degree had company-provided lunch and commuted by company bus. But, we, the [blue-collar] *kinŭnggong* [technician/craftsman], had to bring our own lunch and either walked or commuted by commercial bus. As a factory worker, I didn't complain about this discrimination because the white-collar workers had a higher university degree" (author interview, April 17, 2015, plus several e-mail supplements, May 2015).

Kim's ambition and hard work earned him a string of awards and official honors, including Korean Master Technician (*Kinung Han'gukin*, 2011) and on-site professor of Korean industry (Taehan Min'guk Sanŏp Hyŏnjang Kyosu, 2012), among other credentials. Kim's autobiography, along with that of eleven other outstanding craftsmen, was published in 2011 jointly by the Ministry of Employment and Labor and the Human Resources Development Service of Korea.[25] Kim retired in 2017 after turning sixty. Looking back at his own career, Kim stated: "Looking back on those days, especially when I could have been involved in the militant union movement from the late 1980s onward, I did very well in making the right choice to pursue my career as craftsman. My colleagues around me used to sneer at me a lot then, but now I sense that they praise me" (interview, April 2015).

CONCLUSION

The change in the HCI workers' collective identity from well-disciplined industrial warriors to radical Goliat warriors rising up in the Great Workers' Struggle against authoritarian labor policies and despotic workplace management was revolutionary. Their collective discontent, despite the educational benefits and relatively higher wages they had enjoyed, led them not only to break their reciprocal social contract with the state but also to lead the solidarity movement of the Korean working class, renouncing their initial conservative industrial warrior consciousness and identity. Despite their heroic claim to represent the Korean working class through the radical *minjung* solidarity movement as its leading agency, however, the primary goal of HCI workers as Goliat warriors was to pursue their own parochial interests (such as wage increases, improved working conditions, and other remunerative opportunities) through company-level enterprise unionism, rather than fighting for the broader political issues of the Korean working class within and beyond Korean society. In spite of this obvious flaw, their all-out labor union militancy in the course of the Great Workers' Struggle, in partnership with radical *minjung* intellectuals, was extremely effective in improving the collective image and status of Korean workers. Their all-out labor union militancy and their partnership with *minjung* intellectuals also made a significant contribution to bringing about the radical change in Korean society on labor issues.

The breakdown of the HCI worker-intellectual partnership, however, was unavoidable mainly because, in spite of the HCI workers' radically changed collective consciousness as Goliat warriors, the political issues of class struggle were for most of them a luxury. Hence, when Korea's recession in the manufacturing sector deepened in the early 1990s, these elite HCI workers, especially at the rank-and-file level, readily participated in what became known as the Corporate Culture Movement (Kiŏp Munhwa Undong), which aimed to destroy the labor union militancy that had been out of control since 1987.

CHAPTER 3

Counterrevolution

The Corporate Culture Movement and HCI Workers' Response

How did the incumbent Korean government foster the Corporate Culture Movement, especially with the coercion of the Korean business community, and how did the movement affect HCI workers' attitudes toward their militant unions? What did the Korean capitalist *chaebŏls* achieve through this campaign? Domestically, the period following the inauguration of the Roh Tae-woo transitional government was epoch-making. The spectacular change in Korean society came with dramatic wage increases for Korean manufacturing workers. The unprecedented increases in the average monthly wage in the manufacturing sector, from ₩756,306 in 1987 to ₩854,855 in 1988 and again to ₩965,751 in 1989 (at 2010 prices), were only one aspect of this societal change, brought about mostly by the HCI workers' militant democratic unions (Koyong Nodongbu 1993). Following the eruption of the Great Workers' Struggle, the newly formed democratic unions changed the nature of labor relations on the shop floor by "making collective bargaining into a necessary procedure that managerial authorities had to deal with in order to put the worker on the production line" (Dae-Oup Chang 2002, 18). As a result of these wage increases, about 33 percent of Korean people in 1991 described themselves as "middle class," with disposable income for "non-subsistence purchases and investments" (Cotton and Van Leest 1996, 185, 188), especially for enhancing living standards and leisure time, and for meeting rapidly increased social expectations.

As a major component of Korea's newly won democracy, however, the Great Workers' Struggle generated a serious problem, at least in the short term, for the country's export economy, law and order, and social stability in general. Yet Roh Tae-woo, then chairman of the ruling Democratic Justice Party (DJP), having announced his eight-point democratization package on June 29, 1987, could not repress the struggle ahead of Korea's first democratic presidential election on December 16, 1987, and the thirteenth National Assembly elections, on April 26, 1988. The newly inaugurated Roh administration, together with the ruling DJP, however, failed to secure a parliamentary majority in the April 1988 elections. And this failure opened the way for a tsunami of industrial strikes known as the Great Workers' Struggle, for almost four consecutive years, as discussed in chapter 2. It is important to note that the Great Workers' Struggle overlapped with Korea's economic boom between 1987 and 1989, which initially produced a massive increase in exports and a current account surplus, followed by an economic slump with increasing competitive pressure in global markets from late 1989. Hence, it is not difficult to see why both the government and the Korean business community were so desperate to find ways to cope with the increased competitive pressures in global markets on the one hand, and regain control over the new radical democratic union militancy on the other.

Korea's leading HCI firms, in particular, had invested a huge amount of capital to increase production during the boom, and then found themselves with not only increasing competition, initially from newly industrialized countries and then also China, but also growing protectionism in developed countries, especially the United States, as well as "an upward revaluation of the South Korean *won* by almost 16% in 1988" (Hart-Lansberg 1993, 237). Yet the cost of labor increased over four consecutive years from 1987 to 1990 at an average annual rate of 16.4 percent, whereas working hours decreased from 51.9 per week in 1987 to 47.5 in 1993. This crosscurrent drove up not only production costs but also the difficulty of maintaining quality control, not to mention meeting production schedules amid almost continuous labor disputes. At this point both the Korean state and many leading *chaebŏls*— including Samsung, Hyundai, Daewoo, and Kia—began to actively promote a neoliberal "new management strategy" (*sin kyŏngyŏng chŏllyak*), which was promoted as the Corporate Culture Movement.[1]

The primary aim of this neoliberal new management strategy was to restore the labor management structure by rebuilding management's cultural hegemony, in the Gramscian sense, in order to increase Korea's international competitiveness and to facilitate capital accumulation. The collective term "Corporate Culture Movement" was therefore strategic, advocating a new business culture for Korea focused on a soft approach to mutual cooperation and harmony instead of the old authoritarian approach. In this context, *chaebŏl*s, as the leading agency of the exceptionally united Korean capitalists, engineered Korea's newly adopted neoliberal human resource management system focused on labor flexibility and workplace harmony modeled on Japanese corporate culture. They also convinced the government to implement its own corporate culture policy as a nationwide campaign for neoliberal restructuring to the extent of a counterrevolution. This chapter traces the key features of the Corporate Culture Movement, initially devised by the leading Korean *chaebŏl* firms and then taken up by the government, and analyzes its impact on HCI workers' attitudes, especially in terms of their approach to militant unionism.

THE CORPORATE CULTURE MOVEMENT AS NEW MANAGEMENT STRATEGY

The rise of the Corporate Culture Movement (CCM) began sometime after 1987, and by 1989 seventy-five out of the one hundred largest firms in Korea were engaged in some form of management reform (Pak Chun-sik 1993, 192). Large leading HCI firms, in particular, aggressively sought what was then dubbed "management rationalization" (*kyŏngyŏng hamnihwa*), emulating mainly the Japanese management model, to find a new form of labor relations in the workplace, which had become radically unionized since 1987. Middle management in these firms, in particular, had lost control over worker productivity on the shop floor mainly because the pre-1987 labor control system no longer existed. As early as the mid-1980s, in fact, many leading HCI firms promulgated their own version of the CCM by designating some prominent university research institute and leading experts in humanities and culture to develop and articulate their company's identity and cultural characteristics.

POSCO, then known as Pohang Iron and Steel—as large a firm as Hyundai Heavy Industries, employing about 20,000 workers in 1989—for example, is reported to have begun its own corporate culture development between December 1986 and September 1987. POSCO then engaged the Seoul National University Institute of Social Science to articulate its management principles, organizational structure, value system, and the level of its contribution to the national economy, among other key factors, including its high standard formal education for workers.² By mobilizing the research center of Korea's most renowned university, POSCO articulated its company management principles as a "people-centered [in'gan chonjung] national firm [minjok kiŏp] with a global outlook." Yŏ Sang-hwan, vice president of POSCO, however, stressed that, since its establishment in 1968, POSCO had led its workers with a set of corporate principles without necessarily verbalizing the term "corporate culture," and thus when the Social Science Research Center articulated the firm's character and thus identity, there was already a distinctive set of norms in place at POSCO, representing its own corporate culture (Munhwabu 1992, 1:77–78).

In fact, POSCO was and still is famous for its highly developed corporate culture, loosely known as the "POSCO spirit." This was built on the four personal principles of Pak T'ae-jun, POSCO's founding chairman, known as the "king of steel," who introduced POSCO's centralized military-style labor-management system from the very beginning, by removing the distinction between white-collar and blue-collar workers and managing all workers like soldiers in an army. Although Pak publicly announced on June 28, 1987, that he had "never denied a democratic labor union" and had accepted the establishment of the POSCO workers' democratic union in June 1988, he succeeded in dissolving the POSCO Union in July 1992. Under the firm's carrot-and-stick policy, especially during the two months from January through February 1991, for example, some 16,000 union members withdrew their membership, except for about twenty "pro-company" members (An Sŭng-ch'ŏn 2002, 138).

Inspired by the Japanese turnkey technology and management system, Pak equated the importance of steelmaking with national power, which had essentially represented a personal belief of his mentor, President Park Chung Hee, who publicly declared that "steelmaking is national power" when he officially launched POSCO on April 1, 1968. Within this nation-building framework, Pak's four personal principles were: (1) steelmaking patriotism; (2) responsibility and perfectionism; (3) transparent information management; and (4) the priority of staff welfare (Seok-man Yoon 2011, 56–61). These principles could be regarded as representing Park Chung Hee's nation-building strategy at an enterprise level. In his interview with this author (Kijang, April 23, 2005), Pak said that Park Chung Hee had been his mentor since 1948, when he met him as a twenty-three-year-old cadet at the Korean Military Academy. He has also said that POSCO's motto, "Make steel, serve the nation" (Chech'ŏl poguk), essentially referred to patriotism, which in practice meant "the mass production of quality iron and steel at a lower cost for South Korean industry, especially for the defense industry . . . as a means to strengthening national capacity against North Korean threats" (Seokman Yoon 2011, 56). On this basis, Pak demanded of every POSCO worker patriotism, unbridled loyalty, and absolute obedience to superiors like soldiers in the army. In turn, POSCO treated workers by far the best of all large corporations, with a 63 percent diffusion rate of company housing in the P'ohang area, which was higher than that in Ulsan or Masan in 1989 (Yi Sang-ch'ŏl 1991, 69).

Like POSCO, Daewoo, a leading *chaebŏl* founded in 1980 and with some 28,000 workers in 1984, carried out a radical restructuring in 1989 with its own new management strategy, called "Hope: 1990s Movement" (hereafter "Hope Movement"). Prior to the Hope Movement, Daewoo's shipbuilding had twice carried out labor restructuring, initially focused on what it called TQC (Total Quality Control) from 1981 to 1985, and then again refocused as the MAST (Business Innovation Movement) from 1986 to 1988. These two restructurings resulted in a reduction in the number of workers to about 12,000. By 1992, the Hope Movement had set up five key projects, namely, "harmonious labor management, technology innovation, productivity improvement, cost reduction, and a safe way of life." At the factory level, Daewoo proceeded with fifteen projects corresponding to each area or division as the company's second phase of the Hope Movement program, which included the new shipbuilding concept, modeled on Japanese-style production-control techniques, industrial engineering, standardization, activation of labor management, and management innovation. The aim of this comprehensive Hope Movement was to build the firm into the world's number one shipbuilding company (Pak Tong-Gyu 1994, 9).[3]

Daewoo, like POSCO and many other leading firms at that time, implemented what it called "consciousness reform" (*ŭisik kaehyŏk*) of all the firm's employees, while also implementing a new production management system with strengthened managerial power on the shop floor. This new production management system focused on small group activities, aimed in particular at making labor processes on the shop floor more efficient, especially by enabling labor flexibility. Daewoo management in fact equated its Hope Movement to a productivity improvement campaign that they defined as "endless efforts in striving for a work unit that can be operated with lesser man-hours" (quoted in Kang Sŏk-jae 2002, 45). Here the assumed idea of the productivity improvement campaign, focused on minimizing man-hours for work-unit production, appears to have been similar to the "Vision 92" campaign led by Anam Industry, a semiconductor company founded in 1956, which claimed to have achieved both tangible and intangible results.[4]

In terms of tangible results, Anam claimed to have effected a 40 percent increase in sales by the end of September 1992 compared to 1989, in spite of a 35 percent decrease in the number of workers (Munhwabu 1992, 2:260–61). In terms of intangible results, according to Kim Yŏng-sŏ, director of the Management Strategy Team at Anam Industry, the mind-set of the company's staff members changed from "Anam, an easy place to work" to "the working Anam" (Munhwabu 1992, 2:267), which in effect made them realize the importance of sharing an awareness of risk, as well as the importance of leadership in quality and technology.

As table 3.1 shows, Korean workers, especially in the heavy and chemical sector, underwent radical thought training, or what can be characterized as conscientization education, under the mantra of their companies' Corporate Culture Movement campaigns. The leading *chaebŏl* firms in particular conducted four main program areas of training/education, campaigns, special events, and public relations promotion, which were aimed at changing not only the consciousness of their employees but also that of their family members, including their parents. The slogans adopted by the twenty firms and various institutions and organizations, under various CCM campaigns examined in case studies published by the Ministry of Culture, featured popular phrases like "one mind" (*han maŭm*), "one family" (*han kajok*), and "one-goal movement" (*han mokp'yo undong*), emphasizing the importance of harmonious relations between labor and business, rational thinking, and cooperative manners, among other aspects of corporate culture.[5]

Akin to the mass mobilization of the Park Chung Hee state's New Community Movement (Saemaŭl Undong) of the 1970s, at the center of these four main programs stood the ultimate strategy of the Korean firms' new business management strategy focused on "burden sharing." This new labor management strategy in the Korean business community became a hot issue when Korea was preoccupied with the democratic elections of 1992, especially the presidential election in December. The key policymakers of the departing transitional Roh Tae-woo regime actively responded to the united pressure from the Korean business community, especially the leading *chaebŏls*. In this respect, the government-organized symposium titled "Organizational Innovation and Culture Management" (Chojik Hyŏksin Kwa

TABLE 3.1. Four main program areas of the Corporate Culture Movement

Program area	Specific programs	Focus
Training/ education	Corporate culture and one-mind movement Corporate protocol education History education	Change of consciousness and thinking based on corporate culture Healthy corporate work life Correct understanding of the company's history and tradition Reform of consciousness and harmony
Special events	Company excursions by the staff's children Computer education for the staff's children Summer training Family tours Inviting retirees to participate in events	Integration of families and the company; becoming a lifetime family and expansion of a sense of one large family
Campaigns	One-mind campaign Personal health campaigns Taking the company newsletter home Maintain a "becoming the best" movement Language purification campaign Tidy office; clean desk and workplace management policy	Development of consensus between home and the company Enjoying healthy social lives Publish articles on corporate culture and on related labor-management relations and business ethics in company newsletters Reform of consciousness and habits (etiquette, human relationship, dialogue) Improvement of human relationships and addressing irrationality (irrational language, unpleasant words, etc.) Neat and tidy as a way of life Taking photos of self-regulated enforcement and public announcements of implementation of this policy
Public relations	Corporate culture and one-mind movement One-mind movement PR brochures Findings of inquiry into performance of staff as company (team) players One-mind movement contest	Creating a corporate culture atmosphere and mind-set Publication of company newsletter and pamphlets Sharing of findings of inquiry and improvement based on those findings Encouragement of a sense of fulfillment and participation (posters, slogans, and tributes) Traditional customs and family culture

Munhwa Kyŏngyŏng), held on October 15–16, 1992, represented the official launch of the Corporate Culture Movement, signaling what turned out to be a counterrevolution, especially in the promotion of labor flexibility to bolster Korea's competitiveness in world markets.

THE CORPORATE CULTURE MOVEMENT AS COUNTERREVOLUTION

In the opening address to the "Organizational Innovation and Culture Management" symposium, Yi Su-jŏng, minister of culture, outlined a five-point directive for promoting a "wave of corporate culture" that would be essential for "the development of Korean business, Korean society, and Korea itself as a nation":

1. Through an active promotion of culture within the company, a new vitality must be infused into Korean business while also activating its structure.
2. Cultural thoughts and behavioral patterns of our business organization must be developed.
3. Corporate culture must be developed in close contact with society.
4. Corporate culture must be developed as the best weapon for overseas market development.
5. Corporate culture, through business development, should ultimately play an important role in accelerating national development. (Munhwabu 1992, 9–12)[6]

The participants in the symposium included many leading *chaebŏl* firms and state-funded large corporations, including Samsung, Lotte, Ssangyong, LG, DACOM, POSCO, and Korea Petroleum Development Corporation. The participants also included many heads of leading universities, banks, government investment institutions, and the media, most of whom were members of the Korean Council of Corporate Culture (Kiŏp Munhwa Hyŏbŭihoe), which had been established only a month earlier by some seventy companies.[7] At this symposium Lim Tong-sŭng, director of the Samsung Economic Research Institute, the most influential think tank in Korea, outlined the three main reasons behind Samsung Group's creation of a corporate culture. First, Samsung had become so large that unless a corporate culture was created under which every staff member could make independent judgments and act in accordance with the company's "autonomous management" (*chayul kyŏngyŏng*) principle, thus carrying out their own responsibilities and duties, a top-down management principle alone could not sustain the company's continuous development. Second, generational change in company ownership called for a facilitating corporate culture different from that of the founding generation (*ch'angŏp sedae*). Third, and most importantly, progress in Korea's democratization, along with the internationalization that had occurred in the 1980s, demanded cultural change with an emphasis on respect for humanity.

For Samsung to become a leading global company, therefore, Lim stated that the company would implement a Management Innovation Movement (Kyŏngyŏng Hyŏksin Undong) in stages under Samsung's threefold management principles: to serve the country through serving business (*saŏp poguk*); to respect humanity (*injae cheil*); and to pursue business rationalization (*hamnihwa ch'ugu*) (Munhwabu 1992, 1:87–89). Interestingly, Samsung's management principles were uncannily similar to POSCO's principles. In terms of improving worker productivity on the shop floor, both Samsung and POSCO, like many other leading firms in the HCI sector at that time, relied on so-called small-group quality-control circles, or *p'umjil punimjo*, modeled on Japanese manufacturing system on the shop floor, as part of their new neoliberal management strategy to improve efficiency. The impact of worker productivity improvement through the *punimjo*, which leading firms had introduced into the HCI sector after 1987, was far reaching, especially in terms of driving labor market flexibilization through a massive increase in the casualization of labor.

Many leading HCI firms, including Hyundai Heavy Industries, Daewoo Heavy Industries, Hyundai Motor, and Kia Machine Tools, as a result not only hired few new recruits after 1987, and even less after 1990, but in the case of Hyundai Heavy Industries enforced a "collective punishment system" (*yŏnjwaje*) when hiring. No one without a reference, dubbed later a "slave document" (*noye munsŏ*), from three senior managers—the head of a department (*pujang*) and a director and deputy-director of a section (*kwajang* and *ch'ajang*), for example—could enter the firm. Referees were therefore forced to toughen their control over newly hired workers to avoid any rebuke from the firm. This recruitment process essentially guaranteed the compliance of all newly hired workers.[8] Table 3.2 shows that the proportion of subcontracted workers employed in Korean shipbuilding industries from 1990 to 1993 increased from 17.5 percent of its total workforce (in

TABLE 3.2. Formation of the Korean labor force in the shipbuilding industry, 1990–1993

	1990		1991		1992		1993	
	Ship-building	Non-shipbuilding	Ship-building	Non-shipbuilding	Ship-building	Non-shipbuilding	Ship-building	Non-shipbuilding
No. of skilled workers	25,318	9,320	24,185	9,333	22,920	9,530	21,714	9,923
No. of subcontracted workers	6,456	904	5,620	1,962	6,124	1,654	6,675	2,874

Source: Based on Han'guk Chosŏn Kongŏp Hyŏphoe (1994, 13–14).

1990) to 19.3 and 23.2 percent in 1992 and 1993, respectively, while the total number of skilled workers (*kinŭngjik*) decreased from 34,638 in 1990 to 31,637 in 1993.

Labor Flexibility

To comprehend labor flexibility in today's Korean labor market, it is useful to differentiate two levels of the labor force: regular workers in full-time permanent positions, called ch*ŏ*nggyujik, who receive the full benefits afforded by Korea's labor laws; and nonregular workers, called *pijŏnggyujik*, who do not receive full benefits. The nonregular workers, or *pijŏnggyujik*, include limited-term workers; part-time workers with less than thirty-six hours a week; and atypical workers, including dispatched workers, subcontract workers, specially employed persons, independent contractors, and home-based workers (Kwang-Yeong Shin 2013, 339).

Under these types of work arrangements, the rapid increase in subcontracted workers meant a significant drop in the number of regular HCI workers, especially in Daewoo Heavy Industries, which had adopted the new shipbuilding concept, modeled on the Japanese shipping industry's manufacturing technology. The Daewoo Heavy Industries' new shipbuilding concept primarily aimed to remove the inefficiency and other operational flaws prevalent in the existing production system, especially through systematic application of labor flexibility. By specializing the production organ through the removal of flaws, especially by "categorizing" (*kaebyŏrhwa*) workers on the shop floor, Daewoo aimed to shorten the completion time for shipbuilding from eighteen months to one year by 1993. For this purpose, Daewoo started with the education and training of its rank-and-file workers and their supervisors or foremen (*chikchang* and *panjang*) on the shop floor, while implementing workplace improvement activities, which, according to one study (Pak Chun-sik 1993, 198), increased the firm's productivity by nearly 400 percent in 1993 compared to the early 1980s. This radical increase in productivity was due mainly to the introduction of so-called multifunctionalization (*taginŭnghwa*) of shop floor jobs, which integrated several jobs that had required different workers into one worker with the relevant multi-skills.[9] As a result of this multifunctionalization, many factory jobs that had normally taken the labor of four workers in the past now required just one worker.

An equally radical change to the labor process for increasing productivity on the shop floor seems to have been the then widespread unit-productivity meeting system, similar to what was known in Hyundai Heavy Industries as the "*ture hwaltong*"[10] which, reminiscent of Korea's traditional village co-op system, consisted of three key activities: task improvement, consciousness improvement, and suggestion activity. Consciousness improvement, for example, was divided into six activities: cleaning, safety, timekeeping, teamwork building, ability cultivation, and cooperative manners, all of which essentially aimed to build an enterprise consciousness (*kiŏp ŭisik*), or what many leading Korean firms have referred to as company spirit (*kiŏp chŏngsin*). The Samsung Spirit, the Hyundai Spirit, or the POSCO Spirit tapped into the individual worker's autonomous but mandatory participation in the firm's Corporate Culture Movement. As part of enterprise consciousness, especially by stressing terms such as "autonomy" (*chayul*), "participation" (*ch'amga*), and "tailoring" (*kaebyŏrhwa*), these firms strategically increased the authority and status of middle-ranking supervisors or foremen at the workplace by putting them in charge of quality management and workplace safety management, as well as management of individual workers and the merit-rating process.

This merit rating by supervisors or foremen at the workplace, in particular, directly affected each worker's merit-based wages and promotion, and thus was very effective in implementing workplace labor regulation, even to the extent of workers spying on each other. For this significantly increased authority over their own labor management, Korean firms also conducted systematic leadership education and training courses for their middle-ranking supervisors.[11] Subsequently, supervisors managed their units more effectively by developing various human relations activities while increasing productivity by managing teams to compete with one another in the monthly evaluation, which culminated in either awards or disciplinary penalties. The close involvement of supervisors in social activities, such as informal social gatherings, home visits, weddings, funerals, and even sponsoring of family events, were primarily aimed at building the corporation's Korean-style family ethos, emulating Japanese corporate culture.[12] Ultimately, many leading Korean firms established an effective production network system, especially for building labor flexibility, which, on the one hand, popularized the new corporate culture as "win-win cooperation" and, on the other, brought about change in the collective company-first consciousness of workers.

So successful was the Corporate Culture Movement in the Korean business community at large that by July 1993, leading *chaebŏl*s, such as Daewoo and Samsung Group, awarded special bonuses to their workers to celebrate the three-year no-strike labor-management talks, in the case of Daewoo, and the implementation of a momentous early commuting system and other exceptional measures, including a three- or four-day workweek, in the case of Samsung.[13] The change in attitude of most HCI workers over the course of their company's Corporate Culture Movement, however, led them to expose not only their reluctance to support militant labor unionism and the working-class solidarity struggle, but more notably their incipient class consciousness, perceived by many nonregular subcontracted workers as a "labor aristocracy," as I discuss further below.

Yet, Korea's Corporate Culture Movement has not attracted significant scholarly attention in English. Many scholars, even well-informed observers in today's Korea, tend to think the Korean firms' enterprise consciousness (*kiŏp chŏngsin*) developed in the early 1990s was a false consciousness that covered up the exploitative labor-management relations that relied mainly on a union-bashing strategy to regain control of the shop floor and implement more effective labor management. These views are plausible, especially when one considers that the power of the radical National Council of Trade Unions (Chŏnnohyŏp), under continuous labor repression to the extent of a labor crisis, had lost more than half its membership after one year (An Sŭngch'ŏn 2002, 149–52).

However, to understand the performance-oriented corporate culture of Korean firms, especially of large *chaebŏl*s such as Samsung, Hyundai, and LG, as well as state-owned corporations including POSCO, it is important to go beyond the union-bashing strategy of Korean firms backed by the Korean developmental regimes, as well as views on the Korean industrial workers' changed consciousness. Consideration needs to be given to the Korean model of the Corporate Culture Movement, particularly regarding the productivity management strategy that revived Korea's traditional communal co-op system of *ture* on the shop floor. Hyundai Heavy Industries' *ture hwaltong*, for example, typified how Korean firms, especially the HCI *chaebŏl* management, linked their workers' unit productivity to this traditional system. During the state-led New Community Movement of the 1970s and the *minjung* democratization movement of the 1980s, this system had become a trope symbolizing "one-for-all and all-for one" solidarity. In either case it was anything but democratic.

In fact, no Korean with experience of the 1970s and 1980s can deny that the people worked as "one-for-all and all-for-one" for their country's two consecutive revolutions, initially heavy and chemical industrialization in the 1970s, and then for democratization in the 1980s. Both efforts were spectacularly successful, although each had many inherent flaws and contradictions, not to mention the bitter conflict between Korean conservatives and liberals or progressives. In this sense, it can be argued that the new quasi-cooperative system of productivity management under the banner of the Corporate Culture Movement in Korean firms was at least more efficient and democratic on the shop floor than the old repressive work practices, even though it raised labor intensity and worker surveillance to the extent of becoming the norm in many large HCI *chaebŏl* firms in Korea since the early 1990s, especially after the 1997 crisis.

THE CORPORATE CULTURE MOVEMENT AS A LABOR FLEXIBILITY DEVICE

In terms of achieving flexibility of the labor force, especially through the Corporate Culture Movement, however, nothing was more decisive than the "voluntary" withdrawal of the Kia Machine Tools Union (KMTU) in March 1993 from the Council of Masan and Ch'angwŏn Unions (CMCU; Mach'ang Noryŏn) and the NCTU. On February 17, 1993, the KMTU, known for its record of militant unionism, held an extraordinary general meeting at which it decided to withdraw from the CMCU and the NCTU, with the support of almost 80 percent or 1,209 of 1,512 attending members. In its public statement issued on the same day, the KMTU announced that "the KMTU activities that have ignored the company's critical economic situation caused only the company's contraction" and thus KMT workers had decided to "strive for the normalization of their firm's management."[14]

This withdrawal turned out to be the beginning of a decline in union militancy, with a massive number of workers, including many militant HCI workers, resigning from the union altogether. Shaken by KMTU's announcement, the CMCU newspaper reported that Tan Pyŏng-ho, president of the NCTU, fearing a trickle-down effect throughout the country, desperately sought to stop the KMTU's withdrawal by traveling to Ch'angwŏn the day before the announcement.[15] In observing these activities, newspapers from the southeastern region and Seoul each reported a different story on the KMTU's withdrawal from the NCTU and CMCU, predicting either a "great change in the labor movement" or "smooth sailing in this year's wage negotiations" in the Ch'angwŏn and Ulsan areas.[16] On March 12, 1993, *Chosun Ilbo*, the most influential conservative newspaper in Korea, reported that democratic unions had withdrawn from the CMCU in rapid succession and the total number of unions affiliated with the CMCU had gone from thirty-seven (with over thirty thousand members in 1989) to just nineteen since the KMTU's withdrawal. One major reason for this contagion, as well as for the sea change in the rank-and-file workers' attitude, according to *Chosun Ilbo*, was the surging wave of the workers' "survival instinct" in the face of rising job insecurity and the ongoing economic slump.

According to internal documents of Kia Machine Tools titled *Status Report, 1993* (Hyŏnhwang Pogo, 1993), this radical change was the result of KMT's new management strategy from 1987 to 1992, which focused primarily on "management normalization" of the company, especially by reducing the strength of radical unionism on the shop floor.[17] KMT, an affiliate company of the Kia Group founded in 1976, had started its own new management strategy with the retrenchment of fifty-six managerial staff mainly through reduction in working hours and voluntary retirements. Subsequently KMT set up a new project, "Trans-Mission Production," composed of a three-stage process: (1) normalization of labor relations, (2) management normalization, and (3) improvement of the KMTU from a confrontational organization to a partner organization. Here KMT identified "trust restoration" as its top priority in labor relations. As a preliminary step to implementing this project, KMT analyzed the firm's labor relations, focusing on the major causes of labor disputes led by the KMTU from 1986 to 1993, which included five critical points:

1. The many illegal labor disputes that revolve around the Ch'angwŏn Industrial Park are organized by outsiders, such as students-turned-workers (*hakch'ul*), radical *undongkwŏn* activists, and other dismissed workers turned democratic union movement activists, who, with the rapid rise of the CMCU and its subsequent organizational power backed by the NCTU, have become the leaders of many marginalized workers and their union movement activities since the declaration of democratization on June 29, 1987.
2. Unionized workers' insensitivity to violating laws—and their demand to be paid even for illegal walkouts, wildcat strikes, overtime work refusals, group passes (early leave by groups), slowdowns, and other

illegal strikes—was not offset by any countermeasure or solution to these illegal activities.
3. The KMTU militants had a widespread idea that they could achieve their demands if they fought using Kia Motors' production line as their hostage.
4. The overwhelming management crisis mood was caused by the threat of the firm's demise—due partly to the continuous labor disputes from 1987 to 1990, with a suspension of production for about fifty days annually.
5. There was a loss of management capacity and labor supervisory power under the state of anarchy amid the Great Workers' Struggle.[18]

To normalize company management, the KMT formed an Emergency Planning Committee to enforce a systematic education program that trained executive staff members in leadership skills as a small group activity, while also conducting what the management promoted as "Oneness" (*Hanmaŭm*), an education/training program that was essentially a conscientization campaign. This Oneness program aimed to train every staff member to be in harmony at work "armed mentally, theoretically, and logically" (Kia Machine Tools 1993, 1:8). To this end, the KMT focused on a fivefold strategy that included strengthening the power of managers to control labor autonomously on the shop floor; public relations for sharing information as a norm; staff education as a daily routine, especially focused on sharing information regarding labor relations and promoting policy consistency; the installation of an institutional framework to discipline those who violate company rules using judicial measures while also applying the "no work, no pay" principle;[19] and the practice of exemplary leadership, especially through open company management (Kia Machine Tools 1993, 1:8).

From 1989 to 1993, the KMT systematically educated all managers, including union leaders, in self-improvement through on-the job training, while all workers were sent annually to undertake a course at the Kanaan Farmhand School to cultivate a healthy work spirit.[20] The KMT also sent rank-and-file workers to undertake on-the-job training at motor parts companies in Japan, as well as holding a series of meetings to discuss ways to overcome the company crisis. Regarding public relations on the shop floor for purifying workers' consciousness (*ŭisik sunhwa*), the KMT published in-company PR brochures and the KMT workers' journal, *The Road* (*Kil*), and two other weekly magazines, including *Sound of the Bell* (*Chongsori*), as well as conducting regular briefing sessions on company management. By 1992, according to the *Status Report, 1993* (hereafter the Status Report), KMT's "no work, no pay" rule had been firmly established and the firm had taken strong action against violators by suing five individuals (Kia Machine Tools 1993, 1:8).

In effect, managers on the shop floor responded positively with regained confidence. The Status Report, in its final assessment, noted six key points, including a suggestion that the company must continue its on-the job training for managers to cultivate their alertness, while also uniting the collective will of "warrior-managers" in the firm's efforts to support its workers' recovery of their "industrial warrior consciousness." Handwritten notes on the Status Report by Yu Han-sik, director of KMT's Department of Human Resources Support, showed that the KMT's management normalization project, "Trans-Mission Production," focused primarily on generating "self-awareness" of the KMTU and its rank-and-file members, especially through briefing sessions, open discussions, and many other formal and informal activities, rather than old-style top-down pressure.[21] Yu's handwritten notes stated, "Let's make the KMT rank-and-file workers stop those who are beating their own children," and referred to POSCO as a model of what he described as "a self-awakened company" that had "awakened" its workers to withdraw from the union, which in turn led to dissolution of the POSCO Union in July 1992. As part of its key strategy, KMT, like Daewoo, Samsung, and many other leading HCI firms, actively promoted so-called win-win cooperation within the framework of the Corporate Culture Movement by sponsoring workers' social activities, including sports events, hobby group activities, and recreational tours for workers' parents.

As table 3.3 shows, by March 1993, KMT was running a number of staff-welfare programs, including a scholarship program for the children of workers with a record of more than two years continuous service. KMT also provided various service facilities, including a barbershop, laundry, and gym, free of charge, while also offering workers cheap loans to purchase a house or apartment (₩7 million) or to rent accommodation (₩3 million), at a 3 percent rate of interest, with repayment over ten years for purchases or five years for rentals (Kia Machine Tools 1993, 1:41). These staff-welfare programs were similar to those of the Hyundai Group, Daewoo, and POSCO. Although the Status Report did not remark on the KMTU's withdrawal from both the NCTU and the CMCU, KMT clearly succeeded in "awakening" or changing the hearts and minds of its workers to push for their union's withdrawal from these two widely known militant union organizations. In

TABLE 3.3. Kia Machine Tools employees' benefits and privileges, March 1993

Benefit	Status	Benefit	Status
Scholarship subsidy for children	For children of staff members with more than two years of service, middle and high school fully paid; university half paid	Dormitory	180 persons
Apartment	231 households	Meals	₩800 per meal
Workweek	44 hours	Loans for buying home	₩7 million at 3% interest with repayment over ten years
House lease subsidy	₩3 million at 3% interest; repayment over five years	Barbershop	Free facility near company
Laundry	Free facility at designated locations	Free commuter buses	19 buses (13 company buses and 6 leased)
Regular retirement	At fifty-five	Gym	Installation of a body-building gym
Cooperative Union	Management of a new Cooperative Union building in Yosu with profits and dividends to members	Cooperative store	Co-op offering goods at cost
Other benefits	Filial tours for staff members' aged parents Computer classes for staff members' children Culture classes for staff members' wives	Industrial accident and sick-leave pay	Disability pay at 30% of regular wages Sick leave paid at 60–90% of regular wages for up to four months

Source: Based on Kia Machine Tools (1993, table 6).

fact, many rank-and-file KMT workers, including union leaders, openly discussed the idea that the company might go bankrupt. What was the key factor that generated this company-first attitude among the KMT workers? In his 2015 interview with this author, Yu Han-sik said:

> As a young man who had begun a career as a skilled worker myself, I genuinely understood the rank-and-file KMT workers' grievances and distrust of not just management but also their own militant union leaders' radical approach. So we tried to build our workers' trust of the management by sharing information regarding the company's economic condition, sale

matters, and labor-related problems, among other matters, and by talking openly and regularly about them. So, if I may use one key term to explain the success behind the withdrawal of Kia Machine Tools Union from the National Council of Trade Unions and the Council of Masan and Ch'angwŏn Unions, it was trust restoration through our Trans-Mission Production project. (Ch'angwŏn, April 18)

Here the phrase "trust restoration" ironically reflected the widespread sellout deals between many leading firms' democratic union leaders and management over 1992 wage increases. The militant democratic union leaders of Hyundai Heavy Industries, Halla Heavy Industry, and Hanjin Heavy Industry, among many other large HCI firms, for example, had signed tentative agreements on 1992 wage increases that were rejected at their unions' general meetings in July (in the case of Halla and Hanjin) and September 1992 (in the case of Hyundai Heavy Industries) (An Sŭng-ch'ŏn 2002, 139–41). The testimony of Kim Chun-sik, former president of the KMTU (1987–89), however, provided an alternative perspective on labor repression by management in his lengthy interviews with this author in 2010 and 2011: "The members of the Kia Machine Tools Union were very anxious and worried because its withdrawal from the NCTU (Chŏnnohyŏp) and the CMCU (Mach'ang Noryŏn) had been directed by the company owner. In order to conciliate the workers on the shop floor, KMT further strengthened its shop floor surveillance system while also attempting continuously to neutralize the union" (Ch'angwŏn, November 17, 2010, and November 9, 2011).

Kim recalled that thirteen workers, dismissed in 1990, struggled for reinstatement over the next ten years but failed. Ultimately, they gave up on reinstatement but received some compensation. Kim claimed that Kia Machine Tools' surveillance system scared many rank-and-file workers, and he strongly hinted that the KMTU's "voluntary withdrawal" from the NCTU and CMCU had to be effective for the workers.[22] I heard recollections similar to Kim's during my April and November 2012 interviews with other HCI workers and former union leaders in Ch'angwŏn, Ulsan, and Kyungju in the southeastern industrial belt, especially about the systematic surveillance by HCI firms, even outside the workplace. Surveillance by HCI firms was particularly focused on certain union leaders and hard-core rank-and-file workers who had been blacklisted by management.[23]

One interviewee, under the pseudonym Mr. Shin, recalled that after 1993 his company managed union leaders with a special surveillance system combined with blacklisting. Mr. Shin also said that in this radically changed workplace environment with a new corporate culture, his "bursting dream" to become a "flag-bearer of the modernization of the fatherland" (*choguk kŭndaehwa ŭi kisu*) and an "industrial warrior," had come to nothing since Park Chung Hee was assassinated (author interview, Ulsan, November 26, 2012). In spite of this candid recollection, the transformation of HCI workers into a privileged group, especially with their collective incipient class consciousness as a labor aristocracy, seems not to have been accidental, whether or not the HCI workers consciously planned this transformation.

INCIPIENT CLASS CONSCIOUSNESS AS A LABOR ARISTOCRACY

One of the most radical changes that came out of the Corporate Culture Movement, especially in Hyundai Heavy Industries (HHI), occurred when its rank-and-file workers and their families showed their disregard of the HHI Union's tentative agreement to conduct labor disputes by not showing up at its general meeting on June 16, 1995. As a result, the HHI Union changed its position and signed what became known as a "no-strike, no-dispute labor-management" deal, which would continue for the next nineteen years, from 1995 to November 2014.[24] This remarkable change in the HHI workers' collective position on strikes reflected the steady growth in their incipient class consciousness as a labor aristocracy since the early 1990s. Equally remarkable was that the steady growth in incipient class consciousness as a labor aristocracy occurred not just among the regular shipbuilding workers of the HHI but more broadly among the HCI workers of large *chaebŏl* firms with their union membership composed of regular workers. In this respect, the local newspaper, *Kyŏngsang Ilbo*, in Ulsan, the home base of the majority of Korean HCI workers, including Hyundai workers, first raised the problem of "the tyranny of labor aristocracy," a phrase used by nonregular or often by subcontracted workers of HCI manufacturing firms in the Ulsan area. They publicly expressed their collective grievances against the shifting of the layoff problem by unions at large HCI *chaebŏl* firms onto subcontracted workers in the Ulsan area. On February 25, 1993, the *Kyŏngsang Ilbo* wrote:

> There is concern about the friction between a considerable number of large [*chaebŏl*]-firm unions in the Ulsan area and subcontracted workers over the

large [*chaebŏl*]-firm unions' demand to lay off subcontracted workers first in order to solve the problem of staff [regular workers] reduction following management instability.... The subcontractors have reacted against this by saying, "It is a 'tyranny of labor aristocracy' to shift the main cause of their own layoff problem to subcontract workers who work for low wages under bad working conditions." (Quoted in Yu Hyŏng-gŭn 2012, 221)

The public outcry by nonregular workers against the tyranny of the labor aristocracy had little or no effect on many HCI *chaebŏl* unions and their hard-core rank-and-file members, who appeared to have been preoccupied with their own problems, especially regarding the above-noted new management strategies (*sin kyŏngyŏng chŏllyak*) of their firms. On June 21, 1995, for example, Pak Sam-hun, a production worker at Daewoo's shipbuilding plant, immolated himself on the rooftop of his workplace in protest against his firm's new management strategy while his union, similar to some twenty other unions in the motor industry, including Hyundai Motor, Hanjin Heavy Industries, and Kia Motors, went on an all-out strike against the Kim Young-sam regime's labor control policies, especially against the workers' struggle for the annual wage increase in 1995. Pak, forty-one years old and married with two children, was the second to immolate himself at that time, after Yang Pong-su (thirty-one years) of Hyundai Motor Union had immolated himself about four weeks earlier on May 12.

In discussing the successive immolations of Pak and Yang, An Sŭng-ch'ŏn, former president of Korean Workers' Labor Movement Solidarity (Han'guk Nodongja Undong Yŏndae), argued that the major cause of the immolations of these two hard-core activists of Hyundai Motor Union and Daewoo Heavy Industries Union, which were the vanguard of the Korean workers' democratic labor union movement, was that they had a sense of a crisis regarding the markedly fallen control of the democratic *minju* faction on the production site (An Sŭng-ch'ŏn 2002, 165). An went on to assert that as early as July 1, 1994, the Daewoo Heavy Industries Union, under the leadership of Choi Ŭn-sŏk and his executive team, carried out an "absence strike" (*kyŏlgŭn p'aŏp*), directing their members to be absent from work. But over 90 percent of the union's worker-members ignored this order by coming to work. In June 1995, a dispute resolution submitted by the union's executive branch was rejected at the representatives' convention. An contended that the Hyundai Motor Union, during the two-year period under the leadership of Yi Yŏng-bok and his executive branch, had failed to slow the conveyer belt, which had become continuously faster. Instead of protecting the voluntary struggle led by each department regarding this problem, An argued, the union had ignored these struggles, largely because of the Korean capitalists' dogged attack, which had driven the democratic labor union movement into a crisis. Through their adoption of the neoliberal new management strategy, An concluded, the Korean capitalists had taken control of the unions from below, while also strengthening their control of the production site (An Sŭng-ch'ŏn 2002, 165–66). A personal view, especially regarding union representatives' undemocratic bossiness in disregarding the interests of their rank-and-file members, was articulated by one of my 2012 interviewees, Mr. K. Pak, a master craftsman with a work record of more than thirty-six years at Doosan Heavy Industries (formerly Daewoo Heavy Industries, Ch'angwŏn): "Most of those hardline [kangsŏng] union reps behave the same. They are bullies and don't care about anyone other than their own vested interests. Because I did not attend several meetings as I had training sessions with a special technician from Germany, they expelled me in either 1999 or 2000, and since then they have asked me to register for membership, but I declined" (author interview, Ch'angwon, April 2012).

No wonder the power struggle on the production site (often referred to as the "shop floor") crumbled between 1993 and 1995, effecting a dramatic change in the consciousness of HCI rank-and-file workers that was reflected in the reduction in national union density. It had slid to 14.5 percent by 1994, losing more than one percentage point annually from its peak at 19.8 percent in 1989 (see figure 5.1). The most obvious reasons for this sweeping change in blue-collar Korean workers' consciousness and attitude, especially regarding democratic union activities at the workplace, according to a survey by the Korean Democratic Workers' Coalition (Han'guk Minju Nodongja Yŏnhap), were "the egotistic climate all-round of caring about personal self-interest rather than the interests of the entire union membership" (22.3 percent), "workers' apathy regarding union affairs itself" (15.5 percent), "the opportunistic attribute of some union representatives" (15.5 percent), "company interference and suppression" (13.6 percent), and "governmental authority interference and suppression" (8.7 percent) (quoted in Pak Sŭng-ok 1992, 224). The changing lifestyle of workers reflected in the survey is described in an article in the *Workers' Newspaper* (Nodongja sinmun) of March 6, 1992: "The spread of a bourgeois lifestyle and the flooding of individualism among [white-collar] clerical workers and [blue-collar] skilled workers made it impossible to hold meetings on Saturdays and Sundays, and although they [the white-collar clerical workers and blue-collar skilled workers] acknowledged the necessity of union activity, they themselves became bystanders" (quoted in Pak Sŭng-ok 1992, 221). In this light, it is not difficult to comprehend the extent of the dramatic change in HCI workers' lifestyle, especially their unprecedented wage increases, as nominal wages had more than doubled in the four years from 1987 to 1991, improved working conditions, and the shifting of so-called "3-D" (dirty, dangerous, and difficult) jobs to subcontracted workers, while they also received various benefits secured through their union-led collective enterprise bargaining. Naturally, their social expectations drastically increased. Many newly available company-sponsored family events, cultural programs, and other forms of leisure activities captured the interest of HCI workers and their families, similar to many newly emerged middle-class white-collar workers. Overall, this survey matches the findings of my own in-depth surveys carried out in 2014 and early 2015 (see chapter 5). Well over 30 percent of all respondents, who were HCI workers with more than thirty years of employment in their respective firms in the HCI sector, had come to own their first car by 1992, with some owning one as early as 1986–87.

In fact, about 10–30 percent of workers in some leading firms, predominantly HCI workers, commuted to and from the workplace using their own vehicle at that time (Pak Sŭng-ok 1992, 224). The HCI workers' new consumerism appears to have reflected the emergent new middle class in Korean society in the early 1990s, similar to the emergent rich middle classes in many countries in the Asian region (Goodman and Robinson 1996). Referring to survey data on 1,208 production workers from thirteen large *chaebŏl* HCI firms during February and March 1991, Pak Sŭng-ok (1992, 225), a former labor movement activist and now labor policy analyst, argues, "Ultimately, we can find that the workers at the low-wage level prefer a 'militant union' and 'political unionism' and the workers at the high-wage level, such as HCI workers, prefer a 'cooperative union' and 'economic unionism.'" Some labor experts have viewed the vastly changed attitude of Korean workers, including HCI workers, toward their unions as a new development in exhibiting a "dual consciousness and free-rider mentality," regarding their union as a kind of "employment safety pin" or even as a "vending machine union" for self-help (Kim Wŏn 2007, 104). As if conscious of this view and other similar critical views on the change in HCI workers' free-rider mentality, especially regarding their collective aim of economic unionism, one HCI worker, Mr. Ch'oe, emotionally recalled his experience from the early 1990s in his interview with the author: "It was not easy for us to learn so many new skills and rules in those days. But with four young children..., especially extra study for two boys in a *hagwŏn* [private supplementary educational institute], I could not do anything but work and do whatever the managers told me to do just to hold on to my job. I could have sold anything, even my own soul, for my children's education to go to university, which my two sons eventually did" (Ch'angwŏn, April 18, 2015).

CONCLUSION

The impact of the state/capitalist counterrevolution via the Corporate Culture Movement was overwhelming, especially in terms of restoring a hegemonic labor management structure at the workplace for neoliberal capital accumulation. In response, the majority of HCI workers readily acquiesced to their firm's corporate culture program by transforming their militant labor unionism into a company-first neoliberal mind-set while also preserving their own parochial economic interests through social closure by exposing their incipient class consciousness as a labor aristocracy. In effect, the Korean firms' Corporate Culture Movement laid out a foundation for Korea's neoliberal capitalist system, focused on flexibility of the work force through growth in in-house subcontracting. In fact, this new mode of dual labor management was initiated and normalized by HCI *chaebŏl*s in the shipbuilding, steelmaking, construction, and automobile industries.[25] The success of the Korean firms' Corporate Culture Movement also led to a new culture of performance-based productivity, which increased the power of the *chaebŏl* under the Kim Young-sam government (Lim and Jang 2006, 445). Remarkably, this did not mean that HCI workers and the rest of Korean workers succumbed unconditionally to the state/capitalists by giving up their collective struggle of militant labor unionism altogether. When the Kim government introduced a set of neoliberal labor laws in favor of the *chaebŏls*' united push for economic liberalization, a general strike broke out in late December 1996 and continued into March 1997, a prelude to the Asian financial crisis in late December of that year. Needless to say, the HCI workers were at the forefront of this all-out strike, but not necessarily in support of class solidarity with a wide range of workers as per their earlier Goliat warrior consciousness.

CHAPTER 4

The Asian Financial Crisis

HCI Workers' Social Closure and the Rise of Chaebŏl *Dominance*

THE general strike of 1996–97 was triggered by the ruling New Korea Party (Sin Han'guktang) when it resorted to railroading a set of new labor laws through the National Assembly at 6:00 a.m. on December 26, 1996, without the presence of opposition lawmakers. The labor laws, which were more restrictive than the government's earlier proposal,[1] postponed legalization of the Korean Confederation of Trade Unions (KCTU) until 2000,[2] as well as delaying the legalization of multiple local unions until 2002, among other union restrictions. These new labor laws legalized layoffs in the case of mergers and acquisitions and in firms in danger of bankruptcy, along with other special acts to empower the Agency for National Security Planning to investigate anyone under suspicion of either praising North Korea or of not reporting any activity of North Korean sympathizers.

Regarded by many both nationally and internationally as one of the largest antineoliberal labor protests in the world at that time, some 3.6 million Korean workers participated in this largest general strike in Korean history. Many civic organizations and middle-class white-collar workers joined the protest, not to mention the militant blue-collar elite HCI workers and their radical umbrella organization, the KCTU, as well as workers from the conservative Federation of Korean Trade Unions (FKTU). They were all worried about the new labor laws, which threatened their job security. Clearly, this seventy-five-day general strike, from December 26, 1996, to March 10, 1997, represented not only the Korean workers' long march toward the "final settlement" of their struggle against the state's labor law reforms over the previous ten years, but also class warfare between Korean workers (both white-collar and blue-collar) and the state/capitalist ruling class. The general strike, in fact, turned out to be a prelude to the Asian financial crisis of 1997–98, the most severe national calamity since the Korean War.[3]

The crisis started early in 1997, when Hanbo, the fourteenth-largest conglomerate in Korea at that time, and seven of the thirty largest *chaebŏl* groups, including Kia Motors, Halla, Sammi, and Jinro, went bankrupt, along with a massive number of SMEs. In addition, Hanbo was found to have been embroiled in corruption with regard to preferential loans involving President Kim Young-sam's second son, Hyŏn-ch'ŏl, who was subsequently arrested. The collapse of Hanbo shook the confidence of foreign lenders, and then Kia Motors, the eighth biggest *chaebŏl* in Korea, with twenty-eight domestic and ten overseas subsidiaries, went under legal administration in October 1997.[4] The domino-like bankruptcies quickly led to the collapse of the Korean economy less than one month before the presidential election scheduled in December 1997.

BANKRUPTCY, BUSINESS RESTRUCTURING, AND HCI WORKERS' RESPONSE

Korea's so-called IMF era began when the Korean government signed a massive bailout agreement with the International Monetary Fund on December 5, 1997, and received $58.35 billion, equal to 13 percent of South Korea's GNP of $437 billion (Han'guk Ŭnhaeng 2010, 228). In providing this relief loan, the IMF made the Korean government scrap the requirement that foreign investment be limited to a 49 percent share of Korean companies, and that *chaebŏl*s sell off their subsidiaries to foreign buyers in order to reduce their debt-to-equity ratios. With these preconditions, President Kim Daejung, known as "DJ," newly inaugurated on February 25, 1998, committed to a comprehensive neoliberal restructuring of the finance, business, labor, and public sectors in order to relieve the structural problems of the Korean economy, among other improvements, to match global standards (Shin and Chang 2003, 70–76).

The DJ government's sweeping neoliberal reforms, particularly in regard to the application of the 8 percent risk-asset ratio set by the Bank for International Settlements, led to the closure of sixteen finance companies.[5] In a desperate effort to defend its currency, as advised by the IMF, the DJ government applied a maximum 200 percent debt-to-equity ratio limit to Korean businesses, which resulted in many companies with a higher ratio going bankrupt, including the seven aforementioned *chaebŏl* corporations. As labor shedding became one of the most crucial measures for rescuing Korean firms, the DJ government pushed ahead with reforms enabling companies to lay off employees more freely. As a result, the unemployment rate shot up from 2.6 percent in 1997 to 17.4 percent by January 1999, with the number of unemployed having rapidly increased to 3.68 million (An Sŭngch'ŏn 2002, 226). Table 4.1 illustrates the change in newly employed persons in various job fields from June 1997 to June 2000. The number of craftsmen (*kinŭngwŏn*),[6] one of the two HCI workers' categories, had decreased to 76.9 percent of the 1997 level by June 1998, to 81.5 percent by June 1999, and

TABLE 4.1. Fluctuations in employment by occupational category, before and after the 1997 crisis

Occupation	No. of workers in thousands (% of June 1997 figure)			
	June 1997	June 1998	June 1999	June 2000
Managers	519 (100%)	495 (95.4%)	461 (88.8%)	462 (89.0%)
Professionals	1,008 (100%)	1,118 (110.9%)	1,068 (106.0%)	1,119 (111.0%)
Technicians and semitechnical experts	2,237 (100%)	2,138 (95.6%)	2,351 (105.1%)	2,385 (106.6%)
Clerks	2,652 (100%)	2,481 (93.6%)	2,298 (86.7%)	2,490 (93.9%)
Sales workers	4,860 (100%)	4,704 (96.8%)	4,792 (98.6%)	5,038 (103.7%)
Workers in agriculture and fishery	2,398 (100%)	2,595 (108.2%)	2,431 (101.4%)	2,350 (98.0%)
Craftsmen	3,229 (100%)	2,483 (76.9%)	2632 (81.5%)	2,772 (85.8 %)
Equipment operators, machinists, assembly workers	2,222 (100%)	2,084 (93.8%)	2,105 (94.7%)	2,238 (100.7%)
Laborers	2,398 (100%)	2,316 (86.6%)	2,077 (102.6%)	2,247 (109.6%)
Total employed	21,523 (100%)	20,175 (93.7%)	20,599 (95.7%)	21,475 (99.8%)

Source: Based on Shin Kwang-Yong (2004, table 3).

to 85.8 percent by June 2000, showing that this craftsmen category had suffered a significantly larger than average setback from the crisis. These rates, converted to the number of jobs lost in this category, amounted to 746,000 craftsman jobs lost in the year after June 1997, though 149,000 craftsman jobs had been recovered by June 1999, and another 140,000 by June 2000.

Another HCI category, equipment operators, machinists, and assembly workers, also showed employment decreasing to 93.8 percent of the 1997 level, or an approximate decrease of 140,000 jobs from June 1997 to June 1998. This category of employment, compared to the 1997 level, slightly increased to 94.7 percent, for an approximate loss of 120,000 jobs by June 1999. Clearly the crisis had a disastrous effect on the employment of these two categories of workers.[7] These figures show overall that the decrease in the employment rate resulting from the Asian financial crisis had a serious impact on HCI workers, resulting in a massive number of unemployed skilled and semi-skilled workers. This postcrisis labor restructuring also reflected an oversupply of skilled labor in the Korean automobile industry, which had almost doubled production, from 2.06 million vehicles in 1990 to 4 million in 1998. Not surprisingly, the restructuring of the automobile industry typified the extremely high level of competition among *chaebŏl*s, especially at the top level, as *chaebŏl*s aggressively pushed their own firms' neoliberal restructuring as part of the government's structural readjustment plan through mergers and acquisitions, downsizing, the sale of shares to foreign investors, and other unprecedented policies. The deepening problem of job insecurity amid this "greater employer militancy" (Gray 2008, 116) frightened HCI workers, their families, and even their militant unions, which agreed to no-strike agreements with employers to preserve existing jobs. The case of Kia workers provides a classic example of patriotic unionism or business-first unionism in an effort to save the company before it went bankrupt. The following case studies of the restructuring of Kia Motors, Hyundai Motor, and Hyundai Heavy Industries shed much light on this phenomenon in the course of neoliberal restructuring.

KIA MOTORS' BANKRUPTCY

Kia Motors, the core company of the Kia Group and the eighth largest *chaebŏl* in Korea, was the first victim of the 1997 crisis, due mainly to the company's overinvestment, in an attempt to increase its domestic and export market share by rapidly expanding production capacity. Kia's problem was that it relied heavily on debt financing, especially short-term loans through nonbank financial institutions, to the extent that its debt-to-equity ratio reached 519 percent by the end of 1997, about 130 percentage points higher than a year earlier and considerably higher than the other thirty largest *chaebŏl*s (Nam, Kang, and Kim 1999, 2). Kia's downfall generated heated debate largely because it was seen as having been sabotaged—despite its good public reputation as a "national company" (*kungmin kiŏp*)—by the Kim Young-sam government and Samsung, then the second-largest *chaebŏl* after Hyundai. The primary reason for this speculation of sabotage was that, unlike most other big *chaebŏl* firms, the Kia Group (hereafter Kia) was managed by a professional CEO, Kim Sŏn-hong, who held just 0.1 percent of the firm's shares.

According to Kia management and the Kia Union, Samsung and the government (especially Deputy Prime Minister Kang Kyŏng-sik) brought down Kia Motors by conspiring to have Samsung take over Kia, and to do this, Samsung and the government attempted to purge Kim Sŏn-hong (Cho Sŏng-jae 1998, 83).[8] To stop this sabotage, the Kia Motors Union and twenty-eight Kia subsidiary firms started a wage freeze combined with wage cuts, as well as a nationwide fund-raising campaign to collect ₩1 billion per subsidiary firm to save the corporation (Kim Ki-wŏn 2002, 7–8). Over twenty civic organizations, including the KCTU, played a leading role in the "Save Kia" campaign by forming what they called the Alliance of the Pan-National Movement for Saving Kia (Kia Salligi Pŏmkungmin Undong Yŏnhap) under the slogans "patriotic unionism" and "business-first unionism."

The popularity of this campaign, especially among supporters of the KCTU and other labor movement activists and intellectuals did not, however, mean that there was no opposition even among leftist intellectuals. Chŏng Un-yŏng, a leftist economist, for example, argued in an essay featured in *Hankyoreh Sinmun*, a leading progressive newspaper, on August 5, 1997, that Kia was not a "national company" but a *chaebŏl* and thus should go out of business like any other mismanaged *chaebŏl*. Others argued that the Save Kia campaign, with the involvement of the Korean Automobile Federation and the KCTU, represented inappropriate labor-management cooperation, in which the union was abrogating its responsibility by giving up its own rights and priorities in favor of "labor-management cooperation" or "labor-management harmony" (Ch'ae Man-su 1997). Nonetheless, Kia Motors eventually went under legal administration in October 1997 and was taken over by Hyundai Motor at the end of 1998. Yu Han-sik, then managing director of the machinery division and director of research and development at Kia Heavy Industry, one of the key subsidiaries of Kia Motors, reminisced in 2015: "We cut back 436 out of 2,047 workers in July 1998 and applied for mediation to the creditors, but this was rejected. KHI [Kia Heavy Industry] eventually merged with Hyundai WIA. I resigned from Hyundai WIA in March 2003 after completing my last bit of work required for the takeover force" (author interview, Ch'angwŏn, April 18, 2015).

Hyundai Motor's Restructuring

The restructuring of Hyundai Motor was driven mainly by internal conflicts in the management structure of the Hyundai Group, which comprised many sons under their monarchical father Chŏng Chu-yŏng, the founder of Hyundai Group. Known in Korea as the "Princes' Revolt," Hyundai Motor's restructuring, led by its CEO Chŏng Mong-ku (Chung Mong-koo), was a success, especially in terms of growth in business after it took over Kia Motor, one of Hyundai Motor's three competitors at that time, which also included Daewoo and Ssangyong Motors.[9] From the perspective of Hyundai Motor workers, however, things were not very different from the shattering experience of Kia Motor workers, because they, like the Kia workers, also faced massive layoffs. In fact, through the first and second layoffs, formally announced to the Hyundai Motor Union (HMU) on July 16 and August 10, 1998, Hyundai Motor management laid off several thousand workers, even though some 8,194 workers were already leaving in a form of voluntary retirement (hŭimang t'oejik) in the three months following June 1998 (An Sŭng-ch'ŏn 2002, 219).

Among the workers who were subject to the layoffs were three hundred union leaders, but the negotiations on implementation between the HMU and management fell apart because management insisted that staff redundancies were necessary to attract foreign capital. The massive layoffs were largely an outcome of the controversial "February Agreement" of the labor-business-government Tripartite Commission, in which unions allowed a set of layoff measures, including "the earlier and easier implementation of layoffs by removing the provision of a two-year-moratorium" and the operation of "temporary-work agencies" for the flexible deployment of contingent labor, among other measures (Dae-Oup Chang 2002, 25). Hence, the HMU's thirty-six-day strike starting on July 20, 1998, became the first test of the neoliberal restructuring plans of the newly inaugurated president, Kim Dae-jung, especially in terms of countering his government's autocratic deployment of some ten thousand riot police on the streets of Ulsan, blocking the factory gates of Hyundai Motor.

After several days of intense negotiations between Hyundai Motor management and the HMU, an agreement was reached on August 24, when CEO Chŏng Mong-ku and Kim Kwang-sik, president of the HMU, jointly announced that "277 workers be laid off out of the 1,538 workers who were listed to be laid off" (quoted in An Sŭng-ch'ŏn 2002, 220). Although this agreement was the outcome of government-mediated negotiations,[10] it turned out that Kim had also agreed to the layoff of the other 1,261 workers by forcing them to take eighteen months unpaid leave. Amid these massive layoffs, however, three hundred female nonregular canteen staff members were laid off, whereas the regular male HMU members, including the aforementioned three hundred union leaders, all escaped the dismissal that had been set out in the company's original plan. The outraged striking workers of Hyundai Motor and many other firms, especially Mando Machinery, an American auto parts manufacturer, were struck by a sense of betrayal, mainly because the HMU's thirty-six-day strike, in the eyes of the striking workers, represented a broader labor-capital struggle (Neary 2000, 2) or "a proxy war between Korea's total capital and total workforce" (Yu Kyŏng-sun 2010). Therefore, the striking Hyundai Motor workers condemned their union leaders as "traitorous" and overwhelmingly rejected Kim's agreement with management at the union's general meeting on September 4, with 63.6 percent of the members vetoing the agreement (Cho Hyŏng-je 1999, 74).

Overall, HMU's capitulation concretely showed the underpinning labor aristocracy consciousness and approach of the HCI workers and their *chaebŏl* unions in the crisis. The HCI unions had openly used nonregular in-house subcontractor workers (predominantly female workers) as a buffer to safeguard the existing jobs of their union members. This blatant social closure, by denying access to others, especially in-house subcontractors, to the large *chaebŏl* unions' scarce resources, including membership itself, quickly became the standard union model in big companies, by which HCI workers sought only their own parochial interests of "maximum economic compensation through maximum struggle" (quoted in Cho Hyŏng-je 1999, 64) throughout the booming economy after 1997. What drove the HCI workers was their collective fear of unemployment in the face of declining jobs.

In effect, the Hyundai Motor Union's capitulation to layoffs was the beginning of the Kim Dae-jung government's acceleration of its get-tough policy toward striking workers, in which a massive number of riot police were deployed to regain control over workplaces in Ulsan. By arresting Kim Kwang-sik, president of HMU, and fourteen other union representatives, the government even broke an agreement not to arrest Kim. Moreover, the government took disciplinary action against some ninety other union leaders, among various other measures (An Sŭng-ch'ŏn 2002, 220–21).[11] One recently available research study found that Hyundai Motor had already laid off 1,722 nonregular workers by replacing them with regular workers as a general practice, to avoid the layoff of regular workers prior to beginning its adjustment of regular workers in the postcrisis restructuring (Yu Hyŏng-gŭn 2012, 221). The worst aspect of the HMU's agreement to allow the layoffs was that it set a precedent for other *chaebŏl* unions to make similar deals by reserving scarce resources for their own members through social closure. As a result, many unions of SMEs, which comprised largely in-house subcontractor nonregular workers, ceased their strikes protesting layoffs, even in the brinkmanship situation of redundancies. The fact that overall the HMU's defeat had led to the redundancy of 10,166 workers, about 22 percent of Hyundai Motor's entire workforce, demonstrated not just the union's failure to stop management's restructuring plans, but more seriously the leadership failure of the KCTU, which had broken its promise to members by canceling its planned general strike.

Hyundai Heavy Industries' No Labor Restructuring

Yet the 1997 crisis did not have the same effect on every HCI worker. The HCI workers of Hyundai Heavy Industries (HHI) and their union, in particular, had become a "symbol of labor-management harmony," as exemplified in their twenty-year unbroken no-strike record, from 1995 to November 2014.[12] Despite the crisis, HHI workers were unaffected because their management promised not to enforce any artificial labor restructuring that would affect the economic interests of union members. Furthermore, the HHI workers and their union were publicly praised for their labor-management cooperation, to the extent of developing their company into the world's largest shipbuilding company, and they received many awards, including one from the president.[13] Behind this widely publicized labor-management harmony, however, were two major factors unknown to outsiders until recently. One is that the HHI rank-and-file workers had put forward a petition for a no-strike settlement in wage negotiations in 1995, and the company had accepted it by offering a wage increase of 7.7 percent, plus 210 percent of wages as a performance-based bonus, and 100 percent of wages as a no-strike incentive.[14] In a special report titled "Hyundai Heavy Industries Union, with Its No-Strike Record for 20 Years, Never Gave Way Even Once," published by the daily newspaper *Maeil Kyŏngje* in Seoul on November 20, 2014, Kim Ki-ch'ŏl wrote: "Although the history of no strikes continued, the Hyundai Heavy Industries Union never gave way even once. When the [company's] performance was good, wage negotiation was settled by a high wage increase and performance-based benefits; when the going got tough in achieving performance, [the union] took benefits by obtaining employment guarantees and the expansion of other employee benefits."

Another and perhaps more physical reason for the HHI record of no-strike labor-management harmony, was the company's systematic surveillance system, in which every union activity was controlled by managers, from actively preventing militant unionists from being elected as union representatives to assessing every move in union activities by planting spies on the shop floor and outside the firm. This extraordinary surveillance system was made public in March 2016, when *Pressian*, a leading internet news agency in Seoul, featured an article based on three volumes of a private log book recorded and owned by a former director of the Operations Division (Unyŏnggwa) at Hyundai Heavy Industries from 2004 to May 2011. One entry of the log book, dated November 22 (no mention of the year), states:

1. The meeting of the Tongji Yŏnhap (Comrade Alliance) (in the Chŏnnohoe office), 59 members attended. Let many [of them] be elected— Without a meal [*kyŏlsik*] event. Confident about at least twenty to be elected.
2. Will make a representative from the Marine [Division]—Yi Chŏng-ha [looks] hopeful—[he is] tenacious and has a very strong will—is registered.
3. Ship [Division]—Cho Han-su, Pak Chin-ch'ŏl—very strong—urging them to give up registering—do not express their own thoughts. . . .
6. Must move the members' hearts—need effort.—Use opinion leaders (OL).—persuasive stakeholders be persistent and tenacious.
7. It never is an easy election. Many situations are all slow.[15]

This note and various related articles—including several interviews with Yi Chae-rim, who had been chief of labor management for twenty-four years while working for HHI from 1979 until his retirement in May 2011, according to the reporter (Hŏ Hwan-ju 2016b)—concretely showed how HHI managed the union through its deployment of various control measures, such as mobilizing managers and other "opinion leaders" at the workplace, who in effect carried out multiple activities, from intervening in the union elections, to bribing procompany union representatives, to creating procompany public opinion among rank-and-file HHI worker-members. Here it would be fair to note that the use of various control measures on labor union leaders was not limited to Hyundai Heavy Industries. Similar practices, including blacklisting, were the norm across many large *chaebŏl* firms, and even some SMEs in the HCI sector.

THE KIM DAE-JUNG GOVERNMENT'S CRISIS MANAGEMENT

To implement the comprehensive IMF-mandated reforms, a national negotiation forum called the Tripartite Commission was established in January 1998 by President-elect Kim Dae-jung. The Tripartite Commission involved eleven senior figures, one each from the government, the main political parties, both the radical KCTU and the moderate FKTU, and business. After three weeks of intense negotiations, the commission announced its controversial February Agreement on February 6 with an emphasis on the "grand compromise" of fair burden sharing, which included five main points: (1) the reform of *chaebŏls*; (2) countermeasures against unemployment; (3) the ratification of the legal status of labor unions, including the KCTU, and the dismantling of the old authoritarian restraints; (4) enhanced labor flexibility; and (5) the extension of the social pact into an institutional framework for long-term cooperation (Sun 2002, 260–61; Kong 2000?, 25).[16] On February 14, nineteen articles, including the Labor Standards Act (Kŭllo Kijunbŏp), were passed by the National Assembly, which allowed a more flexible and expansive basis for dismissals while also establishing a legal infrastructure for dispatched labor so that the government's policy of restructuring large *chaebŏl* corporations could be executed more smoothly.

The radical KCTU quickly ran into trouble, however, when delegates overwhelmingly rejected its leadership, which had agreed to the controversial February Agreement. So outraged were the KCTU delegates with their leaders' "traitorous act" in reversing a preexisting resolution made at a KCTU delegates' conference that they passed a vote of no confidence in KCTU's entire leadership, including its acting president, Pae Sŏk-bŏm, by 184 votes to 54 (77–23 percent) at their temporary delegates' conference on February 9, 1998.[17] Accordingly, the KCTU leadership resigned. The delegates argued that what their leadership had agreed to was not a fair burden-sharing agreement based on *chaebŏl* reform and employment stability, but an agreement to impose the burden of mass unemployment on workers and to concede the weakening of their unions (Sun 2002, 275).

The delegates' rejection of the KCTU leadership led to the election on March 31, 1998, of Yi Kab-yong, former president of the militant Hyundai Heavy Industries Union, as the new KCTU president, although by a narrow margin. Supported mainly by those who had rejected the previous leadership, especially striking rank-and-file HCI workers, Yi withdrew the KCTU from the Tripartite Commission, declaring, "The KCTU will not join the Tripartite Commission, unless it be elevated to a binding organization, and renegotiation on equal terms be premised as a prerequisite" (quoted in An Sŭng-ch'ŏn 2002, 212). In June 1998, nevertheless, the KCTU decided to reenter the commission after President Kim directly intervened by holding separate bilateral meetings with the KCTU. In so doing, the KCTU abandoned its earlier commitment to nonparticipation and renegotiation, just as Yi abandoned his pledge to mobilize nationwide militant labor unionism against the mass layoffs. The failure of the KCTU leadership, with its internal problems and identity crisis, was attributed to oscillation between brinkmanship struggle and social compromise (An Sŭng-ch'ŏn 2002, 211–12).

The KCTU officially withdrew from the commission for the second time on February 24, 1999. The government launched its Third Commission in September 1999 with the aim, in theory, of amending national labor relations acts. The commission's social pact functioned in practice as a key apparatus for labor politics, especially to enable the government to revise legislation to fit President Kim's long-held vision of a "mass-participatory economy." With his widespread reputation as a symbol of Korea's democracy movement, Kim in fact publicly equated his vision of a mass-participatory economy with the neoliberal principle of "maximum reliance on the market" (Dae-Jung Kim 1985, 34), which had become a central policy of his government. In so doing, mass layoffs and other newly introduced radical labor flexibility measures were justified to carry out the historical mission of saving crisis-ridden Korea, to the extent of creating a national consensus that industrial strikes against labor flexibility and neoliberal restructuring were unpatriotic, a barrier to advancing Korea as a liberalized civil society.

Ultimately, the beneficiaries of the three Tripartite Commissions were the government and business. The large *chaebŏl*s not only restored their hegemonic control over labor at the workplace, especially through marketized labor control, tapping into Korea's dual labor-market system, but more significantly, increased their dominance well beyond what they would have expected in the postcrisis Korean economy. This amazing development deepened the HCI workers' collective consciousness as a labor aristocracy, transforming militant labor unionism into a device for safeguarding their own vested economic interests through social closure. This seemingly obvious problem ironically exposed the inherently different power relations, especially the rivalry and unresolved conflicts, among several leading militant labor union organizations, even in the precrisis period, which later led to the formation the three leading factions within the KCTU and the democratic labor movement as a whole. To what extent did these factional rivalries and unresolved conflicts influence the HCI workers' transformation from collective militant labor unionism into a device for their own parochial economic interests through social closure during the 1997 crisis and thereafter? To understand this complex question, it is necessary to take a step back and trace the establishment of the KCTU, as well as its constituency and leadership.

KCTU'S FACTIONAL STRIFE AND HCI WORKERS' SOCIAL CLOSURE

Since the Great Workers' Struggle of 1987–91, Korea's democratic labor movement has been led largely by militant HCI workers who—with a relatively higher education (mostly technical high school graduates) than the pre-1987 union leadership, which was composed of relatively low-skilled workers in labor-intense light industry—were distinctive in their collective makeup. They shaped their collective identity as a blue-collar elite using three key characteristics: (1) male; (2) regular skilled workers; and (3) employed mostly in large HCI *chaebŏl* firms. They shaped the overall character of a democratic trade union movement focused on the "on-site" (*hyŏnjang*) interests of economic unionism, akin to "bread-and-butter unionism" in the United States. Their primary interests were local issues of salaries and working conditions rather than the political issues of class struggle to bring about a radical *minjung* democracy in Korean society, as pursued by students-turned-workers (*hakch'ul*) and other radical intellectual labor movement activists (*undongkwŏn*). In terms of ideological compatibility, in particular, the HCI blue-collar workers, with their relatively moderate background, and the *hakch'ul* and other *undongkwŏn* activists, who have mostly become white-collar workers since the 1990s, had little in common. Even during their worker-intellectual partnership of the Great Workers' Struggle, as I discussed in the previous chapter, they differentiated themselves from one another, just as their social perception and treatment in Korean society were and still remain different, although now significantly changed for the better. These incompatible expectations and the associated attitudes were similar at the enterprise union level, where "more than half of manufacturing blue-collar trade unions had bylaws explicitly denying white-collar workers union membership," just as "white-collar unionization was chiefly a non-manufacturing affair" (Suh 2009, 21).

This incompatibility was particularly evident in the deeply rooted rivalry among various democratic labor union movement organizations when the KCTU was formed in November 1995, with *chaebŏl* unions in the HCI sector and white-collar workers' unions exercising hegemony, while the NCTU, based on SMEs with many women workers, lost influence. Furthermore, *chaebŏl* unions organized at the enterprise level provided the organizational basis for pursuing union members' parochial interests, primarily related to job security and wage increases and other financial and welfare benefits. In this regard, enterprise unionism made workers dependent on the performance of their own firm and hindered the formation of inter- and intra-industry solidarity. The KCTU, for example, was built on the Congress of National Trade Union Representatives (Chŏnnodae; formed in June 1993), which comprised four large union organizations: the NCTU, composed mainly of SME unions with many women workers; the white-collar workers' National Council of Occupational Trade Unions (Ŏpchonghoeŭi); the Council of Hyundai Group Unions (Hyŏnch'ongnyŏn); and the Council of Daewoo Group Unions (Daenohyŏp). Within these four major union organizations, HCI blue-collar elite workers, especially the radical HHI workers, posed the most obvious opposition to the white-collar National Council of Occupational Trade Unions.

The rivalry between these two elite workers' union camps became more conspicuous under the Korean state's antiunion labor policy, which targeted militant large HCI unions, from the military Chun Doo-whan regime to the Kim Young-sam administration (1993–97), the first democratically elected civilian government since 1960. The Korean developmental state systematically suppressed militant labor unionism, initially led by the NCTU, while it showed more tolerance toward white-collar unions. According to Yi Kab-yong, then one of the four corepresentatives of the Congress of National Trade Union Representatives and president of the Council of Hyundai Group Unions, he was imprisoned for a third time in August 1994, contrary to the NCTU's original agreement with the police, mainly because President Kim's office wanted to prevent Yi from becoming the first president of the KCTU, which was expected to be established in 1995. As a rule, one of the four corepresentatives of the Congress of National Trade Union Representatives had to become the first president of the KCTU. And Yi was the only member free to take the presidency legitimately at that time because, Yi claimed, the other three corepresentatives were either on the government's most-wanted list or had lost the trust of union members in the Daewoo Group (Yi Kab-yong 2009, 146–52).

In spite of being on the most-wanted list, however, Kwŏn Yŏng-gil, a moderate white-collar journalist and president of the National Council of Occupational Trade Unions, became the KCTU's first president. With his social unionist orientation, Kwŏn represented the rising moderate hegemony in the labor union movement, which focused on working with the new middle-class civic movements under the slogan "labor movement with the people" (Kim Se-gyun 2002, 36–38). This was a time when the Korean capitalist *chaebŏls*' all-out campaign for their newly introduced New Management Strategy under the façade of the Corporate Culture Movement was in full swing as part of President Kim's neoliberal globalization campaign together with political democratization. Hence, it is not difficult to comprehend why Kwŏn's moderate approach, focused on "the people" (*kung'min*) and social dialogue, appealed to President Kim's office, not to mention the burgeoning Korean civil society.

Kwŏn and his supporters became known as the People Faction (Kungminp'a) or moderate faction (*sillip'a*), with over 70 percent of the KCTU's first executive branch were close to Kwŏn. The rivalry between the elite blue-collar and white-collar workers' union camps escalated when the KCTU, dominated by the People Faction, converged with the radical former prodemocracy student activist group of the 1980s, the National Liberation Faction (Minjok Haebangp'a), to support Kwŏn's 1997 presidential campaign, representing the newly established People's Victory 21, a coalition of radical activist groups.[18] Although Kwŏn failed in his campaign, conducted under the auspices of the KCTU, the KCTU itself cooperated with the Kim Daejung government's corporatist neoliberal labor policy by endorsing the controversial February Agreement negotiated under the acting KCTU president, Pae Sok-pom. In this respect, Kwŏn's entering into politics was only the beginning of many union leaders of the People Faction using the KCTU for their own political platforms and activities.

At the provincial elections on June 4, 1998, for example, which was the first opportunity since organized labor was permitted to engage in political activities, twenty-two of forty-nine individuals running for office based on links with the KCTU and People's Victory 21 succeeded in becoming either chief of a local urban office (*kuch'ŏngjang*), or a provincial councilor, or a municipal councilor (An Sŭng-ch'ŏn 2002, 215). These former leaders of the People Faction were mostly white-collar elites with a university degree and often had a labor movement background. These results, combined with acting president Pae's alleged "sellout" agreement, naturally generated a strong sense of alienation and relative deprivation among the KCTU's rank-and-file members, especially elite HCI workers from the On-Site Faction (*hyŏnjangp'a* or the leftist *chwap'a*) striking against the mass layoffs, as shown in the Hyundai Motor workers' thirty-six-day strike and many other militant HCI workers' strikes at that time. These striking On-Site or Leftist Faction HCI workers, in fact, had lost their confidence in the KCTU's leadership under the moderate right People Faction.

Counter to the People Faction, the left-wing On-Site Faction became a force to be reckoned with when Yi Kab-yong was elected, albeit marginally, as the new KCTU president for a one-year fixed term in March 1998. As former president of the Hyundai Heavy Industries Union and of the Council of Hyundai Group Unions (Hyŏnch'ongnyŏn), widely known as an icon of the militant Goliat Struggle in May 1990, Yi's rise to the KCTU presidency led to the KCTU's withdrawal from the Tripartite Commission in May 1998, when he instigated a general strike on May 27–28, 1998. Yi's militant approach to the KCTU's social reform agenda, focused on class-based mobilization was, however, equally disappointing in terms of failing to address the KCTU's internal problems, especially factional rivalry, or in making any impact on the DJ government's neoliberal restructuring. Influenced by the radical People's Democracy or PD Faction (Minjung Minjujuŭip'a) of another former prodemocracy student activist group of the 1980s, the radical On-Site

Faction of the KCTU under Yi's leadership promoted comprehensive reform of the structure of Korean society (*sahoe kujo ŭi chŏnmyŏnjŏk kaehyŏk*), advocating the need for a strong class-based identity and struggle. As a result, the KCTU under Yi became utterly inconsistent in its labor policy objectives with those of the DJ government's Tripartite Commission. The KCTU under Yi's leadership, for example, instigated yet another general strike on July 14–15, 1998, in cooperation with arguably the two most powerful unions in Korea: the Korean Metal Workers' Union (KMWU; Chon'guk Kŭmsok Nodongjohap) and the Korean Federation of Public Services and Transportation Workers' Unions (Chŏnguk Konggong Unsu Nodongjohap). Then the KCTU briefly returned to the commission before withdrawing from it again in February 1999, which led to the moderate FKTU conducting bipartite negotiations with the government. In this process, the severe differences and thus associated conflict between the leading People Faction and the On-Site Faction led to the rise of a centrist group within the KCTU, the Central Faction (Chungangp'a). The Central Faction became public in February 1999 at the election of the members of the executive board of the KMWU. Mun Sŏng-hyŏn, one of the three key figures of the Central Faction and the former vice president of the NCTU, became president of the KMWU, and then Tan Pyŏng-ho, another key figure of the Central Faction and the first president of the NCTU, was elected as the new president of the KCTU in September of that same year.[19]

The Central Faction, like the On-Site Faction, was influenced by the radical People's Democracy Faction, and it too advocated the need for a strong class-based identity and struggle. These three leading factions, in terms of their own strategy and the leadership style of the KCTU, as well as the democratic labor union movement as a whole, were not very different, however, engaging in hostile rivalries mainly for building their own factional power or what many Korean labor union movement leaders and observers loosely referred to as "factional hegemonism" (*chongp'a p'aegwŏnjuŭi*). A new level of factional hegemonism in fact reached its peak in 2004, when the People Faction won a majority at the election of both the Central Executive Committee and the Board of Representatives of the KCTU, winning all of the five vice-president positions. Between 1995 and November 2012, five of the seven presidents of the KCTU were from the People Faction. Similarly, the Democratic Labor Party, which the KCTU established in 2000 to represent the progressive camp in Korean society, was reported to have fielded some forty candidates, which in effect, according to one progressive labor movement activist (Kim Ch'ŏl-ha 2015), meant that "there are over forty factions at least within the KCTU."

The KCTU succeeded in getting ten of its members elected to the National Assembly in 2004. Although this was the first time in Korea's contemporary history that former union members were elected as lawmakers, this did not necessarily mean that rank-and-file members of the KCTU, especially militant HCI workers striking against layoffs, had any less apathy toward the KCTU leadership. This apathy had persisted since their leaders' "treacherous" betrayal amid the 1997 crisis and subsequent restructuring layoffs. The KCTU's failed leadership amid the postcrisis neoliberal restructuring layoffs, in fact, induced HCI rank-and-file workers to transform their collective militant labor unionism into one of social closure, especially by redefining their collective identity as a labor aristocracy focused on their own parochial economic interests rather than on inclusive labor union solidarity concerned with the broad-based issues of the Korean working class as a whole. In the process, the HCI workers drove their unions not only to reinforce a check-off system which, by means of the enterprise union bylaws in Korea, structurally excluded nonregular workers—both temporary and daily—from the protection of the union, but also to consolidate their hitherto incipient consciousness as a labor aristocracy by acquiescing to a two-tier working class of regular and nonregular workers in the Korean labor market, which became a reality especially after around 2003 (see chapter 5).

Overall, the factional strife within the KCTU and its democratic labor union movement camp as a whole reached what Kim Kŭm-su, former president of the Korea Tripartite Commission (2003–6), described as the "death of on-site," whether in the militant KCTU or the moderate FKTU. Kim pointed out that the "FKTU lacks independence, democracy, and militancy," whereas the KCTU "insists only on factional logic but lacks rationality, democracy, and popular appeal" (Yi Yŏng-kyŏng 2013). By this Kim meant that by around 2012, if not earlier, the HCI workers and their unions were not participating in any solidarity struggle at the workplace, thus contributing to the death of coordinated on-site unionism. This also meant, especially from the perspective of management, that *chaebŏl*s increased their capital accumulation to the extent of shifting Korea's economic paradigm from the old state-led capital accumulation during 1961–97, to a new *chaebŏl*-led accumulation, while also changing their power relations with both the government and labor in postrestructuring Korea.

A NEW PARADIGM OF *CHAEBŎL*-LED ACCUMULATION AND CHANGED POWER RELATIONS

According to a report published by *Pressian* (Pak Hyŏng-Jun 2016), during the ten-year period between 1987 and 1996, which preceded the Asian financial crisis, the average aggregate concentration of net profit of the top thirty *chaebŏls* as a percentage of national corporate profit was 14.7 percent, with profit concentration at 10.7 percent for the top four *chaebŏls* and 4.4 percent for Samsung, the largest *chaebŏl* in Korea.

During the ten-year period from 2001 to 2010, the average annual profit concentration of these three groups of *chaebŏls*, namely the top thirty corporations, the top four, and the Samsung Group, increased to 55 percent (top thirty), 34.2 percent (top four), and 17.1 percent (Samsung). In addition, the income from stock dividends of the top ten *chaebŏls* grew almost sixfold, from ₩31 billion in 2001 to ₩178 billion in 2011 (Pak Hyŏng-Jun 2016). This unprecedented growth in the level of *chaebŏl* corporate profit was achieved while the average annual rate of GDP growth dropped to less than half the average rate of that from 1987 to 1996. This inverse growth trend essentially revealed a paradigm shift from Korea's old model of developmental state-led accumulation (1961–97) to a new *chaebŏl*-led accumulation. Some Korean analysts view this paradigm shift in terms of sweeping social change derived from polarized growth as a consequence of Korea's transition from a "high-economic growth model with high investment" to a "low-economic growth model with low investment" (Ryu and Ahn 2010), which occurred after the 1997 crisis. Indeed, Korea's spectacular economic development up until the crisis was due largely to the Korean developmental state's high investment in building "Korea Inc." through export-led industrialization with the power to discipline big business.

Developmental State-Led Accumulation, 1961–1997

The Korean developmental state's uncommon capacity to control the Korean capitalist class was strictly locked into what Vivek Chibber characterized as the "subsidies as contracts" system. This system provided *chaebŏls* with almost unlimited state support and protection, from subsidies to cheap foreign loans, state guarantees, and tax cuts, among a string of other privileges, including protectionist policies. In return, this system required *chaebŏls* to fulfill their commitments, not only achieving their annual export performance targets, but also investing in specified lines of industry in accordance with the state's prescribed investment priorities and benchmark technology. If any firm failed in its set tasks or was proven to be unwilling to support the state's program, the Korean developmental state not only discontinued its support but punished it severely by way of *"chaebŏl* training" (Hyung-A Kim 2004, 82–84).

Here the term *"chaebŏl* training" was based on Park Chung Hee's low opinion of *chaebŏls* as "illicit profiteers" or "rapacious wolves," whose traitorous behavior needed "surgical operation" "in the name of our nation," in Park's words (1962, 201), especially within the state-guidance paradigm. This strictly statist approach of the state's subsidies-as-contracts system changed the very nature of the Korean state into a classic model of the East Asian developmental state, especially in the course of Korea's heavy and chemical industrialization under the authoritarian Yusin system after 1972. The Korean state's inculcation of modern citizenship, based on the highly nationalistic self-discipline of the New Community Movement, was later characterized as "developmental citizenship" (Kyung-sup Chang 2007), "crony capitalism" (David Kang 2002), or "developmentalist mentalité" (Myung-Koo Kang 2011). Developmentalist mentalité, in particular, showed itself most concretely in the resurgence of developmentalism, as embodied in the "Park Chung Hee syndrome" in the early 1990s, which by 1998, amid the financial crisis, had led Park's daughter, Park Geun-hye, to become a member of the National Assembly and then president by December 2012 as the icon of Korea's anticommunist conservative movement.

Given that the unemployment rate fell from 8.1 percent to 2.6 percent during the 1963–97 period (Kyung-sup Chang 2007, 68), it is not difficult to comprehend why most Koreans came to believe that the government could determine the state of their economic livelihoods. For this reason, most Koreans actively participated in the state-led accumulation initiatives, to the extent of integrating almost all economically motivated individuals into the state-led export race focused primarily on heavy and chemical industrialization. The fact that more than two million young people, including some 870,000 graduates of technical high schools between 1972 and 1987, as explained in chapter 1, actively participated in the developmental state-led accumulation, was itself a socioeconomic revolution that ensured Korea's economic success. In this respect, Korea's developmental state-led accumulation model plainly showed how both the Korean capitalist class (i.e., *chaebŏls*) and skilled labor (i.e., HCI workers) actively collaborated with the state, each strictly under their own specified social contracts and each with its own set of reciprocal requirements. This highly collaborative model in the case of Korea, which guaranteed almost full employment for more than thirty years after the country launched its export-led industrialization in mid-1964, abruptly ended with the Asian financial crisis in 1997.

Chaebŏl-*Led Accumulation in Postrestructuring Korea*

Ironically, the 1997 crisis provided a new opportunity for *chaebŏl*s not only to restore their capitalist hegemonic control over Korea's newly marketized labor but also to radically transnationalize their firms by drawing in many powerful foreign investors on the one hand and radically increasing economic granularity on the other, to the extent of constructing a new economic model of what turned out to be *chaebŏl*-led accumulation. Although both the old and new economic models were *chaebŏl*-dominated in Korea's export-led economy, they were and still remain significantly different in two key respects. One is the dramatic change in the state-*chaebŏl* power relationship, which has radically strengthened the power of the *chaebŏl*s, which are now seen by many as representing Korea—the Chaebŏl Republic. The other respect is the phenomenon of jobless growth, as a result of polarized growth tied to Korea's "granular" economy led by the ten biggest *chaebŏl* business groups, which, as early as 2006, accounted for 54 percent of GDP and 51 percent of total exports (Di Giovanni and Levchenko 2012, 1084, 1088–89).

Some argue that the *chaebŏl*s' resurgent concentration of economic power, while national economic growth became polarized as the Korean economy stalled, was due largely to speculative foreign financial capital, which enabled *chaebŏl*s to diversify their business domestically and globally (Ha-Joon Chang 2007). Others blamed this polarized growth on the *chaebŏl*s' cronyism and outmoded monopolies (Kim Ki-wŏn 2001; Kim, Yu, and Hong 2007), which had become the main barriers to the entry of new firms into the Korean market, even at a small scale in the case of venture businesses. A more recent research study by Hyeng-joon Park (2015), however, argues that the *chaebŏl*s' accumulation of capital, especially after the post-1997 restructuring, was and still remains essentially based on strategic sabotage by capitalists, in the Thorstein Veblenian sense. Such strategic sabotage, he contends, has involved "a deliberate limitation on the productive capacity of society" while excluding "other capitalists from business opportunities" through their "politics of exclusion" (Hyeng-Joon Park 2015, 306). Park's argument is persuasive, but I would argue that the *chaebŏls'* strategic sabotage, especially through their counterrevolution of the Corporate Culture Movement as part of the Korean government's economic liberalization during the 1990s (discussed in chapter 3), not only enabled them to consolidate their hegemonic power to build the "state-banks-*chaebŏls* nexus" (Shin and Chang 2003), but also consolidated their version of neoliberal corporate culture (*kiŏp munhwa*) focused on labor flexibility as the norm in Korean society.

With their consolidated power, especially through "winner-take-all politics," to borrow a term from Hacker and Pierson (2010), the *chaebŏls* succeeded in advancing the government's restructuring program to the extent of what Korean sociologists Lim and Jang have characterized as "democracy hijacked by neoliberalism" (2006, 448). In this highly complex socioeconomic and political process, the *chaebŏls* exploited or perhaps sabotaged the Korean people's developmentalist mentalité or "economy-first" national psyche, which was endemic among the Korean middle class in the post-1997 crisis period. The domestic elite, such as economic bureaucrats, the media, and many influential civic groups, including the Citizens' Coalition for Economic Justice and People's Solidarity for Participatory Democracy, actively promoted neoliberalism in the postcrisis period as "anti-authoritarian and anti-*chaebŏl* democracy based on market principles" (Lim and Jang 2006, 448.). In this context, it is reasonable to argue that the paradigm shift from the old developmental state-led accumulation model to a new *chaebŏl*-led accumulation model in postcrisis restructuring Korea was due largely to the *chaebŏls'* strategic maneuvering of the restructuring program under both liberal and conservative governments amid neoliberal globalization, with vital support from both economic bureaucrats and civic groups, as well as the middle class, who came to believe in the idea similar to that prevalent in Southeast Asia, that "democracy may not be essential to capitalism" (Reich 2007, 9).

The resulting unbridled *chaebŏl*-led accumulation since then, even in the most recent years, has been distinct in the deepening of Korea's labor market polarization as *chaebŏls* systematically employed a massive number of contingent workers. According to data collected from 3,019 large firms by the Ministry of Labor in March 2015, 490,000 or 37.7 percent of 1.3 million workers who were employed in the top ten *chaebŏl* corporations were nonregular workers (*pijŏnggyujik*) who, unlike regular workers, do not receive the full legal benefits afforded to Korea's labor.

One of the major reasons for the small number of quality new jobs has been the low level of new investment by *chaebŏls*. The size of internal reserves of the thirty largest *chaebŏls* increased by more than ₩170 trillion from ₩330.1 trillion in 2010, then to ₩500.2 trillion in 2014, which was a 51.5 percent increase during this five-year period. Yet the rate of real investment by these thirty *chaebŏls* compared to their internal reserves decreased from 18.9 percent in 2010 to 12.9 percent in 2014, even though their overall investment increased by ₩2.2 trillion (or 3.5 percent) during the same period, mostly for the acquisition of facilities, equipment, and research and development. The rate of Samsung's real investment compared to its internal reserves, in particular, was only 10.7 percent, lower than the average 12.9 percent of real investment by the thirty *chaebŏls*. Fifteen other top-ranking *chaebŏls*, including Hyundai Motor (8.4 percent), Lotte (8.6 percent), Hyundai Heavy Industries (7.5 percent), Hanhwa (6.5 percent), and Doosan (6.2 percent) were also lower than the average of the thirty *chaebŏls* (Yi Chu-yŏng 2015).[20]

Changed Power Relations

The *chaebŏls*' extraordinary accumulation of internal reserves with a conspicuously low level of new investment reflected to a large extent the dramatically changed power relations not only between the Korean government and capitalist *chaebŏls* but also in labor-management relations, especially in terms of unions forging so-called labor-management cooperation (*no-sa hyŏmnyŏkchuŭi*). What needs to be noted here is that HCI workers at large had long adopted "company-based economism" (No Chung-gi 2011, 47) by acquiescing to a two-tier labor management system at the workplace while consolidating their collective status and identity as a labor aristocracy, especially in the postcrisis period. At the same time, the *chaebŏls* were even more systematic in effecting changed power relations with successive Korean governments, whether conservative or progressive. With their private power closely linked to state power, in other words, *chaebŏls* have influenced the government's economic policymaking processes and key policymakers to rearticulate the national trends of Korean society itself, referred to as the "competition state" (*kyŏngjaeng kukka*).[21]

As is generally known in Korea, the Roh Moo-hyun government's key economic policies, including its goal to achieve US$20,000 per capita in GDP, were devised by the Samsung Economic Research Institute. Several key members of the Roh government (2003–7) were in fact former employees of Samsung, and many officials and senior-ranking bureaucrats of various ministries, including the prime minister's office and the Ministry of Finance and Economy, among other institutions, undertook "reeducation" courses at the Samsung Educational Research Center (Kim Yŏng-bae 2007). Not surprisingly, Samsung has come to be referred to as "the Republic of Samsung" (Harlan 2012). Even President Roh publicly stated that "all the power has moved to the market" soon after his inauguration. Just five months before he committed suicide in May 2009, Roh stressed that "[the] power lay within the strong players in the market, and media power was aligned with that market power, and thus political power also served those successful players in the market in our reality."[22]

The exceptional power of the *chaebŏls*, especially in influencing the government's economic bureaucracy, was further strengthened under President Lee Myung-bak (2008–12), who, as a former executive of Hyundai Construction, transformed Korea into a so-called corporate country (*kiŏp kukka*) or *chaebŏl* republic (*chaebŏl konghwaguk*) (Kim Tong-ch'un 2015, 243–67), where systematic corruption in the *chaebŏls* through their political-economic elite cartel and other "affective networks" (Seok-choon Lew 2013) became a key feature. In this respect, former president Park Geun-hye's bribery scandal involving a string of *chaebŏls*, including Samsung, Hyundai Motor, Lotte, SK, and POSCO, was only partly why many Koreans, both conservatives and progressives, including young Koreans with progressive-leaning tendencies, became so passionately involved in the candlelight protests for almost two months and removed Park from office in March 2017, when the Constitutional Court upheld her impeachment, passed by the National Assembly in December. The sad reality is that Park is not the only president who has fallen into disgrace because of bribery scandals combined with abuse of power. Every other democratically elected president since 1987 has also been disgraced because of bribery scandals that have involved either their family members or close relatives, while most top-ranking *chaebŏls* and a string of cabinet ministers, high-ranking policymakers, and judges, prosecutors and other power elite have also had their share of disgrace connected to bribery and other forms of political-economic corruption.[23]

CONCLUSION

Korea's post-1997 restructuring brought about an amazing paradigm shift from state-led to *chaebŏl*-led accumulation, in effect transforming Korea into a *chaebol* republic, thanks largely to the IMF, which turned out to have led Korea into "ill-advised liberalization" (Crotty and Lee 2002, 3). While the *chaebŏls*, as the leading agency of Korea's economic liberalization since the mid-1980s, have since surged as a ruling capitalist class with markedly increased power, HCI rank-and-file workers and their unions radically transformed the militant labor unionism of the late 1980s into a device for consolidation of an incipient class consciousness and identity as a labor aristocracy through social closure. In so doing, they effectively excluded other workers from scarce militant labor union resources by formally agreeing with management to institutionalize a dual labor market of upper and lower tiers of Korean labor.

CHAPTER 5

The Rise of HCI Workers

A Labor Aristocracy vis-à-vis Nonregular Workers

THE sweeping transformation of Korea into a *chaebŏl* republic encouraged HCI workers to consolidate their collective position as a labor aristocracy. They differentiated themselves as upper-tier regular workers of the large *chaebŏl* corporations from other regular workers of SMEs and contingent nonregular (*pijŏnggyujik*) workers of the lower tier in Korea's dual labor-market system, which had been institutionalized since the Asian financial crisis. The institutionalization of Korea's two-tier system, especially in large manufacturing *chaebŏl* corporations, quickly spread after the Hyundai Motor Union formally signed the Agreement to a Full Employment Guarantee (Wanjŏn Koyong Pojang Habŭi) in June 2000. This formal agreement between the Hyundai Motor Union and management had in fact set a new precedent for Korea's labor market flexibility, using contingent *pijŏnggyujik* subcontract workers as a buffer for large *chaebŏl* corporations' regular workers' unions, which further encouraged HCI workers' incipient class consciousness as a labor aristocracy since 1993. Hence, "labor aristocracy" refers here to HCI regular workers' and their unions' newly elevated collective position of privilege in the workplace, predominantly in heavy industry, especially in terms of job security, superior wages and welfare provisions, as well as the privilege of what the Korean people have dubbed "employment inheritance" (*koyong sesŭp*) for the children of regular HCI workers retiring with over twenty-five years of service.

This extraordinary development of structural categorization within the Korean labor force, especially in privileging regular workers in large *chaebŏl* firms as the core upper tier and other regular workers of SMEs and nonregular workers as the peripheral lower tier in a dual labor market, not only undermined the social foundations of class solidarity, but also confirmed the collective status and thus identity of HCI regular workers as a labor aristocracy in the age of today's globalized Korea.[1]

The changed status of HCI workers and their unions as a labor aristocracy makes little sense, however, unless one considers the precarious employment status of SMEs and other nonregular workers within the context of the dual labor-market system of upper and lower tiers of Korean labor, or a newly emerged two-tier working class, especially in terms of the nonregular workers' low wages, little or no union protection, and economic and social discrimination, including daily discrimination at work. In this context, this chapter discusses the labor segmentation of HCI workers, whose collective status had risen to that of a labor aristocracy in contrast to the dire situation of the massive number of irregular workers, while also illuminating the HCI workers' own views and attitudes toward unions, as well as their changed outlook and self-image as a labor aristocracy.

HCI WORKERS' POLITICS IN PURSUIT OF WAGE INCREASES AND JOB SECURITY

The HCI workers' economic unionism, or "bread-and-butter unionism," had long been a weapon in the pursuit of wage increases, job security, and other economic and welfare benefits, especially through their militant union's collective bargaining since the late 1980s. Since the early 1990s, however, the strategy of HCI workers and their unions' militant labor unionism, focused exclusively on their social closure, has widened the gap between core and peripheral labor markets. Table 5.1 provides a comparison of average monthly salaries and fixed bonuses at the main industrial parks in Ulsan, where the workers employed in the Petrochemical Industrial Park earned the highest level of wages and bonuses, followed by Hyundai workers at the Hyundai Industrial Park. But the wage level of workers at the Hyomun-Yŏnam Industrial Park, where mostly subcontracting SMEs with their subcontract workers of Hyundai Motor were located, was about 75.0 percent that at the Hyundai Industrial Park in 1990. This had been reduced to

TABLE 5.1. Average monthly salary and fixed bonus at main industrial parks in the Ulsan area, 1990 and 1993

	Petrochemical Industrial Park	Hyundai Industrial Park	Hyomun Yŏnam Industrial Park
No. of firms	32	20	158
(No. of workers)	(9,890)	(85,113)	(9,976)
1990 monthly wage	₩791,000	₩619,000	₩464,000
bonus rate	700–800%	500–600%	300%
1993 monthly wage	₩1,145,000	₩1,033,000	₩711,000
bonus rate	700–800%	600%	500%

Source: Yu Hyŏng-gŭn (2012, 152).

68.8 percent by 1993, and was further reduced to less than 60 percent by about 1996 (Yu Hyŏng-gŭn 2012, 151).

It should be noted, however, that HCI workers' collective sense of labor solidarity or comradeship (*tongnyo ŭisik*), especially with their firm's nonregular in-house subcontract workers during the immediate pre- and post-1987 period, up until the early 1990s, had been strong. The widespread utilization of nonregular workers in Hyundai Heavy Industries (HHI) around 1987 and 1988, is a classic example. In June 1988, of the 18,985 members of the HHI Union, 14,590 were regular or *chŏnggyujik* craftsmen, whereas just 1,040 were nonregular subcontract workers (Han'guk Sahoe Yŏn'guso 1989, 234). And the wages and working conditions of the *chŏnggyujik* craftsmen, who were employed directly by Hyundai Heavy Industries, and nonregular subcontract craftsmen employed indirectly by a small subcontracting firm affiliated with HHI were not significantly different. Many HCI workers, including more than a dozen Hyundai workers whom I interviewed, commented that many highly skilled workers had been nonregular contract workers prior to 1987 mainly because, by working as nonregular contract workers, they were paid more, freely choosing better paid work with flexible work hours and freedom to move about accordingly.[2] According to them, there was no real difference between employment via direct management (*chigyŏng*) and via subcontracting (*hach'ŏng*), and thus both the regular and nonregular subcontract workers of HHI participated together without any difference in their collective employment status or identity as blue-collar HCI workers when the Great Workers' Struggle erupted in 1987.

Moreover, they both joined the newly established democratic Hyundai Heavy Industries Union (in 1989), which, through collective bargaining, changed the status of many nonregular subcontract workers to regular (*chŏnggyujik*) full-time employment (Shin Wŏn-ch'ŏl 2001, 356).[3] In the case of Hyundai Synthetic Timber Company (Hyundai Chonghap Mokjae), not only did nonregular subcontract workers join the union just like the firm's regular workers, but a nonregular worker hired by a subcontractor became the first president of the union (Chŏng I-hwan 1992, 113–14).

Yet the HCI workers' collective identity as blue-collar workers, not to mention their collective sense of labor solidarity, dramatically decreased in the early 1990s when Korean firms succeeded in their own neoliberal New Management Strategy, focused on flexibility of the workforce through an increase in in-house subcontract workers under the mantra of the Corporate Culture Movement, as I discussed in chapter 3. The Corporate Culture Movement ultimately led to the institutionalization of labor market flexibility, especially in the post-1997 restructuring period, when nonregular subcontract workers were systematically deployed into the so-called "3-Ds"—difficult, dangerous, and dirty jobs—which most HCI workers avoided (Kang Sŏk-chae 2002, 205–7). In some areas, entire lines of production were contracted out or direct production lines were staffed with subcontract workers.

The rapid expansion of in-house subcontract workers into direct production lines, in particular, moved to a new level when many HCI unions, especially the Hyundai Motor Union, used it as a basis for their collective enterprise bargaining. After the bitter experience of their thirty-six-day strike of 1998, however, the Hyundai Motor Union signed the Agreement to a Full Employment Guarantee in June 2000, which guaranteed full-time employment to every regular worker with union membership at Hyundai Motor, as well as promising that the company would not unilaterally implement either layoffs or voluntary retirements. It also guaranteed that when a job-threatening situation occurred, such as the introduction of new technology, automation, outsourcing, or platform integration, the regular worker-members' jobs would be guaranteed by changing existing operational plans for in-house subcontracting, outsourcing, and infrastructure development. The key points of the agreement relevant to regular workers were:

- The company will maintain the present level of its regular workforce and employment as at the end of April 2000 and will not unilaterally implement either layoffs or voluntary retirements.

- The company, when it anticipates a surplus of manpower, must secure jobs and the amount of work by managing subcontracting, outsourcing, and infrastructure development as a top priority within the factory (at the workplace).
- Whenever regular workers are absent for reasons of industrial accidents, leave of absence, business trips, education, dispatch, etc., replacement is permitted with either contracted or service contract labor.
- When the term and number of workers involved are certain, as in the case of the discontinued production of certain car models, parallel production turns between new and old model cars, temporary special events, and the occurrence of odd jobs with limited output, the deployment of nonregular workers will temporarily be permitted, but the job placement process will be agreed between labor and management.
- Regarding shortages of workers in the supply and demand manpower plan after 2000, additional nonregular workers will be deployed in the order in which those subcontract workers' jobs had been converted into jobs under direct management [i.e., regular workers] prior to 1998, and then other recruitment processes will be undertaken to meet unavoidable increases in the workforce. But the job placement processes will be agreed between labor and management.
- As a rule, the ratio of nonregular workers at the entire factory will be limited to that under management before August 1997, except in cases where there is labor-management agreement. (Quoted in Yu Hyŏng-gŭn 2012, 214)

The core of this agreement was that Hyundai Motor could maintain 16.9 percent subcontract labor (i.e., nonregular workers), which was the same level as in August 1997. In his interview with this author, Chŏng Kap-tŭk, president of the Hyundai Motor Union (1996–97 and 1999–2000), said that it was his union's strategy to agree to the 16.9 percent of subcontract labor in order to prevent Hyundai Motor from bringing in a 30 percent level of subcontract workers (interview, April 27, 2012). Chŏng was reported to have publicly claimed that "subcontract workers are a buffer for regular workers and thus we will let the company bring in subcontract labor, even if I have a knife put to my throat" (quoted in Cho Kye-wan 2011). Chŏng's statement summed up the rationale behind Korea's widespread direct (*chigyŏng*) and subcontracting (*hach'ŏng*) dual labor market, in which the regular workers' unions have pushed their wage levels since the 1990s "disproportionately higher than the wages of workers employed in smaller, nonunionized enterprises" (Yoon-Kyung Lee 2011, 113), as well as higher than the wages of nonregular in-house subcontract workers.

This outcome may appear puzzling to many, especially to those who are not familiar with Korea's development of enterprise-based unionism, which, although not common in advanced and newly industrialized countries,[4] was explicitly specified in Korean labor law even after the 1987 amendments eased restrictions. Furthermore, the Hyundai Motor Union was and still is leading the Korean workers' democratic labor union movement with its almost unbroken record of annual strikes, except in four years as part of its collective enterprise bargaining tactics since its establishment in 1987.[5] In this process, the HCI workers' enterprise-based collective wage bargaining has certainly "vitiated labor's socio-political potential and solidarity" (Suh 2009, 7) to the extent of splitting the Korean working class into a labor aristocracy of regular workers and "inferior classes" (*yoldŭng kyegŭp*) of nonregular workers.

THE HCI WORKERS' CLASS TRANSFORMATION

To illustrate the significantly improved standard of living enjoyed by regular HCI workers, table 5.2 shows data from a survey carried out in January 2000, which compared objective life conditions, by company scale and industrial classification, of the union members of the Korean Metalworkers' Union at Ulsan.

This survey illustrates the consistent differences in living conditions of HCI workers, depending on either the size of the firm or the rank of the firm, such as, in the case of the automobile industry, between firms that manufacture completed vehicles (*wŏnch'ŏng ŏpch'e*) and subcontractors (*hach'ŏng*) that produce auto parts. For example, the larger the firm, the lower the rate of employment of workers' partners (only 10.5 percent in companies with one thousand workers or more, and 23.4 percent in firms with less than three hundred workers), but the higher the rate of home ownership (68.2 percent in firms with one thousand workers or more and 47.7 percent in firms with less than three hundred workers), the larger the average deposit or *chŏnsegŭm* for an HCI worker's housing lease (₩24.22 million) compared to deposits lodged by workers employed in firms with less than three hundred workers (₩20.62 million) or auto parts subcontractors (₩18.34 million). The ownership of vehicles by those employed in large HCI firms of one thousand workers or more and manufacturers of completed vehicles (*wŏnch'ŏng*)

TABLE 5.2. Living conditions of members of the Korean Metalworkers' Union, Ulsan, January 2000

Employee characteristic	By size of company			By type of company		Overall average
	More than 1,000 persons	301–999	Less than 300 persons	Auto manufacturers	Auto parts	
Average years of service	12.7	9.8	9.3	11.4	7.1	12.3
Partner employment rate (%)	10.5	13.4	23.4	8.6	18.7	11.3
Property ownership rate (%)	68.2	49.2	47.7	67.3	45.4	65.3
Avg. housing lease deposit amount (₩10,000)	2,422	2,366	2,062	2,439	1,834	2,397
Avg. monthly rent (₩10,000)	17	11	9	19	9	14
Vehicle ownership rate (%)	83.6	81.8	64.5	86.5	61.7	82.6
Vehicle ownership rate pre-1995 (%)	57.2	38.4	45.2	59.3	32.6	55.1
Share investment rate (%)	79.9	43.4	29.1	74.2	13.4	74.6
Property tax (₩10,000)	7.9	6.0	5.3	7.5	4.3	7.6
No. in sample (N)	4,905	591	248	2,660	219	5,744

Source: Based on Yu Hyŏng-gŭn (2012, 154).

was far greater (83.6 percent and 86.5 percent respectively) than that of the employees of SMEs, or that of auto parts subcontractors (64.5 percent and 61.7 percent, respectively).

The exceptionally high rate of investment in shares by those employed in large firms of one thousand workers or more and manufacturers of completed vehicles (79.9 percent and 74.2 percent, respectively), compared to other workers, however, seems to illustrate most concretely the difference in economic conditions to the extent of a segmented standard of living between regular HCI workers of large firms and nonregular workers employed in SMEs or subcontractors of many affiliated SMEs in the same heavy and chemical industry at the end of the 1990s. How did these substantial differences come about? And what was the significance of the level of skill and training in the segmentation of labor? This dramatic change had very little to do with skill and training, especially whether one graduated from a technical high school or vocational training institute, or one's length of employment in many cases. The greatest contributing factor to the change in socioeconomic conditions of regular HCI workers, especially their economic mobility to the level of middle stratum (*chungsanch'ŭng*), has been systematic wage increases through their union's enterprise bargaining power, in which, as one researcher noted, they had been almost exclusively engaged for more than a decade since 1987 (Lee and Lee 2004).

The HCI workers and their unions' collective bargaining power, embedded in the institutionalized dual-market system in post-1997 restructuring Korea, brought about two radical changes, especially after 2000. One was the adoption of the HCI unions' wage maximization policy based on a payment-by-results system, which essentially meant abandoning the HCI unions' wage policy of the 1990s based on workers' living costs. Instead of the previous policy, the HCI unions adopted a new wages policy based on the firm's performance. The other radical change was the HCI workers' systematic exclusion of nonregular in-house subcontract workers from membership in regular workers' unions, while also in effect maintaining a restricted wages policy in the HCI sector for nonregular in-house subcontract workers. In its wage proposals up until the early 2000s, for example, the Hyundai Motor Union had stipulated the principle of the workers' "cost of living" as its basis for wage negotiations but after around 2003 changed its wage policy, arguing:

> Since the HMU's establishment until now, the union has suggested request proposals for wage increases based on the concept of the cost of living. . . .

In order to secure the workers' minimum subsistence wage, [however,] the rate of wage increases can only maintain the net wage level when it secures a level of increase that includes the rate of inflation and the economic growth rate.... In addition, it is necessary to propose an alternative model through a new approach regarding the concept of the standard cost of living. (Quoted in Yu Hyŏng-gŭn 2012, 237–38)

The outcome of this argument was wage maximization. As table 5.3 shows, the Hyundai Motor workers' average total remuneration, when tied to a payment-by-results system, increased continuously from 2001 to 2010, even in 2009, when their base pay rise was frozen as a consequence of the US-led global financial crisis.

In 2014, the average monthly wage of regular workers in large firms (with more than three hundred workers and with unions), which comprised 7.4 percent of all wage workers in Korea, was three times more than that of nonregular workers of SMEs without unions, who received an average of ₩1.34 million per month in comparison to an average of ₩3.92 million received by the employees of large firms (Ch'oe Chong-sŏk 2014). The average monthly wage of regular workers in large firms, mostly in the privileged HCI sector, was also double the average monthly wage of all wage workers in Korea. Regular workers at Hyundai Motor, in particular, each earned an

TABLE 5.3. Results of Hyundai Motor's wage negotiations, 2001–2010

Year	Wage increase resulting from negotiation (₩)	Rate of increase compared to standard wages (%)	Bonuses (lump sum allowances, including incentives)
2001	96,750	8.3	300% + ₩1.6m
2002	95,000	7.5	350% + ₩1.5m
2003	98,000	7.1	300% + ₩1m
2004	95,000	6.5	400% + ₩1m
2005	89,000	5.7	300% + ₩2m
2006	85,000	5.0	300% + ₩2m
2007	84,000	4.7	300% + ₩2m + 30 bonus shares
2008	85,000	4.6	300% + ₩4m
2009	30,117	1.6	300% + ₩5m + 40 bonus shares
2010	79,000	4.0	300% + ₩5m + 30 bonus shares

Source: Hyundai Motor Union, Business Report; quoted in Yu Hyŏng-gŭn (2012, 236).

average of almost ₩100 million (approx. US$89,000 at the 2014 midyear exchange rate) annually, including basic wages and additional overtime payments and other financial awards, such as end-of-year bonuses. By distributing stock bonuses to regular workers from 2007 onward, Hyundai Motor openly boosted its workers' collective sense of identity as shareholders or investors holding the same interest in the firm's growth and profit as any other shareholder. Four out of eight HCI workers whom I interviewed in April 2012 told me that they each owned over one thousand of their company's shares and that they considered themselves "a keen shareholder."[6]

Hyundai Motor workers tended to resemble most of Korea's white-collar workers, with a typical "enterprise-union consciousness," which, according to one study, was most marked in firms with "high incomes and job autonomy, [and] well-established internal labor markets, among other characteristics" (Suh 2009, 7). It must be said that this extraordinary development, especially in terms of HCI workers' enterprise-union consciousness, together with their collective class consciousness as a labor aristocracy, was not limited to Hyundai Motor workers, but also applied to other blue-collar elite HCI workers at large firms, including Hyundai Heavy Industries, Hyundai WIA (formerly Kia Machine Tools), Kia Motors, and Doosan (formerly Daewoo), as well as to many workers at state-owned companies. My 2015 survey of the HCI workers found they had a similar sense of collective identity based around their *chaebŏl* firm and their private disposable wealth and associated expectations as a labor aristocracy, especially regarding their high wages and job security, among other welfare benefits, achieved through enterprise unionism and collective bargaining.

In 2015, one in every three large *chaebŏl* firms with three hundred or more paid workers was reported to be practicing a job inheritance provision for their employees, although the specific terms and conditions varied, as negotiated by the relevant union through its collective agreement with its respective firm.[7] It is no wonder that the HCI workers and their unions' social closure, especially in postcrisis and neoliberal restructuring Korea, has increasingly deepened collective grievances and antagonism among millions of nonregular subcontract workers. The nonregular subcontract workers in Ulsan, in particular, have publicly protested against "the tyranny of labor aristocracy" since 1993, criticizing the HCI workers' unions that shifted their regular member-workers' layoff problem onto subcontract workers.

LABOR SEGMENTATION

In fact, the issue of the tyranny of labor aristocracy was fully exposed nationwide when, more than ten years later, in February 2004, Pak Il-su, a fifty-year old subcontract worker at Hyundai Heavy Industries, immolated himself on the shipbuilding drydocks in Ulsan, leaving a powerful legacy akin to that of the legendary Chŏn T'ae-il, the martyr of the South Korean workers' labor movement. In his suicide note Pak wrote, "Subcontract workers are also human. No one is a labor aristocrat or a subcontract worker by birth" (quoted in Pak Chŏm-gyu 2014). Pak's death exposed the tyranny of the labor aristocracy—not just that of the leadership of the Hyundai Heavy Industries Union at that time, which turned a blind eye to his death,[8] but more broadly that of regular workers' unions in other large companies owned by *chaebŏl*s and state-owned enterprises, public institutions and organizations, and even universities. In these companies and public institutions, a large number of nonregular subcontract workers and various types of temporary workers struggled for their marginalized labor rights.

Since Pak's death, there has emerged a string of nonregular workers' unions in the HCI manufacturing sector, initially started prior to his death, by in-house subcontract workers at Hyundai Motor, who established a union in July 2003, which then mushroomed into a network of nonregular workers' unions at Rex-LENG (formerly Kiryung Electronics), GM Daewoo, Kia Motors, and Hyundai Hysco, among others. These new nonregular workers' unions have certainly aroused public awareness of the dangerously increased number of nonregular workers and their problematic socioeconomic situation. By August 2016, for example, there were about 6.44 million nonregular workers in Korea, or 32.8 percent of the country's total wage earners, according to Statistics Korea, or KOSTAT (T'onggyech'ŏng 2016). This figure, however, was interpreted differently by Kim Yu-sŏn, a leading Korean labor analyst, who argued, based on his analysis of KOSTAT's figures, that the total number of nonregular workers by August 2016 was in fact 8.74 million or 45 percent of the country's total wage earners, which was an increase of 60,000 nonregular workers from 8.68 million in August 2015 (Kim Yu-sŏn 2016b). Kim further pointed out an even more concerning fact: the actual proportion of nonregular workers would be over 50 percent, as the figures from the government's survey inaccurately categorized in-house contract workers as regular workers (*chŏnggyujik*), and workers in the special employment category of owner-operators (Kim Yu-sŏn 2016a).

These nonregular (*pijŏnggyujik*) workers received 53.7 percent in the case of males, or 36.3 percent in the case of females, of the wages that male regular workers (*chŏnggyujik*) received (Kim Yu-sŏn 2016b). Hence the wage disparity between regular and nonregular workers had become fixed at a ratio of about 2:1, while wage discrimination based on gender and employment status was harshly concentrated against female nonregular workers. What makes this wage disparity and employment inequality even more discriminatory is that the nonregular workers received no job security or comprehensive legally mandated benefits, or even minimum protection from receiving less than the minimum wage, mainly because of the light "cotton-wool punishment" of employers who did not pay the stipulated minimum wage. KOSTAT reported a third of all employees to be nonregular workers, including part-time, fixed-term, and dispatched workers, and the share of "temporary workers (22%) was more than double the Organization for Economic Cooperation and Development average" (OECD 2016, 42). The problem of nonregular workers in Korea thus remained much worse than that of nonregular workers in Japan or the United States in 2014.[9] According to the *Han'guk Ilbo,* which cited the Bank of Korea's analysis on August 16, 2016, the number of nonregular workers who received less than the legal minimum wage had increased from 2.12 million in 2013 to 2.5 million in 2015, and their number was predicted to exceed 3 million in 2017, after increasing to 2.8 million in 2016 ("Som pangmangi ch'ŏbŏl" 2016).

In this light, the "tyranny of labor aristocracy" clearly affected not only the rapid increase in the number of nonregular subcontract workers but also the predicament of HCI workers and their unions, in terms of their radically strengthened enterprise unionism through social closure, which became synonymous with the collective egotism of large *chaebŏl* unions, as well as the Korean Confederation of Trade Unions dominated by the Korean Metal Workers' Union (Chŏn'guk kŭmsok nodongjohap). Still, it is important to remember that the HCI workers had been virtually guaranteed job security up until the 1997 financial crisis, which alarmed them to the extent that they radically transformed their militant labor unionism by consolidating their class position as a labor aristocracy in Korea's emergent upper- and lower-tier labor-market system, or two-tier working-class system. Through their institutionalization of social closure, the HCI workers as regular workers and their *chaebŏl* unions, in other words, have benefited from their companies' superior access to capital and technology, while workers in SMEs have languished in poorly paid jobs in undercapitalized enterprises, a characteristic similar to that of the dualism of the Japanese labor market, which, notwithstanding, has significantly diversified since the 1990s (Watanabe 2017). Overall, Korea's labor-market dualism, which has widened the split between the HCI workers as a labor aristocracy and nonregular subcontract workers as so-called second-class citizens (*idŭng kungmin*) or an inferior class (*yŏldŭng kyegŭp*), has ultimately led to extreme forms of labor protest, especially aerial sit-in protests. Since the famous aerial protest for 309 days by Kim Chin-suk on top of Crane No. 85 at Pusan's Yŏngdo shipyard to protest the mass layoffs by Hanjin Heavy Industries and Construction in 2011, aerial sit-in protests have turned into life-threatening warfare.[10]

The 408-day sit-in protest on top of a 45-meter-tall chimney by Ch'a Kwang-ho (Ja Gwang-ho), from May 2014 to July 2015, against the unfair dismissal of union workers by the then defunct Star Chemical, a manufacturer of synthetic fibers, was the hitherto longest sit-in protest in the world.[11] In his 2015 article "The Hope Bus Is Leaving Again on 12 September," Ch'a Kwang-ho criticized the illegal practice by large firms of engaging subcontract workers: "I have barely returned to the ground after 408 days, but there are people climbing up to the sky.... However, Hyundai-Kia Motors ignores even the Supreme Court ruling that in-house subcontracting is clearly illegal and thus they should 'regularize' those in-house subcontract workers. Despite the fact they illegally employ tens of thousands of [in-house subcontract] workers.... They split the workers by using the new recruitment system as bait, and pressure the in-house subcontract workers to sell their souls."

At the workplace level, labor exclusion and discrimination by regular HCI workers and their union aristocracy led to a so-called system of worker-exploit-worker. Ha Pu-yŏng, former vice president of Hyundai Motor Union, openly appealed for sweeping attitudinal change at both Hyundai Motor and the Hyundai Motor Union:

> Ten years have passed since nonregular workers formed their union at Hyundai Motor in 2003 and the Ministry of Labor adjudicated that the Hyundai Motor in-house subcontractors were illegal dispatch agencies....
>
> As long as nonregular workers who are being paid half the regular workers' wages exist, there is no escape from labor aristocracy.... The regular workers' sense of justice, which used to distinguish right from

wrong, has vanished and their conscience . . . has decayed and been corrupted to become a spot where workers exploit workers. . . . This is the reason why regular workers of large factories, who have no place to stand as a result of their social isolation, must lead in solving the problem of nonregular workers.[12]

The nonregular workers' all-out strikes illustrate Korea's deepening social crisis, especially unemployment among young people aged fifteen to twenty-nine, reported to have increased to 410,000, a fifteen-year high, in August 2015, up from 330,000 in 2013 (Hyung-A Kim 2015). In this light, leaders of the five leading young people's associations have publicly demanded that the FKTU and KCTU, which typify the militant union aristocracy, take responsibility for young people's unemployment because, according to these associations, their union militancy has become the main adversary preventing the employment of young people ("Ch'ŏngnyŏn ilchari" 2015).

Parallel to this view, other proponents of the labor union movement argue that the concept of a labor aristocracy in Korea was propagated by the government, the conservative media, and the *chaebŏl*s as a strategy to break up the Korean working class by splitting workers into regular and nonregular camps. The supporters of this view contend that although there are firms where wages and working conditions of nonregular subcontract workers and workers at SMEs are half those of the regular workers of large firms, the true inequality lies in the massive gap between the wealth of the *chaebŏl*s and workers' incomes in general (Paek Nak-ch'ŏng 2015, 222–26).[13] In light of these competing arguments, especially concerning the vastly changed collective attitude of regular workers in large *chaebŏl* firms as a labor aristocracy, let us consider the HCI workers' views on democratic unions in their society over the past four decades.

HCI WORKERS' VIEWS ON THEIR UNIONS AND STATUS AS A LABOR ARISTOCRACY

We turn now to HCI workers' views on their unions and their new collective identity and public image as a labor aristocracy, along with their vastly changed attitudes over time, based on in-depth interviews I conducted in 2014 and 2015 with a sample of thirty-nine HCI workers in three HCI *chaebŏl* firms: (1) Hyundai WIA (formerly Kia Machine Tools) with ten respondents; (2) Doosan Heavy Industries (formerly Daewoo Heavy Industries) with nine respondents; and (3) Hyundai Heavy Industries (HHI) with twenty respondents.[14] These thirty-nine HCI workers had either graduated from technical high schools or completed vocational training programs through public or private institutes, as well as undertaking in-plant training courses, between 1972, when Korea commenced its third Five-Year Economic Development Plan, focused on heavy chemical industrialization, and 1987, when Korea began its democratic transition.

Most of these HCI workers, born between 1954 and 1969, are now in their late fifties to early sixties and thus are mostly Korean baby boomers (1955–63) who started to retire four or five years ago. Having generally worked well over thirty years in their areas of technical expertise in the HCI sector, the respondents were highly skilled regular workers with established careers in their respective firms. As explained in chapter 4, HHI workers had been publicly known for their record of not striking for almost twenty years, from 1995 until November 2014, when they staged several partial strikes. Thus HHI interviewees had mostly worked for the previous nineteen years without any threat of layoffs. Juxtaposed to this record is that of Hyundai WIA, formerly Kia Machine Tools until its merger with Hyundai Motor amid the 1997 crisis.

In order to compare this volatile takeover experience with the unaffected experience of HHI workers, my interview respondents were selected from those former Kia Machine Tools workers who had been under real threat of retrenchment. For the same reason, my respondents from Doosan Heavy Industries were selected from former workers of Daewoo Heavy Industries, which had merged with Doosan amid the 1997 crisis. Thus, twenty of the thirty-nine respondents, namely HHI workers, had no experience of the threat of layoffs, whereas the other nineteen had experienced real traumas in the pre- and post-takeover periods of their respective companies. The questionnaire, focused on this first generation of HCI workers, was used to identify their socioeconomic background and their views, especially on the militant labor movement and enterprise unionism, as well as their personal background, duration of employment, current yearly income, and views on their collective identity and public image as a labor aristocracy, as well as their sense of social class[15] and social stratum.[16]

Table 5.4 shows summary data on the demographic and socioeconomic backgrounds of the thirty-nine respondents. Their average age was 55.2; the average length of their employment was 34.3 years;[17] and their annual income averaged about ₩78 million (approx. US$76,500). This annual income was 2.4 times higher in 2014 than the average income of all Korean regular

TABLE 5.4. Characteristics of the thirty-nine respondents from three corporations, 2014 and 2015

Corporation (N)	Average age	Average length of employment (years)	Average annual income (₩10,000)[a]	Subjective class[b]	Subjective stratum[c]
Hyundai Heavy Industries (20)	56.3	35.5	8,375	Middle (13) Working (3) NR (4)[d]	MH (1) MM (14) ML (4) NR (1)
Hyundai WIA Machine Tools (10)	55.0	32.9	8,670	Middle (8) Working (1) NR(1)	MH (3) MM (5) ML(1) L (1)
Doosan Heavy Industries (9)	53.0	33.1	7,080	Middle (3) Working (4) NR (2)	MM (1) ML (7) NR (1)
Total (39)	55.2	34.3	8,152	Middle (24) Working (8) NR (7)	MH (4) MM (20) ML (12) L (1) NR(2)

[a] US$1 = about ₩1,100 as of January 2015.
[b] Subjective class was identified as working, middle, or upper.
[c] Subjective stratum was identified as high (H), middle high (MH), middle middle (MM), middle low (ML), or low (L).
[d] "NR" = no response.

workers, who earned an average of ₩32.4 million.[18] In terms of working conditions, my surveys found that variables such as age, whether they graduated from technical high school or a vocational institute, or length of employment made little difference, though there were relatively large differences in their annual incomes. Regular workers at Hyundai WIA and HHI, for example, earned an annual income of around ₩87 million (approx. US$85,260), whereas Doosan Heavy Industries regular workers' annual income stood at around ₩70 million (approx. US$68,600). While respondents from the three *chaebŏl* corporations received a relatively high annual income, they also enjoyed many additional benefits that were not identified in the surveys, including bonuses and allowances for housing, education, and medical insurance, as well as stock options based on performance.

As a result, twenty-six out of thirty-three respondents considered themselves middle class, while seven saw themselves as working class, and the remaining six did not respond to the question. This relatively middle-class-oriented attitude among the respondents was further underscored in their subjective identification of social stratum. In responding to the question that categorized social stratum into five levels as high, middle high (MH), middle middle (MM), middle low (ML), and low (L), thirty-six out of thirty-nine respondents, the vast majority, identified themselves as located in the middle strata, with four MHs, twenty MMs, and twelve MLs, while only two respondents did not respond to this question.[19] The other three respondents identified themselves as being in the low stratum. Interestingly, four of the seven respondents who identified themselves as working class earned high annual incomes, between ₩60 million and ₩98 million,[20] and each owned a sizable house or apartment (averaging 31.2 *pyŏng*, approx. 103 square meters) and a car. Three of these four had two grown-up children each, one graduated and the other still studying at university, and one had two children in high school. Hence, these respondents' annual incomes together with their assets and their children's education level, in reality, fitted more into the middle class than the average Korean working class, considering that, in 2014, the average middle-class Korean earned ₩3.74 million monthly (i.e., ₩44.9 million annually) with net assets worth ₩230 million, including a house or apartment worth ₩200 million.[21]

When asked about their personal experience during the 1997 crisis, many responded that they had felt the threat of unemployment, reflecting the sentiments and memories of former Kia Machine Tools and Daewoo Heavy Industries workers who were then employees of Hyundai WIA and Doosan

Heavy Industries, respectively. These respondents indicated that they had felt threatened when they saw their coworkers made redundant. They also indicated that they had experienced difficulties in maintaining their households, which inevitably led to economization in domestic spending. One had closed an installment savings account due to a temporary layoff and went through an economic crisis, while others recounted that they had felt great anxiety while their company merged into Hyundai Group, with mass layoffs resulting from restructuring, frozen wages, and other mental and physical trauma.

In contrast, most Hyundai Heavy Industries respondents indicated that they did not experience considerable change in their lives during the crisis. One noted that there had not been much difficulty because his company was unaffected, even though the entire nation was going bankrupt. Another stated that he had profited from his savings by earning higher rates of interest, because the Korean government had implemented a high-interest rate policy at that time. The HHI respondents did not display symptoms of unemployment threat or associated pain that workers from merged companies experienced. The most striking response was the moral criticism that only common folk had participated in the gold collection campaign during the crisis, when the whole nation should have participated.

Given that this was the double-sided perspective of HCI workers, depending on the threat of layoffs or otherwise, my survey asked whether the respondents had experienced any change or setbacks during the 1997 crisis with the question: "Did you have any change in your point of view, especially regarding the labor-management relationship, since the IMF crisis?" If they had formed a different point of view, I asked how that exhibited itself in terms of the direction of labor-management relations. Nearly half the respondents did not reply to these questions, perhaps because of the sensitivity, not to mention the complexity behind their own company union's controversial labor-management relations. Of those who responded, half answered that they did not experience a huge change. In particular, HHI respondents, who had maintained no-strike and no-dispute labor-management relations throughout the crisis and afterward, tended to reply that their view on labor-management relations was little affected. In fact, some HHI respondents stressed that labor and management should continue to coexist (*sangsaeng*), while also giving priority to the development and success of the company, and that labor union executives needed to be rational and cooperative with management. In this regard, the respondents from both Hyundai WIA and

Doosan Heavy Industries, with lived experience of their own companies' mergers and the associated threat of layoffs, among other related economic and social trauma, also stressed the importance of coexistence in the labor-management relationship for the prosperity of the company. In particular, they argued that unions needed to focus on welfare expansion for workers rather than wage increases, stressing that the system should move toward rewarding "hardworking and able workers," instead of rewarding all equally based on the principle of distribution regardless of whether one works hard or not.

On the Issue of Labor Aristocracy

Concerning the respondents' views on their collective identity and public image as a labor aristocracy, fifteen of the thirty-nine respondents did not respond to the survey question "What is your opinion on the so-called labor aristocracy of large-firm unions today?" The individual views of the remaining twenty-four respondents, however, indicated three notable characteristics that showed conflicting views on the issue of labor aristocracy. The first was the need to change the current policy of large-firm unions, which they regarded as being exposed to "moral risks." Sixteen of twenty-four respondents, for example, expressed the need to change union policy, which some noted as being "self-serving" for union leaders. Others pointed to unions as a "biased force" (*p'yŏnjungdoen seryŏk*) that pursues the benefit of the corporate and union executives rather than focusing on universal labor rights. Some stressed, in particular, that their union's policy ran counter to national development, especially counter to the interests of nonregular workers, such as temporary and daily subcontract workers.

The second notable characteristic was their annoyance at their collective identity and public image as a labor aristocracy. Six out of twenty-four respondents expressed their annoyance by noting, "It is a media trick [*nonggan*]" (D-13 and D-16), or rejecting the term as being of "no particular interest" (H-1 and H-15) or being "capitalist logic to slander the unions of large [HCI] firms" (K-5 and K-7).[22] Others linked the term to the self-interest of union executives of large firms. Comments like "The union executives are known as 'iron rice-bowls' [*ch'ŏlbapt'ong*] of which we, the ordinary shop floor workers, are envious" (D-14), and the agreement of several respondents with the public image of both themselves and their unions as a labor aristocracy (H-5, H-6, H-7, H-17) seemed to show that they were well aware of their collective privileges, such as high wages, job security, and other welfare benefits. It was equally noticeable that some respondents saw their aristocratic union as a "biased force of vested interests that seeks profits only for business and union leaders" (H-14 and H-20). This view, especially expressed by one former union leader, somewhat overlapped with other responses, which expressed the third notable characteristic of a labor aristocracy as having "moral risks" (todŏkjŏk haei; K-9 and K-10, D-17, H-2, H-8, H-9, and D-18). These respondents demanded the "need for active change," not just for workers at large firms such as themselves, but also for workers at SMEs (K-8, H-18, and D-11).

Overall, the HCI workers' view of their collective identity and the new public image of their unions and themselves as a labor aristocracy was ambivalent at best and conflicting. In fact, thirty-three out of a total of thirty-nine respondents, including the fifteen respondents who did not answer this particular question, can be regarded as viewing their public image and that of their unions rather negatively, but for different reasons. Curiously, more respondents from the former Kia Machine Tools and Daewoo Heavy Industries expressed more critical views on the issue of labor aristocracy than the respondents of Hyundai Heavy Industries. Nevertheless, none of these respondents linked the public image of their unions and their collective image as a labor aristocracy to the structure of Korea's chaebŏl-oriented economy and its dual-market system, in which HCI workers and their unions have become isolated from the rest of the Korean workforce. This isolation is due largely to their exclusive enterprise unionism, focused on their own parochial economic interests rather than on solidarity with all workers in today's Korean society and beyond.

HCI WORKERS IN SURVEYS ON LABOR UNIONS

What was HCI workers' view of labor unions in the past? As discussed in chapter 1, many skilled workers entered the labor market starting in the mid-1970s. They initially began as a kinŭngsa (craftsman/technician) or even chikkong (factory worker) with or without a class II skills license. And as young male workers in the HCI sector, they instigated the Great Workers' Struggle of 1987, establishing democratic labor unions (minju nojo) in most of the large HCI chaebŏl factories in cities of the southern industrial belts, including Masan, Ch'angwŏn, and Ulsan. Subsequently, HCI workers strategically exploited their militant unionism to the extent of so-called maximum economic compensation through maximum struggle. During the 1997 crisis, however, HCI workers came to realize that the labor unions, no matter how militant they were, could not ensure job security, and that the survival and development of the company were as important as, or even more important for their own survival than, that of the union.

In this process, their collective sense of betrayal among many leaders of the Korean Confederation of Trade Unions particularly encouraged them to transform their militant labor unionism into a device for conserving their own vested economic interests through social closure. This section therefore traces the changed thinking and attitudes of Korean workers regarding labor unions by focusing on survey data published by the Korean Social Science Data Archive (KOSSDA). I selected a set of three surveys, conducted in 1978, when the HCI policy had become most active, especially in terms of export growth; in 1987, when the Great Workers' Struggle erupted; and in 2005, when the gap between the regular workers and nonregular workers had become a major cause of labor conflict, especially the gap that stemmed from the then newly emerged labor aristocracy of both the regular HCI workers and their unions.[23] In fact, the labor aristocracy issue had emerged as a major cause of social conflict in 2003, and for this reason I included an examination of the 2005 survey question regarding labor aristocracy. By comparing data from these three periods of 1978, 1987, and 2005, I examined the change in HCI workers' attitudes toward labor unions from a historical perspective.

The first data I reviewed were sourced from the "Survey on Korean Workers' and Managers' Work Ethic and Labor-Management Policy" (Han'guk nodongja wa kwallija ŭi chigŏp ŭisik kwa nosa chŏngch'aek e kwanhan chosa) conducted by the Seoul National University Institute of Social Science in 1978 (KOSSDA no. A1-1978-0001). These data were collected by mail survey with a nationwide sample of 984 production and office workers. Two survey questions asked about the necessity of labor unions and the respondents' assessment of labor-union activities. One question asked, "How necessary do you think labor unions are for the welfare of the workers in a company?" with five choices of response offered: (1) not necessary at all, (2) not often needed, (3) so-so, (4) somewhat necessary, and (5) absolutely necessary. I simplified these choices by combining (1) and (2), and (4) and (5) into two response categories, "rather unnecessary" and "rather necessary," respectively. The second question—"What is your general opinion about the labor union to which you are affiliated or which you often observe even if you are not affiliated?"—offered three choices: (1) it [the union] is an organization that was established to improve the workers' wages and working conditions, while also endeavoring to undertake such tasks; (2) it benefits only the union executives or employers, but is not beneficial for the workers; and (3) I do not know what the union does exactly.

Table 5.5 shows the results of the survey, which I analyzed by examining cross tabulations in accordance with the respondents' occupations, largely because occupation as a trait variable can differentiate our key subject, HCI workers. In analyzing the 1978 data, I understood that HCI workers may have been included in the category of factory workers (*chikkong*), rather than skilled workers (*sungnyŏn'gong*). This was highly likely due mainly to the fact that HCI workers had only newly entered the workforce with about six years or less work experience, even if they had been employed in HCI firms straight after high school graduation in 1972 or 1973 at best.

Tables 5.5 and 5.6 show that in every occupational group, 61.9 percent of respondents regarded labor unions to be necessary, while 53 percent of respondents considered union activities to be beneficial to the workers. In particular, 70 percent of the factory worker (*chikkong*) respondents answered that labor unions were necessary, while 61 percent regarded union activities as beneficial to the workers. Hence, it can be argued that HCI workers, even as young workers in their twenties who would have been generally treated as *chikkong*, held a more positive view of labor unions than respondents in all other categories in the late 1970s, although labor unions and their activities were under the control of the government's tyrannical antilabor policies.

TABLE 5.5. Survey results: On the need for labor unions, 1978

Occupation	Responses on necessity of labor unions (%)			
	Rather necessary[a]	Neutral	Rather unnecessary[b]	Total
Service/clerk	147 (58.3)	58 (23.0)	47 (18.6)	252 (100.0)
Factory worker	197 (70.1)	45 (16.0)	39 (13.9)	281 (100.0)
Skilled worker	122 (62.2)	33 (16.8)	41 (20.9)	196 (100.0)
Professional/ managerial	111 (54.7)	47 (23.2)	45 (22.2)	203 (100.0)
Total	577 (61.9)	183 (19.6)	172 (18.4)	932 (100.0)

[a] "Rather necessary" is a combination of "absolutely necessary" and "somewhat necessary" in the original survey.
[b] "Rather unnecessary" is a combination of "absolutely unnecessary" and "somewhat not necessary" in the original survey.

TABLE 5.6. Survey results: Workers' views on labor unions, 1978

Occupation	Responses on labor unions (%)			
	It is an organization that actively attempts to improve the workers' income and working conditions	It only benefits the union executives and employers, not the workers	I do not know what it is exactly	Total
Service/clerk	116 (48.1)	80 (33.2)	45 (18.7)	241 (100.0)
Factory worker	173 (61.1)	81 (28.6)	29 (10.2)	283 (100.0)
Skilled worker	101 (53.4)	69 (36.5)	19 (10.1)	189 (100.0)
Professional/managerial	97 (47.8)	68 (33.5)	38 (18.7)	203 (100.0)
Total	487 (53.2)	298 (32.5)	131 (14.3)	916 (100.0)

The 1987 survey, conducted again by the Social Science Research Institute, under the title "Survey on Industrial Relations and Professional Ethics in Korea, Workers" (Han'guk ŭi nosa kwan'gye mit chigŏp yulli chosa, kŭlloja; KOSSDA no. A1-1987-0008), was based on a survey sample of 1,667 production and office workers in three key industrial areas: Kyŏng-in (Seoul, Puch'ŏn, Inch'ŏn, Anyang, and Sungnam), where light industries were concentrated; Ch'angwŏn, in southeast Korea, where the Heavy and Chemical Industrial Park was newly constructed; and Yŏngwŏl, in the eastern Korea mining district. The question I chose to examine from this survey was "How necessary do you think labor unions are for improving wages and working conditions, grievance settlement, and respectful treatment at the workplace?" Four response choices were offered: (1) not necessary at all; (2) not often needed; (3) somewhat necessary; and (4) absolutely necessary. I again simplified these four choices by combining (1) and (2) into "rather unnecessary," and (3) and (4) into "rather necessary," and I analyzed the cross tabulations in accordance with the respondents' occupations.

Table 5.7 reflects the revolutionary mood of Korean workers in 1987, the year in which the Great Workers Struggle erupted. It shows that 91 percent of respondents, for example, replied that labor unions were "rather necessary," and this overwhelming viewpoint was spread across all occupational groups, with each group scoring around 90 percent in agreeing to the necessity of labor unions. HCI workers were no exception regardless of whether they were classified as simple labor or as skilled workers. As explained in chapter 2, HCI workers' militancy, especially in leading the democratic

TABLE 5.7. Survey results: On the necessity of labor unions at the workplace, 1987

Occupation	Responses on the necessity of labor unions at the workplace (%)		
	Rather necessary[a]	Rather unnecessary[b]	Total
Simple laborer	312 (92.0)	27 (8.0)	339 (100.0)
Technician	356 (89.0)	44 (11.0)	400 (100.0)
Skilled worker	187 (91.2)	18 (8.8)	205 (100.0)
Clerk	532 (91.7)	48 (8.3)	580 (100.0)
Total	1,317 (91.0)	137 (8.9)	1,524 (100.0)

[a] "Rather necessary" is combination of "absolutely necessary" and "somewhat necessary" in the original survey.
[b] "Rather unnecessary" is combination of "not necessary at all" and "somewhat not necessary" in the original survey.

unionization movement and the movement of the Korean working class at that time, drew phenomenal support from workers throughout the country, well beyond the industrial cities of Masan, Ch'angwŏn, and Ulsan. As a result, union density shot up, reaching a peak of 19.8 percent in 1989, with almost two million members. This rapid rise in union density, however, was short lived, and by 1992 density had dropped to 16.4 percent (see figure 5.1), and then to as low as 9.8 percent by 2010. Although the rate of union density rebounded to above 10 percent after 2011, with 10.1 percent in that year, and then remained at 10.3 for three consecutive years, from 2012 to 2014, and again in 2016,[24] the holders of union membership have been predominantly regular workers of large firms, especially HCI workers, who do not necessarily support the union activities of nonregular subcontract workers or industrial action by other workers with no union membership.

The survey of 2005 that I examined was titled "Korean General Social Survey 2005" (Han'guk chonghap sahoe chosa 2005). Conducted by the Survey Research Center, Sungkyunkwan University (KOSSDA no. A1-2005-0001), this survey was carried out by way of face-to-face interviews with a nationwide sample of 1,613 male and female respondents over eighteen years old. The 2005 survey was noteworthy, especially in terms of considering the rapidly deepening nonregular workers' problem, which had become Korea's biggest cause of social polarization, together with the labor-market segmentation between regular workers at large firms—broadly seen as a labor

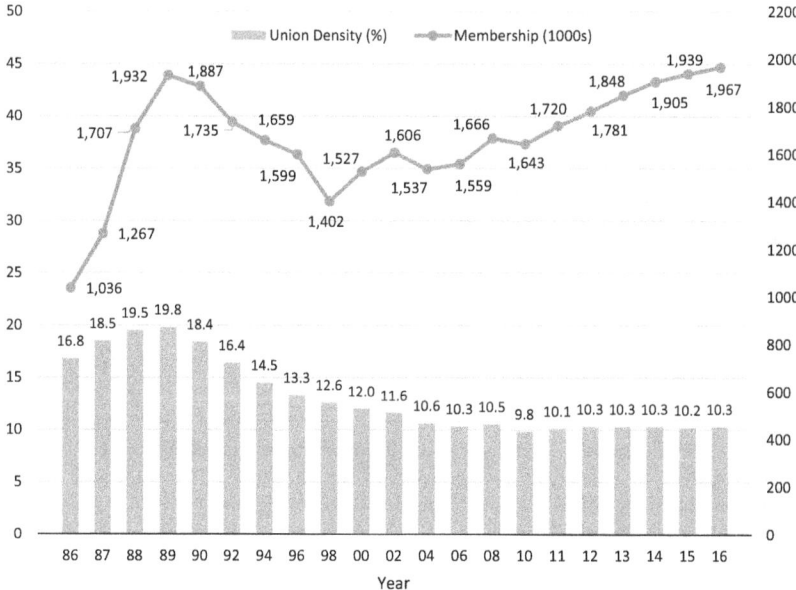

FIGURE 5.1. Union density and membership in South Korea, 1986–2016. *Source:* Kukka T'onggye Pot'ol (2017).

aristocracy with superior wages and job security, among other welfare benefits—and precarious nonregular workers in various categories.

The Korean-style labor aristocracy, as one Korean sociologist noted (Cho Kye-wan 2012, 567), enjoys a monopoly of benefits based on the excess profits that flow out of the relationship between large firms (*wŏnch'ŏng*) and their subcontractors (*hach'ŏng*). This does not mean that regular workers and nonregular workers in today's Korea do not cooperate at all in labor movement activities. On the contrary, there have been distinct cases where regular and nonregular workers have cooperated in challenging the precarization of labor and layoffs, although such cases have tended to be in the service sector, including the case of E-land, a Korean retail *chaebŏl* company. What was and still remains characteristic of the Korean nonregular workers' struggle is that they have been exploited by the regular workers of large firms, most notably the HCI workers and their unions, who have transformed their militant labor unionism, focused on their vested economic interests through social closure by excluding others from using their scarce resources while also differentiating their group as a labor aristocracy in Korea's dual labor-market system.

THE RISE OF HCI WORKERS 139

TABLE 5.8. Survey results: On the militancy of Korean labor union activities, 2005

Occupation	Responses on the militancy of Korean labor union activities (%)			
	Rather militant[a]	Neutral	Rather moderate[b]	Total
Manager/professional	260 (73.5)	68 (19.2)	26 (7.4)	354 (100.0)
Clerk/semiprofessional	237 (67.3)	89 (25.3)	26 (7.4)	352 (100.0)
Service/sales	168 (66.2)	48 (19.4)	31 (12.6)	247 (100.0)
Technician/assembly	128 (64.9)	42 (21.3)	27 (13.7)	197 (100.0)
Simple labor	60 (69.8)	18 (20.9)	8 (9.3)	86 (100.0)
Total	853 (69.0)	265 (21.4)	118 (9.5)	1,236 (100)

[a] "Rather militant" combines "strongly militant" and "somewhat militant" in the original survey.
[b] "Rather moderate" combines "strongly moderate" and "somewhat moderate" in the original survey.

To reflect on this phenomenon, I chose to examine a question asked in the 2005 survey that is very different from those asked in 1987 and 1978: "How militant or moderate do you think the activities of Korean workers' unions are?" Five response choices were offered: (1) very militant; (2) somewhat militant; (3) neither militant nor moderate; (4) somewhat moderate; and (5) very moderate. As before, I restructured the responses by combining (1) and (2) as "rather militant," and (4) and (5) as "rather moderate." Table 5.8 shows the response data for this question. As in earlier cases, I analyzed cross tabulations in accordance with the respondents' occupations.

As table 5.8 shows, the method by which this 2005 survey categorized occupational groups was slightly different from the other two surveys I examined. The main reason for this change of method was because of two new occupational categories, managers/professionals (*kwallijik/chŏnmunjik*) and sales in service ventures (*ssŏbisŭ p'anmaejik*), while the old category of skilled workers (*sungnyŏn'gong*) was newly categorized as technicians/assembly workers (*kinŭngjik/choripchik*). The old Korean term *sungnyŏn'gong*, used mainly prior to 1987, in other words, seems to have been reclassified into the two new categories of labor, *kinŭngjik* and *choripchik*, in the post-1987 period, the former indicating an industrial skilled worker or technician and the latter an assembly worker.

Despite this reclassification, which obviously reflected the change in labor market conditions over almost two decades since 1987, the cross tabulation showed that 69 percent of respondents tended to consider union activities as "rather militant." This response, however, exhibited slight variations across each occupational group. Thus the category of managers/ professionals, who were the object of union activities, had a higher percentage of responses of "militant" (74 percent), whereas technicians / assembly workers, who were stakeholders in union activities, had a relatively lower rate (65 percent) describing workers' unions as "rather militant." In addition, 69.8 percent of respondents in the category of simple labor considered Korean union activities to be rather militant, reflecting their inequitable position in the workforce and their frustration with the lack of union support for this category of workers.

CONCLUSION

Overall, the majority of HCI workers over almost four decades, from the late 1970s to the era of neoliberal globalization in the 2010s, have been consistently strong in their collective expectations regarding the welfare of workers through union activities. Their views on labor union militancy, however, showed a strong preference for radical change to an approach that would be inclusive of both regular and nonregular workers. Regarding their new collective status or identity as a labor aristocracy, the HCI workers' views appeared to be uncomfortable at best. Many rank-and-file HCI workers whom I interviewed openly expressed annoyance, as did our survey respondents, arguing that the term "labor aristocracy" was a product of capitalist *chaebŏls*' strategic maneuvering, especially through the media, which has been closely linked to several top-ranking *chaebŏl*s.

The change in Korea's economic paradigm to a new *chaebŏl*-led accumulation model needs modification, especially to stabilize the labor market through the creation of jobs and more equitable income distribution. Korea has become the country with the highest rate of worker turnover among member states of the Organization for Economic Cooperation and Development. Almost a quarter of full-time workers in 2012, for example, earned less than two-thirds of the median wage according to a 2014 report, which was "the second-highest share [of less than the median wage] in the OECD" (OECD 2014). In this light, the HCI workers' collective identity as a labor aristocracy manifests the inevitable result of Korea's unrelenting industrial capitalism campaign since the mid-1980s, especially since 1997.

Conclusion

HCI workers are isolated in Korean society today, even within the labor force. As the leading force of Korea's democratic labor movement, not only HCI workers and their unions, but also their umbrella authority, the Korean Confederation of Trade Unions, are being criticized by many rank-and-file Korean workers both for being the core of Korea's militant labor unionism, through which they have elevated their collective status to a labor aristocracy, and for isolating themselves by denying others access to union resources. Their social isolation contradicts their own democratic trade union movement philosophy as articulated in the KCTU manifesto, which promotes the achievement of "fundamental labor and trade union rights" while also "eliminating all kinds of discriminatory practices at the workplace."[1] In practice, however, HCI workers and the unions under the KCTU have played a key role in Korea's development of a dual labor-market system by acquiescing in the split between regular workers of large firms with vested rights and nonregular workers of various types and other nonunionized workers at the workplace, including female, young, and migrant workers. Through their militant labor unionism combined with social closure over thirty years since the mid-1990s, the HCI workers not only have increased their total incomes to more than double that of the many nonregular workers but have also dramatically transformed their collective status and thus identity into a labor aristocracy.

The HCI workers' trajectory in pursuing their collective goal of a "better life" (*chal sanŭn kŏt*), especially through better wages and various economic and social welfare benefits, as well as virtually guaranteed job security through union protection over time, has led, however, to a vast wage gap between regular HCI workers at large *chaebŏl* firms and other regular workers of SMEs and nonregular workers. This gap, according to a report by the progressive online outlet *Pressian* (Yi Nam-sin 2017), has doubled from an average gap of ₩780,000 per month in 2001 to ₩1.56 million per month in 2016. It is no wonder that most nonregular workers argue that the KCTU and its member unions represent "only the interests of regular workers of large firms and those of the KCTU itself, which is in conflict with their own interests" (Chu 2017).

This extremely unequal labor-market structure has damaged Korea's competitiveness in the international market, which, according to the Geneva-based World Economic Forum's *Global Competitiveness Report 2016-2017*, was ranked 26th of 138 countries,[2] while Korea's hiring and firing practices were ranked 113th, and cooperation in labor-employer relations, despite the impact of the Corporate Culture Movement, 135th of 138 countries ("Kukka kyŏngjaengryŏk" 2015). Korea's rank of 113th for hiring and firing practices, in particular, reflects the overprotection of unionized regular workers, especially HCI workers, by their militant unions, just as Korea's rank of 135th for cooperation in labor-employer relations reflects the hopelessness of labor-management relations, as well as the pugnacious relations between regular workers and their unions in large firms, and the plight of nonregular subcontract workers under the dual labor-market system of worker-exploit-worker.

The rate of union membership of wage workers in Korea, however, has only been about 10 percent for over a decade, ranging from 10.6 in 2004 to 10.3 percent in 2016, with 1,966,000 of a total of 19,172,000 wage workers with union membership, leaving the remaining 90 percent of wage workers not unionized at all. This low rate of union membership reflects the fact that the membership of both the KCTU and FKTU, Korea's two umbrella labor organizations, is made up almost entirely of unions representing regular workers at large firms, most notably HCI workers, and employees of public sector bodies, to the exclusion of the vast majority of wage workers in small enterprises. In June 2017, unions affiliated with the radical KCTU consisted of 734,369 members, including about 181,087 or 24.7 percent nonregular workers. Similarly, the unions affiliated with the FKTU comprised a total of 954,546 members, of whom about 60,000 or 6-7 percent were nonregular workers. The rate of union membership in Korean firms with 300 or more employees in 2016 was 55.1 percent; in firms with 100-299 employees, it was 15 percent; in firms with 30-99 employees, it was just 3.5 percent; and in those with less than 30 employees, it was 0.2 percent, with virtually no unions. The rate of union membership in the public sector was 67.6 percent, compared to 9.1 percent in the private sector.³

Overall, this lopsided prevalence of union membership illustrates a desperate need for labor-market reform. Both the radical KCTU and the moderate FKTU have long lost public support, to the extent of being viewed as the self-serving "enemies" of the majority of Korean workers. Five leading groups of university students in their twenties and thirties, in particular, have publicly condemned the union militancy exercised under these two umbrella union organizations, referring to them as the main enemies (*chujŏk*). They argue that the KCTU and FKTU no longer represent labor because they block the employment of young people, and thus must take responsibility for the youth unemployment crisis ("Ch'ŏngnyŏn ilchari" 2015). The jobless rate among Korean young people aged between fifteen and twenty-nine hit a record yearly high of 9.9 percent in 2017, with total unemployed topping one million (around 4 percent), according to Statistics of Korea (XinhwaNet 2018); and the OECD's 2016 report on the employment rate of the same group confirmed it as "one of the lowest in the OECD." With fulltime regular work scarce and hopes in ruins in the face of severe economic inequality in both the Korean workforce and Korean society at large, many young people in their twenties and thirties are referred to as the "seven give-ups generation" (*ch'ilp'o sedae*), which has allegedly given up love, marriage, childbirth, employment, home ownership, interpersonal relationships, and hope.⁴

THE ROOT OF HCI WORKERS' SOCIAL ISOLATION

The root of the social isolation of HCI workers and their unions as a result of their narrow and selfish economic unionism, however, lies much deeper than what is apparent on the surface. This is so because their social isolation is not rooted just in the *chaebŏls*' unbridled capital accumulation in the course of Korea's state-led development, followed by economic liberalization focused primarily on neoliberal restructuring, especially in the postcrisis Korean economy. More specifically, the root of the social isolation of HCI workers and their unions lies in the Korean government's failure to reduce income inequality while also failing to effectively coordinate corporation policy to increase investment in the era of neoliberal globalization. Many *chaebŏls*, especially the top ranked, have grown into global corporate giants in postrestructuring Korea. The combined internal cash reserves of the thirty top-ranking *chaebŏl*s, including Samsung, Hyundai Motor, Lotte, and SK Group, increased by more than ₩170 trillion, from ₩330.1 trillion in 2010 to ₩500.2 trillion in 2014. In June 2016, these thirty top-ranking *chaebŏl*s' internal reserves, according to some civic groups, have exceeded more than ₩754 trillion (approx. US$630 billion),[5] which was more than double Korea's annual budgeted fiscal expenditure. Yet the rate of these *chaebŏl*s' real investment was a mere 12.9 percent. Their exorbitant pile of cash reserves with minimal trickle-down effect starkly resembles the winner-take-all political economy of the United States, which, according to Hacker and Pierson (2010, 3), has become the defining feature of American economic life, in which "the top 0.1 percent—one out of every thousand households—received over 20 percent of all after-tax income gains between 1979 and 2005."

Just as winner-take-all politics has aroused much public fury in America, the *chaebŏl*s' record cash reserves have aroused public fury in Korea, not only in regard to their monopoly of the country's economic growth gains, but also in regard to their abuse of economic power in securing the government's favoritism, which has in effect generated many social ills, including income inequality and a lack of startups, while economic unionism without the solidarity of workers has become the norm in most HCI *chaebŏl* firms in today's Korea. This is not to overlook, however, the collective positive role of either the *chaebŏl*s or HCI workers in Korea's rapid development. Under their reciprocal subsidies-as-contracts, they spearheaded Korea's rise to economic affluence prior to the 1997 financial crisis following the Park Chung Hee era, and then again paved the way for Korea to restart its economy as a global player over the two decades since that crisis. In this sense, the *chaebŏl*s' overpowering dominance in Korea's economy, in which trade accounts for more than three-fourths of GDP (Premack 2017), seems to have resulted in part in the *chaebŏl*s' widely known bossism, or monopolistic control over economic resources, together with the authoritarian work culture known in Korean society as *kapchil*.[6] Based on their intricately built power-elite networks,[7] especially through the traditional networks of blood (*hyŏryŏn*), locality (*chiyŏn*), and school ties (*hagyŏn*), the *chaebŏl*s have ascended as a ruling class that has dominated not only the Korean economy but also Korean society by shaping it into a "*chaebŏl* republic" with its winner-take-all values largely unfettered by law and regulation. Indeed, since 1987 no convicted big-name *chaebŏl* chief executive has served his full prison sentence. Yi Kŏn-hŭi (Lee Kun-hee), chairman of Samsung Electronics, for example, was pardoned by President Lee Myung-bak (2008–12),[8] who also pardoned several other *chaebŏl* chief executives, including Chŏng Mong-ku of Hyundai Motor, Ch'oe T'ae-wŏn of SK,[9] and Kim Sŭng-yŏn of Hanhwa Group (Sherisse Pham 2017).

In terms of Korea's political power elite getting away without serving full jail sentences as a result of presidential pardons, the media *chaebŏls* have been no different. Hong Sŏk-hyŏn, CEO of a leading conservative newspaper, *JoongAng Ilbo*, and brother-in-law to Yi Kŏn-hŭi, was pardoned and reinstated by progressive president Kim Dae-jung in 2000; Pang Sang-hun, owner of *Chosun Ilbo*, the most influential conservative newspaper in Korea, was also pardoned and reinstated in 2008 by President Lee Myung-bak (Kim Tong-ch'un 2015, 263).[10] What makes these top-ranking *chaebŏls*' political-economic elite cartel so distinctive in Korean society is that it has become a mechanism for the *chaebŏls*' supremacy above the law, mainly through their close ties with a wide range of powerful people, from national leaders and government officials to High Court judges and prosecutors, from National Tax Service officials to the police, and from the media to academic, cultural, and social opinion makers. No wonder the Korean people are skeptical of their country's judiciary system as "one law for the rich and another for the poor" (*yujŏn mujoe, mujŏn yujoe*). In this respect, the court drama of Samsung heir Yi Jae-yong (Lee Jae-yong), who walked free after his four-year jail term on charges including bribery and embezzlement was suspended in February 2018 (Australian Broadcasting Commission 2018), is a clear example of the reasons for this cynicism, although in a rather absurd way. Unlike Yi, former president Park Geun-hye was sentenced to thirty-three years on multiple corruption charges and abuse of power, including receiving bribes from Samsung (Salmon 2018).

It is in the context of the *chaebŏls*' dominance of Korean society, as well as being in effect above the law, that the majority of the Korean people, as the laboring classes,[11] struggle against economic inequality in their country, which young Koreans popularly refer to as "Hell-Chosŏn" or a "hell-like Korea." In hell-like Korea, in the eyes of many Koreans, especially young people, the *chaebŏls* have become the dominant capitalist class at the top as the *kap*, who exploit ordinary Korean workers, the *ŭl*, at the bottom, as parodied in the popular phrase "Kap and Ŭl Country" (Kang Chun-Man 2013). Ironically, the *chaebŏls* that "ate Korea," resulting in the Asian financial crisis of 1997–98, were strategically nurtured to grow into global corporate giants after the crisis, thanks to the Korean government's adoption of the

International Monetary Fund's neoliberal policy prescriptions and the subsequent restructuring. It is equally ironic that the blue-collar elite HCI workers at large consolidated their collective position as a labor aristocracy in postrestructuring Korea by securing for themselves employment security, superior wages, and various welfare benefits, most notably the privilege of job inheritance for their offspring, which contradicts the HCI workers' participation in the democratic labor movement struggle of the 1980s for fair work practices, social justice, and workers' rights as citizens.

It would be hard to argue convincingly that this highly controversial achievement of HCI workers and their unions was no more or no less accidental than the spectacular growth of the *chaebŏls* in postcrisis restructuring Korea. From the perspective of the HCI workers, however, their collective goal, from the very beginning of their technical high school or vocational training days, was to build an economically sound better life (*chal sanŭn kŏt*) for themselves. Sharing this common goal throughout their working life, the HCI workers radically transformed their labor union militancy of the 1980s into a device for consolidating their collective status and identity at the workplace, focused especially on safeguarding their common economic interests through social closure while also collaborating with their monopoly *chaebŏl* firms. This highly selective collaboration initially took place in the early 1990s, when the capitalist *chaebŏls* as the leading agency pioneered their new Business Management Strategy, focused on labor flexibility and workplace harmony modeled on Japanese corporate culture. The *chaebŏls* then successfully convinced the Korean government to implement labor flexibility as its core means for reviving Korea's competitiveness in the global market. The Korean state's campaign to implement the Corporate Culture Movement during the 1990s was in fact specifically aimed to break down radical militant labor unionism at the workplace, which ultimately led to adoption by the HCI workers and their unions of a collective self-seeking *sauve qui peut* approach.

Only through their highly selective collaboration with their *chaebŏl* employers have the HCI workers and their unions been able to consolidate their enterprise unionism and upward social mobility. Thus they readily used nonregular in-house subcontract workers as a buffer in their collective bargaining, especially by collaborating with their *chaebŏl* firms' systematic shifting of market risk from employers to subcontractors. This collaboration between HCI workers/unions and their *chaebŏl* firms in effect deepened the antagonism not only of the capital-labor divide but also of the labor-labor divide within the democratic labor movement, especially in the past twenty years. In this context, HCI workers, who are predominantly Korean baby boomers now in their mid to late fifties or more, are wedged between their *chaebŏl* employers' managerial and corporate culture domination (*kapchil*) in the labor market on the one hand, and the public's animosity—especially from the young "seven-give-ups" generation, with their massive unemployment or underemployment problem and related income inequality—toward the union aristocracy under the umbrella of the KCTU, on the other.

THE CONSEQUENCES OF KOREA'S RAPID DEVELOPMENT

By reflecting on the immensely complex current situation, I draw the major conclusion of this study on the HCI workers' collective character from the consequences of the multiple factors underpinning Korea's rapid development. The shift from state-led accumulation to *chaebŏl*-led accumulation as a result of neoliberal restructuring effectively destroyed broad-based labor solidarity, especially in the context of the Korean state/capitalist counterrevolution, as discussed in chapter 3. In this regard, the collective character of the HCI workers' economic unionism since the rise of the democratic KCTU reflects a change not only in the capital-labor relationship but also in the state-*chaebŏl* relationship in the course of Korea's "growth-first" development. From their initial master-servant relationship as industrial warriors under the three generals-turned-presidents Park Chung Hee (1963–79), Chun Doo-whan (1980–87), and Roh Tae-woo (1988–1992), not only did HCI workers change their capital-labor relationship of domination and subordination, but the capitalist *chaebŏl*s also transformed their relationship with the state into one based on mutual interest.

The outcome of this fundamental change in the *chaebŏl*s' relationship with Korea's power elite, including national leaders and government officials, especially since the early 1990s, shaped the defining feature of Korea's *chaebŏl*-led economy, combined with *chaebŏl* power, which had dramatically increased. This far-reaching change in the state-*chaebŏl* relationship is arguably the most obvious consequence of Korea's *chaebŏl*-oriented rapid development, which has in effect changed HCI workers' collective character over the past forty-eight years, even though this change essentially reflected the intricate nature of Korea's development starting from state-led rapid industrialization to bottom-up democratization concomitant with neoliberal globalization. All of these changes naturally shaped and reshaped the political and social trajectory of HCI workers as they have played their changing role at the center of each development stage: initially as semi-drafted conservative industrial warriors for the state's heavy and chemical industrialization program under reciprocal subsidies-as-contracts for their technological education and skills training at the high school level; then as a newly emerged militant labor union force under their newly articulated collective identity as Goliat warriors in leading the Korean working-class movement jointly with radical *minjung* intellectuals in the transitional period from 1987 to the early 1990s; and finally as a labor aristocracy, collaborating selectively with *chaebŏl*s in postrestructuring Korea. Against this highly complex yet controversial rapid development, HCI workers' collective role in each of these three historical periods has had its own motives and rationales. Hence, each historical period shaping their sociopolitical trajectory warrants a separate narrative.

The first narrative is about HCI workers as the beneficiaries of the Korean state's heavy and chemical industrialization policy, which provided them with subsidies for education and vocational training at the high school level. A good education in Korean society, as in many other societies and countries, has been the most effective means to upward mobility throughout Korea's contemporary history. The state's subsidies and other assistance for technical education and postschool skills training therefore offered many bright and highly motivated young people, predominantly males from economically poor families in rural and coastal areas, an unprecedented social opportunity. However, it also imposed strict reciprocal terms and conditions. Yet these young people readily accepted the state's requirement of mandatory reciprocity as part of their contract, which required them not only to prove their individual commitment and ability to perform during their education and skills training, but also to reciprocate with their skilled labor later as a core prerequisite for state-led heavy and chemical industrialization in accordance with the state's terms and conditions as its industrial warriors.

Under this strict subsidies-as-contracts system, some two million young people completed their technical high school education or skills training/upgrading between 1972 and 1987. The majority of these newly trained young people became well-disciplined skilled and semiskilled workers with close ties to their state's nation-building project, especially the HCI program, as its main army-like industrial warriors. In fact, they popularized economic nationalism focused on values such as mission-oriented discipline, patriotism, and cooperation, while also promoting an "economy-first" national psyche to generate a new modern citizenship as a precondition to Korea's export-led industrialization. The most notable characteristic of Korea's first generation of skilled workers is that, as the pioneers of Korea's rapid industrialization, they grew into one of the most conservative groups in Korean society, especially in their collective support for state-led development with its "economy-first" approach. In this regard, the revival of the so-called Park Chung Hee syndrome in the 1990s, which ultimately led to the rise of Park's daughter, Park Geun-hye, as Korea's president in 2013, was not entirely unrelated.

The second narrative is about the radical change in HCI workers' collective attitude and character, from their initial docility as industrial warriors to becoming articulate, militant Goliat warriors by breaking their reciprocal social contract with the state and instigating the democratic labor unionization movement and the militant *minjung* solidarity movement of the Korean working class through their leadership of Great Workers' Struggle for almost four years in the transitional period. This revolutionary change was fueled primarily by their accumulated grievances against authoritarian management practices together with their collective sense of resentment, especially their sense of relative deprivation. Here two key factors that drove HCI workers are noteworthy. One was the eruption of the Great Workers' Struggle within a week of the declaration of political democratization on June 29, 1987.

The other factor was the rise of new labor militancy in male-dominated heavy industries in the southeast Ch'angwŏn Industrial Park in April 1985, which, while inseparable from the *minjung* democratization movement led by radical university students, especially students-turned-workers (*hakch'ul*) and intellectuals, ultimately led to the rise of HCI workers as the leading force of the Korean workers' solidarity struggle. Under their newly articulated collective identity as Goliat warriors, following the Korean workers' general strike in May 1991 led by the NCTU, the HCI workers' partnership in the solidarity struggle of the Korean working class with radical *minjung* intellectuals, including the *hakch'ul* and other *undongkwŏn* activists,[12] however, was utilitarian at best, sharing little in terms of collective vision, approach, or ideological commitment. From the perspective of HCI workers, especially at the rank-and-file level, the sudden change of their initial collective identity from industrial warriors to Goliat warriors did not necessarily alter their individual attitude or character, not to mention their individual aim for a better life, especially economic security. The HCI workers' changed character as Goliat warriors, in this sense, primarily showed their pragmatism, especially through their new labor union militancy, focused on individual and collective economic unionism to acquire better wages and better working conditions, among various other welfare benefits.

The radical *minjung* intellectuals, in contrast, sought a proletariat revolution, especially in terms of pro-Marxist-Leninist and pro–North Korean *chuch'e* ideology and political power. In order to pursue this lofty goal, a massive number of *hakch'ul* migrated to factories in the mid-1980s. Their collective aim at the workplace was to educate workers but not to become blue-collar factory workers themselves. Unlike low-skilled workers in labor-intense light industry, where worker-student solidarity (*no-hak yŏndae*) was strong, however, they failed to build strong ties with blue-collar elite HCI workers, who were not necessarily dependent on outside activists to carry out their company-based industrial strikes and other labor union activities. The conflict between the blue-collar elite HCI union leaders and radical *minjung* intellectuals, as I discussed in chapter 2, was profound, even at the height of the famous 128-day strike of 1988, when members of the Hyundai Heavy Industries Union openly demanded that the intellectual "dissident activist force" (*chaeya seryŏk*) stop interfering in their industrial action and leave immediately. Nevertheless, despite their fundamental differences and conflicting goals, the HCI worker-intellectual partnership made a significant contribution to Korean democracy by bringing radical change to Korean society, especially in dismantling Korea's oppressive labor system and wage structure, while also improving public perception of blue-collar factory workers as a whole.

HCI workers' changed character as Goliat warriors was very successful in leading social transformation, even though the idea of their working-class movement serving as a vehicle for revolutionary social transformation had been sown by the radical *minjung* intellectuals. Similarly, the idea of articulating the Korean workers' collective identity as Goliat warriors was an invention of *minjung* intellectuals, just as they invented the radical term *minjung* for the collective identity of the Korean masses in the early 1970s. While the revolutionary image of Goliat warriors unquestionably boosted the collective confidence of the Korean working class at large, it was nevertheless sustained only briefly, even among HCI workers, except for some very committed on-site (*hyŏnjang*) militant democratic union leaders and rank-and-file unionists on the shop floor.

Ultimately, the split between the two elite forces of HCI workers and *minjung* intellectuals, including the students-turned-workers (*hakch'ul*), was no surprise, especially when Korea fell into an economic slump with increasing competitive pressure in global markets from late 1989. Thus the majority of HCI rank-and-file workers readily transformed their militant labor unionism into a company-first consciousness, especially in line with their company-led Corporate Culture Movement, while safeguarding their own collective economic interests to the extent of exposing their incipient class consciousness as a labor aristocracy. Just as the blue-collar elite HCI workers readily transformed their militant labor unionism into a company-first consciousness focused on their vested economic interests rather than the solidarity of the Korean workers as a whole, a massive number of radical *hakch'ul*s and other *minjung* intellectuals also shifted their collective interests from the militant labor-*minjung* movement to other fields, either finding a new career in academia or a management position in the public or private sector, or even joining the rapidly mushrooming progressive social movement as its leading agents. Overall, it would be hard to argue that the collapse of the HCI worker-intellectual partnership in the early 1990s was unrelated to the rise of the subsequent democratic labor movement crisis.

The third narrative is about the rise of the HCI workers' collective identity and employment status as a labor aristocracy in postrestructuring Korea's dual-market system, especially after 2005, the year the Korean economy had become the eleventh largest in the world. The dramatic change in the collective character and employment status of HCI workers underscores the paradox of Korea's rapid development, which had resulted in fundamental change in Korea's economic system, from state-led accumulation to *chaebŏl*-led accumulation. The former system, despite or perhaps because of the state's highly centralized and authoritarian labor policies without basic social security benefits from the government, generated rapid economic growth by creating a massive number of jobs and thus integrating into the workforce almost every economically motivated individual for nearly four decades, from the mid-1960s until the Asian financial crisis of 1997.

The latter system of *chaebŏl*-led accumulation, especially after the Asian financial crisis, in contrast, not only propelled Korea's neoliberal globalization with an unprecedented level of labor flexibility but also drove Korean businesses, especially top-ranking HCI *chaebŏl* corporations, to become extremely powerful global players with transnational capital and amassed political power akin to or even surpassing that of the state, with Korea coming to be seen as the *chaebŏl* republic. In this regard, the phenomenal growth of capital among the thirty top-ranking *chaebŏl*s, including many HCI *chaebŏl*s since the crisis, was not the result of another miracle, but largely of the government's neoliberal economic policies and its indispensable support for those powerful *chaebŏl*s well beyond the boundaries of any mandate. As a result, Korea's GDP had tripled shortly after the financial crisis, while Samsung had surged to the top of Korea's *chaebŏl*s and has remained there since 2000 (Peter Pham 2018). In this process, the HCI workers and their unions swiftly consolidated their economic unionism by institutionalizing their collective bargaining system through social closure, using subcontract in-house workers as a buffer.

Just as the *chaebŏl*s were single-minded regarding their own capital accumulation with little concern for the welfare of Korean working people at large, HCI workers and their militant unions were also hooked on a narrowly focused economic unionism, which dramatically weakened the social basis for the solidarity of the Korean working class with or without union protection. Ultimately, the HCI workers' collective aim to achieve their personal life goals and aims for a better life contradicted their ideals of social justice and democracy, as well as their democratic "*minju*" unionism. Yet their plight deserves compassion, as until 1997 they had been guaranteed job security, initially through their reciprocal social contract during the Park and other military authoritarian regimes, and even under democratically elected governments, thanks largely to their militant labor unionism after the Great Workers' Struggle. This job security nevertheless began to crack after 1989, when Korea's competitiveness in the international market rapidly fell while labor costs rose. The growing number of nonregular in-house subcontract workers during the 1990s under the Corporate Culture Movement, in particular, convinced HCI workers and their unions to transform their militant labor unionism into a device for safeguarding their own collective survival, especially job security. In this context, the 1997 financial crisis drove the HCI workers and their unions to radically consolidate their collective position in Korea's dual labor market as upper-tier regular workers of large *chaebŏl* firms, distinguishing themselves from other lower-tier workers of SMEs and contingent nonregular workers.

Herein lies the dual consequence of Korea's rapid development, marred by the unresolved contradictions of neoliberalism, especially since the 1990s. With the government incorporating a variety of export-led development policies focused on labor flexibility, Korea's productivity dramatically transformed the country into a global industrial powerhouse with an average annual GDP growth rate of "4.6 percent over 1995–2014, nearly three times the OECD average" (OECD 2016, 29). Yet income inequality caused by the dual labor-market system intensified the polarization of Korean society, with nonregular male workers paid about 46 percent less than regular male workers, and nonregular female workers about 64 percent less (see chapter 5). The chronic problem of the income gap that separated the majority of workers in small and medium-size enterprises and millions of other nonregular workers with an ever-present threat of job insecurity and minimal wages, from the HCI workers of large *chaebŏl* firms with their guaranteed job security and high incomes, among other benefits, cannot be resolved under the current winner-take-all economic system in today's Korean society.

The zeitgeist of the moment in South Korea, apart from critical concerns about threats from North Korea, in fact, involves the challenges facing South Korea's winner-take-all economy, dominated by the *chaebŏl*s on the one hand and the labor-market bifurcation that is driving winner-take-all inequality on the other. In this respect, the political trajectory of HCI workers over the past four and a half decades shows that Korea desperately needs radical reform not only for long-lasting economic democratization, but also to redirect itself from a corporate country filled with a rapidly aging population together with working poor, a phenomenon that has spread throughout the world in the neoliberal twenty-first century.

Appendix 1

Characteristics of Hyundai WIA Corporation Respondents (N = 10, August 2014)

Case #	Age	Kia Machine Tools year of hire (length of employment, years)	Annual income (₩10,000)[a]	Subjective social class[b]	Subjective stratum[c]
HW1	58	1975 (36)	8,500	Middle	MM
HW2	55	1987 (27)	9,000	NR[d]	L
HW3	54	1986 (28)	8,500	Middle	ML
HW4	55	1978 (36)	8,800	Middle	MH
HW5	58	1977 (37)	8,000	Working	MM
HW6	51	1983 (31)	8,700	Middle	MM
HW7	54	1978 (36)	8,400	Middle	MH
HW8	57	1978 (36)	9,800	Middle	MM
HW9	52	1988 (26)	8,000	Middle	MH
HW10	56	1978 (36)	9,000	Middle	MM
Average or Summary	55.0	(32.9)	8,670	Working (1) Middle (8) NR (1)	MH (3) MM (5) ML (1) L (1)

[a] US$1 = about ₩1,100 as of January 2015.
[b] Subjective social class was identified as working, middle, or upper.
[c] Subjective stratum was identified by five levels: high (H), middle high (MH), middle middle (MM), middle low (ML), and low (L).
[d] "NR" = no response.

Appendix 2

Characteristics of Doosan Heavy Industries Respondents (N = 9, August 2014)

Case #	Age	Doosan Heavy Industries year of hire (length of employment, years)	Annual income (₩10,000)[a]	Subjective social class[b]	Subjective stratum[c]
DH1	55	1978 (36)	6,500	Working	ML
DH2	56	1977 (37)	NR[d]	Middle	ML
DH3	55	1978 (36)	NR	Working	ML
DH4	51	1981 (33)	8,900	Middle	MM
DH5	48	1987 (27)	7,000	NR	ML
DH6	56	1978 (36)	7,000	Middle	ML
DH7	55	1983 (31)	6,000	Working	ML
DH8	55	1978 (36)	NR	Working	ML
DH9	46	1988 (26)	NR	NR	NR
Average or Summary	53.0	(33.1)	7,080	Working (3) Middle (3) NR (3)	MM (1) ML (7) NR (1)

[a] US$1 = about ₩1,100 as of January 2015.
[b] Subjective social class was identified as working, middle, or upper.
[c] Subjective stratum was identified by five levels: high (H), middle high (MH), middle middle (MM), middle low (ML), and low (L).
[d] "NR" = no response.

Appendix 3

Characteristics of Hyundai Heavy Industries Respondents (N = 20, January–February 2015)

Case #	Age	HHI year of hire (length of employment, years)	Annual income (₩10,000)[a]	Subjective social class[b]	Subjective stratum[c]
HH1	59	1981 (34)	7,800	NR[d]	MM
HH2	60	1979 (36)	9,000	Middle	MH
HH3	60	1981 (34)	9,000	Middle	MM
HH4	58	1974 (41)	9,000	Middle	MM
HH5	60	1973 (42)	7,600	Working	MM
HH6	58	1981 (34)	8,000	Middle	ML
HH7	59	1981 (34)	9,000	NR	ML
HH8	55	1979 (36)	9,600	Middle	MM
HH9	58	1975 (40)	9,000	Middle	ML
HH10	53	1979 (36)	8,900	Middle	MM
HH11	56	1979 (36)	8,500	Middle	MM
HH12	55	1979 (36)	9,000	Middle	MM
HH13	58	1981 (34)	7,000	Middle	MM
HH14	55	1979 (36)	7,000	NR	NR
HH15	58	1979 (36)	9,000	NR	MM
HH16	57	1982 (33)	8,000	Middle	MM
HH17	50	1982 (33)	8,300	Middle	MM

(continued)

Case #	Age	HHI year of hire (length of employment, years)	Annual income (₩10,000)[a]	Subjective social class[b]	Subjective stratum[c]
HH18	54	1981 (34)	8,700	Middle	MM
HH19	48	1983 (32)	6,400	Working	ML
HH20	55	1982 (33)	8,700	Working	MM
Average or Summary	56.3	(35.5)	8,375	Working (3) Middle (13) NR (4)	MH (1) MM (14) ML (4) NR (1)

[a] US$1 = about ₩1,100 as at January 2015.
[b] Subjective social class was identified as working, middle, or upper.
[c] Subjective stratum was identified by five levels: high (H), middle high (MH), middle middle (MM), middle low (ML), and low (L).
[d] "NR" = no response.

Appendix 4

Korean Educational Institutions by Type, Age at Entry, and School Year

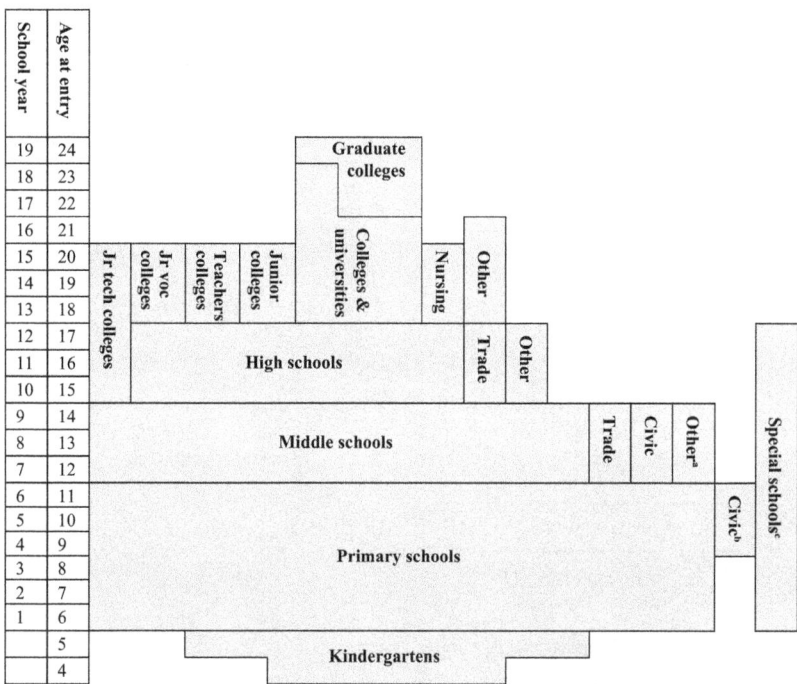

Source: Planning Office (1976, 126).
[a]"Other" includes a range of miscellaneous private institutions.
[b]Civic schools operate at two levels: primary, for those who have not completed six years of primary education; and middle/high school, for those who have completed six years of primary or three years of civic primary education.
[c]Special schools are for students with special needs, such as disabilities.

Appendix 5

Training and Ranks of Engineers and Craftsmen

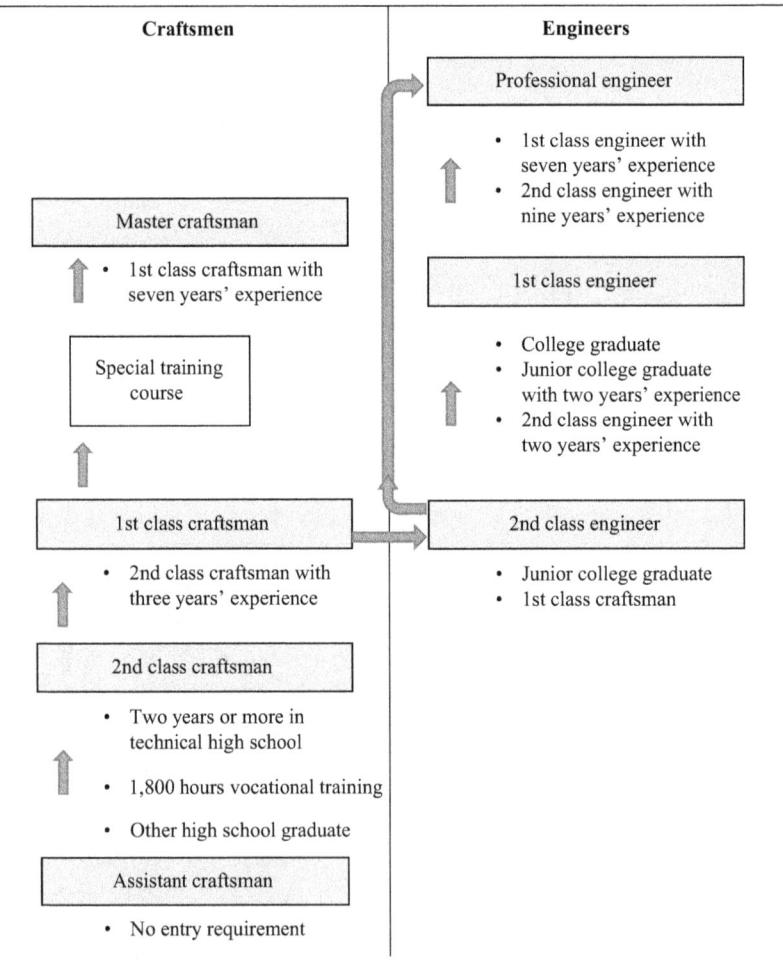

Source: Planning Office (1976, 138).

Notes

INTRODUCTION

1   Korea's per capita (nominal) GDP in 2016 was the eleventh-largest in the world, whereas in 1960 it was at a "record low of 1102.53USD." *Trading Economics*, February 2, 2017, www.tradingeconomics.com/south-korea/gdp-per-capita.
2   The Korean media use the term "labor aristocracy" to refer to regular workers of large firms in heavy industry, or what I characterize in this study as HCI workers and their HCI *chaebŏl* unions. See chapter 5 for a detailed discussion of the issues of labor aristocracy in today's Korean society and its definition.
3   The term "Goliat" is derived from the name of a mammoth crane of Hyundai Heavy Industries, the world's largest shipbuilding group. See chapter 2.
4   Some scholars use the term "first generation" mainly to refer to Korean industrial workers before the 1980s, as Hwasook Nam does in her 2009 book. My use of this term is specific in terms of their technical education and vocational training having been between 1972 and 1987, with that training strategically planned and managed within the Park state's HCI Plan.
5   I use the term "class politics" in the sense of "emergent class difference in politics" in capitalist modernity noted by Weakliem and Adams (2011).
6   Benjamin Selwyn (2016) critically discusses a number of elite development theory traditions, including the *Washington Post*–Washington consensus, statist political economy, modernization Marxism, and varieties of pro-poor growth.
7   In her 2003 book, Beverly Silver coins the phrase "workplace bargaining power," based on Erik Olin Wright's concept of structural power, to refer especially to one of the two subtypes that result "from the strategic location of a particular group of workers within a key industrial sector" (Wright 2000, 962).
8   Here I distinguish my use of the phrase "reciprocal social contract" by emphasizing the strict terms and conditions attached to the HCI workers' technical education and vocational training subsidized by the Park and Chun regimes. These terms and conditions, as I discuss in detail in chapter 1, were far stricter than the terms and conditions attached to the "egalitarian social contract" in Korea's educational policy.
9   The term *Saemaŭl* means "new village." Park initially unveiled this nationwide campaign with the specific aim of improving rural living conditions in

October 1970. After the declaration of the Yusin Reform under martial law in October 1972, the New Village Movement converged into a national campaign of mass mobilization for Yusin Reform that the Park state promoted as the New Community Movement.

10   These workers were born between 1954 and 1969, and thus a vast number of them are baby boomers (1955–63) who, if they were employed in the 1970s, would have a work record well over thirty-nine years in 2018.

11   See Johnson (1982); Dayo (1989); Amsden (1989); World Bank (1993); Wade (1990); Evans (1995); Ha-Joon Chang (2002); Kohli (2004). The terms *kinŭngsa* and *kinŭnggong* have the same meaning, but the former has been used since the late 1980s, whereas the latter term was used prior to 1987. *Kinŭnggong* or *sungnyŏn'gong*, among other similar terms, appeared in particular in government documents, including archival material during the Park regime. For consistency, I use the term *kinŭngsa* in this book.

12   Here Koo specifically referred to those Korean labor analysts who had mostly "close ties with the union activists and social movement communities," pointing out that their writings were "primarily interested in highlighting the extraordinary degree of labor exploitation and harsh state oppression of labor actions" (2001, 15). In so doing, many of these Korean writings focused on both the developmental state view and the radical Marxist view of class warfare.

13   During the 1970s, there were three large-scale industrial strikes by HCI workers, all at shipbuilding firms: the KSEC (in July 1970), Hyundai Shipbuilding (in September 1974), and Hyundai Mip'o Shipbuilding (in April 1978). These strikes demanded mainly wage increases and improvement in working conditions, and were not linked to the democratic labor union movement of the 1970s led by female factory workers. Regarding male workers' strikes in the heavy and chemical industries in the pre-1987 period, see chapter 2.

14   For a critical analysis of the concept of the East Asian developmental state, see Stubbs (2009).

15   On crony capitalism, see David Kang (2002); on developmentalist *mentalité*, see Myung-Koo Kang (2011); and on "*chaebŏl*-centered developmentalism," see Kyung-sup Chang (2007). Terms like "Beijing consensus" and "China model" are intended to replace the Washington consensus (Ramo 2004; Halper 2010), and the term "Chinese authoritarian capitalism" represents "a system in size and structure that is unique and unlike the world has seen" (McGregor 2012, xiii).

16   This plan, known loosely as *kaep'yŏnnon* (a restructuring plan) was initially drafted by O and became the key source of my 2004 study, *Korea's Development under Park Chung Hee: Rapid Industrialization, 1963-1979*. O also provided me with many invaluable personal papers and a seven-volume autobiography, as well as many hours of discussion on his personal knowledge and experience of the Park state's HCI project, especially the master plan.

17   Like O, Kim also provided many invaluable copies of various documents on skilled manpower development, especially *Kisul kyoyuk chedo kaesŏnan, 1973* and "Heavy and Chemical Industry Development Plan, June 1973" (written in English), and

engaged in several long discussions on skilled worker training during my visits to Seoul in 2012 and 2013.

18 In his 2006 New Year's speech (see https://www.youtube.com/watch?v=7asvdaqS70Q), Roh said that the problem of social polarization was the key agenda of his administration in 2006.

19 My first survey was carried out during May and June 2014 and involved workers from Hyundai WIA and Doosan Heavy Industries, with ten workers participating from each firm, but as one of the participants from Doosan did not meet one of the essential criteria of my survey (he had joined the firm in 1988), his responses were not included.

20 These autobiographies were published by the Human Resources Development Service of Korea. They include *Ŏmŏni ŭi naengsu han kŭrŭt* (Mother's bowl of water; 2007), *Hayan komusin* (White rubber-shoes; 2008), *Nae sarang Yasaenghwa* (My love, wild flower; 2009), and *Yŏlchŏng ŭi ondol ŭl nop'yŏra* (Increase the heat of passion; 2011). These autobiographies can be found at www.hrdkorea.or.kr.

21 Three autobiographies published since the 1980s include *Uridŭl kajin kŏt pirok chŏgŏdo* (Although we own very little), ed. Na Po-sun (Seoul: Tolbegae, 1983); *Kat'ŭn sidae, tarŭn iyagi: Kuro tongmaeng p'aŏp ŭi chuyŏkdŭl, salm ŭl malhada* (The same era, a different story: The leading actors of the Kuro joint strike talk about their lives), ed. Yu Kyŏng-sun (Seoul: Mayday, 2007); and Sin Sun-ae, *Yŏlsesal yŏgong ŭi salm* (The life of a thirteen-year-old factory girl) (Seoul: Hakyoreh ch'ulp'an, 2014).

CHAPTER 1: THE CREATION OF INDUSTRIAL WARRIORS

An earlier version of this chapter, especially the content on the mass training of skilled manpower, was published in 2013 as "Industrial Warriors: South Korea's First Generation of Industrial Workers in Post-Developmental Korea," in *Asian Studies Review*.

1 Park, then a major-general, initially seized power through a military coup on May 16, 1961, and was assassinated by his confidant Kim Chae-gyu, director of the Korean Central Intelligence Agency, on October 26, 1979.

2 The Korea Shipbuilding and Engineering Corporation, founded in 1937 under the name Chosŏn Chunggongŏp (Korea Heavy Industry), was the largest shipyard in Korea, and one of very few, until the Hyundai Heavy Industries shipyard was constructed in 1974. For detailed background on the company, see Hwa-sook Nam (2009).

3 The Yusin system, for example, enabled Park to appoint one-third of the National Assembly's lawmakers while also restructuring the government by concentrating power, especially to carry out forced-draft industrialization and the improvement of military defense.

4 O Wŏn-ch'ŏl used this term in his seven-volume autobiography, initially published under the title *Chŏryak Sanŏp Kundansa* (A history of the Strategic Industrial Corps) in *Maeil Kyŏngje*, a conservative daily business newspaper in Seoul, in the early 1990s. O's autobiography, which is generally regarded by the Korean media as a

history of Korea's rapid development under Park, reflected most convincingly Park's concept of Korea's heavy and chemical industrialization.

5. For a detailed analysis of the New Community Movement, especially regarding the role of *pansanghoe*, see Hyung-A Kim (2004), ch. 5.

6. This operation was carried out by the Agency for Defense Development (Kukpang Kwahak Yŏn'guso), founded in August 1970.

7. Alice Amsden (1989, 222) notes that by 1970 the number of primary school graduates and those with no schooling in Korea's labor market was as high as 67.4 percent of Korea's workforce, while only 26.4 percent had secondary schooling.

8. The term "science and technology manpower" was first introduced in a report titled "A Survey Report on Manpower Resources in the Science and Technology Field," produced in 1962 by the military junta administration. Korea's first and second Five-Year Technology Development Plans (1962–66 and 1967–71), especially in regard to the supply of skilled manpower, were drawn up on this basis. The state's predictions of change in labor supply and demand, as well as its changed policy direction from 1967 to 1986, were also drawn up on this basis.

9. In addition to providing funds for purchasing new technical equipment for skills training in various technical high schools, many large firms built new technical high schools as a result of Park's direct intervention. Daelim Technical High School, P'ohang Tech, and Dong-A Tech were some examples of such high schools.

10. The development of a science and technological labor force for the HCI program was a top priority of the third Five-Year Human Resource Development Plan (1972–76) and complemented the third Five-Year Economic Development Plan.

11. For details on the formation of technical engineers and craftsmen, see appendix 5.

12. O and his deputy Kim Kwang-mo separately told me that this restructuring was possible mainly because of Park's Yusin Reform. Author interview with O, June 18, 2010, and Kim, April 18, 2013. O died in May 2019 at the age of ninety.

13. Korea's education system was then based on a 6-3-3-4 system for primary–middle school–high school–university, as it is today. In addition to this system, however, there were a variety of technical schools ranging from three-year junior technical high schools to five-year vocational colleges, which combined the three-year high school curriculum with two-year college courses or three-year middle school plus five-year industry/business special high schools, among others. This study, however, examines the mainstream technical high schools only.

14. In addition to these four categories of technical high schools, there were also three-year higher-level technical schools, which provided the same level of high school curriculum, as well as five-year junior technical colleges (see appendix 4). These schools, however, were not mainstream and are thus omitted in this study.

15. The Korean school system then was strikingly similar to that of Japan, especially in terms of both its highly egalitarian structure (including lottery-based placements allocated by the Ministry of Education) and overheated competition for credentials, excessive private tuition, and so on.

16. These technical high schools were placed in each province.

17 Other research suggests that a total of 10,020 new students were admitted in 1979. See Cho Hwang-hŭi et al. (2002, 152).
18 The official title of these schools was Designated Experimental Technical High Schools for the Priority Training of Advanced Craftsmen, *kinungsa*, for the Middle East.
19 The training facilities of the eleven experimental technical high schools were funded mostly with the first and second loans from the International Development Association; thus they were equipped with relatively plentiful facilities.
20 In the case of Chinju Technical High School, 350 students passed the National Technical Qualification Test, exceeding their allocated target of 150 by 200.
21 It should be noted that other three-year technical high schools, such as *kodŭng kisul hakkyo*, advanced technical colleges, and other five-year vocational high schools, were not included in the state's selection of specialized technical high schools. Hence, this study does not include these schools.
22 KTHS was built in Kumi, Park's birthplace, with a repatriation fund of ¥394 million from Japan. Japan also provided a range of technical equipment for skills practice by students, while also providing many teachers to build KTHS as one of the best technical high schools in Asia.
23 The President's Office not only closely monitored the KTHS annual admission but also used it as the state's model for showing its technological and science education at the high school level to 132 heads of technical high schools and university heads throughout the country, including 12 chairmen of boards of universities in May 1973. See PS 1973b.
24 The period from 5 p.m. to 11 p.m. was set for students to undertake "unsupervised learning by themselves and thus not only the students but also teachers went through practical skills training exercises [*silsŭp*] especially for various skills competitions both nationally and internationally, including the International Vocational Training Competition and the International Youth Skill Olympics." Author interview with Kim Kŭn-tae, retired deputy principal of KTHS, November 16, 2010.
25 Yi managed KTHS for seven years, until 1980, the year after Park's assassination.
26 After graduation, each individual student's performance was reported to the President's Office, especially regarding entry to university and current state of military service.
27 Dr. Yŏng-Ho Park, regarding the KTHS class of 1976. Author's e-mail correspondence with Park, December 2, 2013.
28 During this study the author interviewed over fifty skilled workers in addition to surveying an extra thirty-nine survey respondents (see chapter 5) in the HCI sector. Nearly all had been academically high achievers, and their primary reason for entering technical high school had been to overcome economic difficulty.
29 Interview with Master Kim Ki-ha, Ch'angwŏn, April 26, 2015. For Kim's life story, see chap. 2.
30 The Ministry of Education stated that in 1979 all graduates of machinery technical high shools, experimental technical high schools and specialized technical high schools, totaling about 25,000, plus 72 percent of graduates of the regular technical

high schools, had passed the National Technical Qualification Test before graduation. See Mun'gyobu (1979, 313).

31 In the shipbuilding area, however, a small number of females found employment after 1980. Kim Chin-suk, a well-known union movement activist, who had found her employment as a welder in Hanjin Heavy Industries and Construction in July 1980, was one of those few females.

32 The most notable vocational training centers of the 1970s were Chung-Ang Vocational Training Institute (two years), Chŏng-Su Vocational Training Institute (one year and one and a half years), and Han-Baek Vocational Training Institute (one year), established in 1972, 1973, and 1978, respectively, with funds from Germany, USAID, and Belgium. The founder of Han-Paek Vocational Training Institute was Park Guen-hye, Park Chung Hee's daughter, who in 2013 became South Korea's president but was impeached and ousted from office in March 2017.

33 In 1975, all students of technical high schools were required to sit for the National Technical Qualification Test. The success rate in the test, set by the Korean Ministry of Education, increased from 69 percent in 1976 to 85 and 95 percent in 1979 and 1981, respectively (Mun'gyobu 1977, 171).

34 The thirteen members included, in plumbing, Kim Ŭn-p'il, Kim Hyŏng-sŏp, Song Mun-gu, Pang Chin-wŏn, Kim Chong-man, and Ko Yŏng-sŏk; in canning, U Che-song, No Sŏng-je, Paek Mun-ho, Kim P'il-je, and Chŏng Hong-gi; and in welding, Kim Chae-hwa and Cho Yŏng-ŭn.

CHAPTER 2: FROM INDUSTRIAL WARRIORS TO GOLIAT WARRIORS

1 These new labor policies were initially issued in July 1980 and then codified in December 1980.

2 The term *minjung* included not only workers but also farmers, students, urban poor, intellectuals, women, the middle class, and small- and medium-size businesses. For a critical analysis of the concept of *minjung*, see Van Leest (1992).

3 This data is published in the Ministry of Labor's "Labor Statistics Monthly Report" (Maewŏl nodong t'onggye chosa pogosŏ), from 1987 to 1990.

4 The POSCO workers' residential community, which evolved around their company in P'ohang, a port city located in the southern industrial belt, is also well known for its soldier-like discipline, patriotism, and solidarity, but they are not included in this study because the POSCO workers' union, with more than twenty thousand members, saw the withdrawal of most of its members by January 1991, leaving only some fifty hard-core members before it was totally dismantled at the end of 1991. For the development of POSCO's corporate culture, see chapter 3.

5 As early as 1971, the Jeunesse Ouvrière Chrétienne founded a chapter in Masan, shortly after the establishment of the Masan Free Export Zone and two years before Korea launched its HCI program in 1973.

6 The FKTU, formed in March 1946 with US military backing, was changed to Han'guk Noryŏn in November 1960, as an outcome of the merger between the

FKTU and the newly created National Council of Trade Unions, before it was changed again to Noch'ong in 1961. For a detailed discussion of Chŏnp'yŏng and the FKTU, see Koo (2001, 25–27).

7   Estimates of the number of dead in this uprising vary to up to six hundred. According to the 1994 Kwangju City Government statistics, for example, there were 147 dead, 47 official missing persons, and 2,710 injured. For detailed background and critical analysis of the May 18 victims, see Byun and Lewis (2000).

8   I use this term to describe both individual activists and the democratization movement as a whole, whose articulated goal was "to bring democracy, justice and reunification to Korea" (Nam-Hee Lee 2005, 911).

9   The female-dominated electrical parts manufacturing firms in the Masan Free Economic Zone, however, were one exception. According to Seungkyung Kim, female workers between seventeen and twenty-two years were most likely to be employed here, as companies only hired women within this age group, and anyone older than twenty-six found they no longer fitted comfortably into the factory structure. See Seung-Kyung Kim (1997, 28).

10 Two authors, An Sŭng-ch'ŏn (2002, 87–88) and Nam-Hee Lee (2007, 263–64), wrote about the role of Mun Sŏng-hyŏn, a well-known *hakeh'ul* union leader, and members of his small group, White Pebble, in their wage struggle of 1985.

11 Kwŏn graduated from Ch'ŏnan Technical High School in 1974 and entered Hyundai Heavy Industries in 1978 under the category of "special soldier" (*t'ŭngnyebyŏng*). In April 1986, he formed a special six-member book club in which he is said to have taught labor law to its members for six months, while also conducting discussion sessions on labor problems at the factory site. He was dismissed from his company in 1988 because of his role in the Hyundai workers' 128-day strike led mainly by the Hyundai Heavy Industries Union. Kwŏn was struggling in poverty when he died in February 2009. Author interview in February 2014 with Kwŏn's wife, Mrs. Sa Kyŏng-ae, and Mr. Sa Yŏng-un, who with Kwŏn founded the Hyundai Engine Union.

12 This was declared by Roh Tae-woo, leader of the ruling Democratic Justice Party, who had publicly promised an eight-point democratization package.

13 As the leader of the 128-day struggle, Yi was arrested even before he took up his presidency, mainly as a preventive strategy prior to the 1990s annual wage negotiation by Hyundai management.

14 For detailed background to the HHI workers' Goliat Struggle, see "1990-nyŏn hyŏndai chunggongŏp koliat t'ujaeng" (Hyundai Heavy Industries Goliat Struggle of 1990).

15 By November 1995, when the Korean Confederation of Trade Unions was founded, these two factions were known also as the "on-site faction" (*hyŏnchangp'a* or *chwap'a*) and the "people's faction" (*kung'minp'a*), within the KCTU and the labor union movement as a whole. For a critical analysis of the factional strife, including these two factions, see chapter 4.

16 The POSCO Union's sudden collapse leaving less than one hundred pro-company members encouraged many other large firm unions to follow suit, including Kia

Machine Tools Union, one of the most militant democratic unions, which also saw its workers dissolve their union in February 1993 (discussed in chapter 3).

17 For a critical analysis of the worker-student alliance of the 1970s up until the mid-1980s, see Koo (2001, 104–19).

18 Views similar to this were some of the most frequently expressed views of the HCI workers whom I interviewed during this study.

19 The term *chaeya* literally means "out of office." It originally described the *yangban* literati during the Chosun Dynasty, who were former officials of the court and thus the government. This term resurfaced in the early 1970s to describe intellectual dissident activists, including opposition politicians, especially during the authoritarian Yusin era (1972–79).

20 Ironically, Sŏ was dismissed from the HHIU on January 6, 1989, as a consequence of his complicity with HHI management's unilateral decision to declare a resumption of normal work, which in effect drove 95 percent of the 9,636 HHIU members to pass a vote of no-confidence against Sŏ. For detailed background on Sŏ, see Hyundae Chunggongŏp Nodongjohap (1991, 114–60).

21 This self-taught lesson seems to have encouraged rivalry within the democratic labor union movement camps between the militant "democracy faction," popular among on-site HCI workers, and the moderate faction led white-collar intellectuals after 1995 (discussed in chapter 4).

22 Kim was one of about hundred or so women who were hired between 1977 and 1981 as welders or metal cutters. For a detailed background on Kim, see Hwa-Sook Nam (2009, 211–12).

23 This general strike was in protest against the government's introduction of the Special Law for the Public Servants' Union, which the PSU viewed as limiting their rights of collective bargaining and action.

24 During this period Mun contacted many leaders of militant unions and labor movement activists in Pusan, Ulsan, and Kŏje, including Hŏ Yŏn-do of Kia Machine Tools; a member of Jeunesse Ouvrière Chrétienne, Kwŏn Yong-mok (Hyundai Engine); and Kim Chin-suk of Hanjin Heavy Industries and Construction.

25 This compilation is titled *Increase the Degree of Passion* (Yŏlchŏng ŭi ondo lŭl nop'yŏra), which is the same title as Kim's autobiography.

CHAPTER 3: COUNTERREVOLUTION

1 This particular terminology came into vogue in Korea June 1993, when Yi Kŏn-hŭi (Lee Kun-hee), chairman of Samsung, declared his "new management strategy" at the company's executive meeting of some two hundred representatives held in Frankfurt, Germany. Yi's "new management strategy" was reported to have been based on the Fukuda Report, created by Tamio Fukuda, a Japanese researcher at Kyocera Research Institute, who had become a professor at the Kyoto Institute of Technology. Since then, this terminology has become a dictum of Samsung, the largest *chaebŏl* in Korea, especially symbolizing Yi's idea of company management's

emphasis on innovation, to the extent of "changing everything except wife and children." With Samsung's spectacular success as a global star company since 1993, this terminology also became generic terminology for the adoption by Korean firms of their own style of "new management strategy."

2   As noted in the previous chapter, POSCO workers have been known for their high level of education, together with their high level of workmanship and workplace discipline, as well as their collective consciousness of being elite HCI workers for their nation-building project of steelmaking. POSCO workers were and remain known for their low rate of job hopping. In 1989 about 60 percent of the entire POSCO workforce were between twenty-five and thirty-four. For a detailed outline of the POSCO workers' internal composition, see Yi Sang-ch'ŏl (1991, 53–74).

3   For a detailed outline of the fifteen projects, including the Hope Movement, see Kang Sŏk-chae (2002, 44–46).

4   In 2006, Anam Industry became Dongbu Electronics.

5   These twenty Corporate Culture Movement case studies were published by the Ministry of Culture in October 1992.

6   This is a summary of Yi's four-page address. To highlight his key message on each point, I have summarized his supporting statement.

7   Forty-seven large firms, both private and state-invested or state-funded corporations and other institutions, initially participated in the Korean Council of Corporate Culture.

8   *Workers' Solidarity*, February 28, 2004.

9   For a critical analysis of the Japanese-style skilled labor formation system, see Yi Ho-ch'ang et al. (2012).

10 Under the *ture* system, for example, farm laborers traditionally formed a cooperative work team, especially at rice planting time, and then later divided up their earnings at the end.

11 In early 1994, a total of 2,020 supervisors undertook three days of education and training in organizational activation.

12 The supervisors' expenses to attend these social activities were paid by their firms as part of their business operational expenses.

13 *Hankyoreh Sinmun*, July 10, 1993, 6.

14 *Pusan Ilbo*, February 19, 1993, 14.

15 *Mach'ang Noryŏn Sinmun*, February 22, 1993.

16 See *Kyŏngnam Newspaper*, February 18, 1993; *Pusan Ilbo (Daily)*, February 19, 1993; and *Seoul Economic Newspaper*, February 19, 1993.

17 This comprehensive report and several other important internal documents regarding the KMT's New Management Strategy were copies privately kept by Mr. Yu Han-sik, then-director of Department of Human Resources Support in the KMT. In regard to the KMT's strategic planning, especially for the hierarchical role of building cooperative labor-management relations, KMT management divided the nine-year period from 1986 to 1994 into five stages, identified as the periods of innovation (1986–87), confusion (1988–90), sorting out (1991–92), adjustment (1993–94), and maturation (1994).

18 This is a brief summary of the *Status Report, 1993*, regarding the main causes of industrial strikes from 1986 to 1993. It contains forty-two pages in volume 1 and sixty-three pages in volume 2, including KMTU-related media reports.
19 This principle was established initially in a worker settlement with Hyundai Motor in December 1989.
20 The Kanaan Farmhand School, established in 1962 by Kim Yong-gi (1909–1988), played a key role in the Korean state-led New Community Movement during the 1970s, when the Park Chung Hee state conducted a comprehensive campaign for what Park termed the Saemaul spirit of self-reliance, diligence, and cooperation as a prerequisite for Korea's industrialization through mass mobilization, as discussed in chapter 1. Ironically, but not surprisingly, most large and even medium-size companies actively used this particular private institution for the attitudinal training of their staff members in the 1990s and beyond.
21 I would like to thank Mr. Yu, president of Energy and Machinery Korea, a medium-size firm in Ch'angwŏn, for giving me his personal copy of *Status Report, 1993*, as well as many other important materials, including some rare papers regarding KMT's merger and acquisition of Hyundai Motor Group in 1998. KMT, which changed its name in 1996 to Kia Heavy Industry, merged with Hyundai WIA, an engine and transmission supplier, in 1999 (see chapter 4).
22 Kim further explained his view of KMTU's withdrawal from the NCTU and the CMCU in our in-depth interviews in 2014 and 2015 (see chapter 4).
23 The HCI workers I interviewed during these particular interviews included those of Doosan Heavy Industries, formerly Daewoo Heavy Industries (in Ch'angwon), and Poongsan Corporation (in Kyungju), the first ammunition developer in Korea, commencing production in1973. The Poongsan workers' union was well known for its union militancy. For a comprehensive study of Poongsan Corporation focused on its company culture development, see Choong-soon Kim (1996).
24 On November 27, 2014, the Hyundai Heavy Industries Union, under the militant leadership of Chŏng Pyŏng-mo, began a strike demanding a 6.51 percent increase in the basic wage and performance-based benefits of 250 percent, among other financial benefits. Since then, the union has conducted several partial strikes in 2015 and 2016, including simultaneous strikes with Hyundai Motor Union on July 19, 2016.
25 Although in-house subcontractors were employed by these HCI manufacturing firms since the 1960s and 1970s, it was poorly developed in the 1980s mainly because small-scale business, unlike the HCI *chaebŏl*, did not have access to the capital and technology necessary to become high-tech subcontractors. For more discussion on in-house subcontracting nonregular workers, see chapter 5.

CHAPTER 4: THE ASIAN FINANCIAL CRISIS

1 In April 1996, President Kim Young-sam announced the "New Thought on Industrial Relations for Leaping into a First-Class Nation in the 21st Century," which proposed labor-law reform focused on fair exchange to allow greater employer

flexibility in exchange for the recognition of labor in politics, but this proposal failed to garner labor support.

2   The KCTU was established on November 11, 1995, with a membership of some 400,000 from 866 unions, which by November 1996 had increased to 496,908 members from 929 unions.

3   In this general strike, the KCTU emerged as the leading labor union organization, surpassing the conservative FKTU, through its mobilization of 528 unions with over 403,179 participants. The strike involved on average 168 unions with 189,119 participants per day. For detailed background on this general strike of 1996–97, see An Sŭng-ch'ŏn (2002, 183–99).

4   For a critical analysis of the Korean crisis, see Ha-joon Chang (1998).

5   The Bank for International Settlements requires the capital-asset ratio of central banks to be above a prescribed minimum international standard for the protection of all central banks involved in international settlements. This norm was adopted in 1988. Total eligible regulatory capital must be at least 8 percent of total risk-weighted assets (loans).

6   The term *kinŭngwŏn* has the same meaning as *kinŭngsa* used in the previous chapters.

7   The technicians category, consisting of semitechnical experts, could well be those with a university or college education in record only, but without any specific certified skills. Therefore, the impact of the crisis on this category was equally disastrous.

8   As evidence of this conspiracy, Kia management and the Kia Union presented internal documents from both the government and Samsung that had been leaked before and after the Kia Motors bankruptcy protection campaign (Kim Ki-wŏn 2002, 6).

9   For detailed background on this revolt and the related dispute among Chŏng's sons, see Kim Ki-wŏn (2002, 9–11).

10 For this negotiation, the Minister of Labor came to Ulsan on August 17, 1998.

11 Subsequently, Kim's executive branch of the seventh HMU resigned in March 1999.

12 For the detailed story behind this change, see "Kwagyŏk t'ujaeng ŭi sangjing koliat 19nyŏn twi 'hwahap ŭi sangjing ŭro" (Goliat, the symbol of militant struggle [transformed] into a symbol of harmony nineteen years after), *Chungang Ilbo*, October 20, 2009, https://news.joins.com/article/3832752. On November 27, 2014, however, the HHI Union, under the militant leadership of Chŏng Pyŏng-mo, began a strike demanding a 6.51 percent increase in basic wages, and performance-based benefits of 250 percent, among other financial benefits. Afterward, the union conducted strikes annually for five consecutive years until October 17, 2018, when HHI workers conducted partial strikes against a proposed 40 percent pay cut to employees of the firm's troubled offshore division who opted to go on paid leave. For detailed background on this strike, see "Report: Hyundai Heavy Industries' Workers Strike Again," *World Maritime News*, October 19, 2018, https://worldmaritimenews.com/archives/262922/report-hyundai-heavy-industries-workers-strike-again.

13 *Chungang Ilbo*, October 20, 2009.

14 *Maeil Kyŏngje,* November 20, 2014.
15 *Pressian,* March 18, 2016. This whistle-blower, under the pseudonym "A," is reported to own three volumes of work notebooks. Please note that the names of many members that appeared in sections 1 and 5 are not included. For a critical analysis of this report, see Hŏ Hwan-ju (2016a).
16 As a result of the February Agreement, the Korean Teachers and Educational Workers' Union was legalized. The election law was also amended as early as April 30, 1998, permitting labor unions to participate in real politics.
17 Pae replaced Kwŏn Yŏng-kil, who resigned from the KCTU's presidency to run in the 1997 presidential election as a candidate of what was called People's Victory 21, a transitional organization supported by the National Alliance for Democracy and the Reunification of Korea.
18 The National Liberation Faction, commonly referred to in Korea as NL or Chusap'a, in opposition to the People's Democracy Faction (Minjung Minjujuŭi), or PD or P'yŏngdŭngp'a, were two leading radical prodemocracy student groups in the 1980s. The National Liberation Faction, which had been inspired by the Marxist-Leninist theory of national liberation, represented a philosophy of revolution based on North Korea's Juche ideology, aimed at a revolution in South Korea. The People's Democracy Faction, in contrast, stressed the class contradiction between workers and capitalists. Despite their differences in approach, however, the NL and PD were indistinguishable in terms of political strategy. The National Liberation Faction's principal organization, National Alliance for Democracy and Reunification of Korea, in particular, played a leading role in the 1997 presidential election, as it was a member of People's Victory 21. For background on the National Liberation and People's Democracy Factions, see Chŏng Si-a (2012).
19 By then, Sim Sang-jŏng, the third key figure of the Central Faction, had been serving as assistant secretary-general of the Korean Metal Workers' Union since 1996. Both Mun and Sim were former students-turned-workers (*hakch'ul*), whereas Tan was a blue-collar worker with a high school background. This mixed makeup of leaders' backgrounds—in addition to Tan being located in Seoul, unlike most militant union leaders of the On-Site Faction, who were mostly located in the southeast industrial belt—seems to have worked for the Central Faction in forming alliances, when necessary, with both the People Faction and the On-Site Faction, with a lesser degree of rivalry and confrontation.
20 During 2015, the low rate of real investment, counter to the astronomical increase in the internal reserves of the top *chaebŏl*s, became a hot issue, arousing public disgust and anger, especially as it related to the massive increase in irregular workers and youth unemployment. For detailed discussion of the thirty largest *chaebŏl*s' internal reserves, see Yi Chu-yŏng (2015).
21 The term "competition state" was coined by the Samsung Economic Research Institute, and the status of Korea as a competition state was made official in March 2008 under the newly inaugurated conservative Lee Myung-bak government.
22 On May 23, 2009, Roh threw himself from a cliff behind his home at Ponghwa, Kyongsangnamdo. For the details of Roh's last interview, see Hyung-A Kim (2016).

23 For a critical assessment of the "accumulated evils," especially in the context of the Moon Jae-in administration's anticorruption reform, see Rowan (2018).

CHAPTER 5: THE RISE OF HCI WORKERS

1 The idea of *nodong kwijok* used in today's Korea is somewhat similar to Eric Hobsbawm's idea of a labor aristocracy, which distinguished members using six different factors: *the level and regularity of a worker's earnings, prospects of social security, conditions of work, relations with the social strata above and below him/her, general conditions of living, and prospects of future advancement and those of his or her children.* See Hobsbawm (1964, 273).
2 Five skilled workers from Hyundai Heavy Industries, Ulsan, who had worked for HHI since 1982, told me they had changed their employment status in 1998 from nonregular to regular. They did not wish to reveal their identities. Author interview, April 12–13, 2012.
3 Even in the mid-1960s, according to Hwasook Nam, regular workers and their union at the Korea Shipbuilding and Engineering Corporation actively embraced temporary workers joining their union. In those days, however, the phrase "temporary workers" had the same meaning as *pijŏnggyujik*, which became widespread especially around 1995–96 and after. For an analysis of the regular skilled workers' collective sense of labor solidarity, especially in regard to temporary workers, see Hwasook Nam (2009, 128–32).
4 As noted in chapter 2, the Chun Doo-hwan regime mandated a change from industry-level to enterprise-based unionism in 1980. Korea was one of the few advanced countries with this form of unionism, along with Japan. Enterprise-based unions in Japan, however, are generally known for their cooperation with management, despite their not so cooperative early experience (Benson 2008).
5 In these four years, 1994, 2009, 2010, and 2011, Hyundai Motor Union did not conduct a strike in the process of its annual enterprise bargaining.
6 These four workers included two Hyundai Motor workers and two Hyundai Heavy Industries workers.
7 Eleven, or 36.7 percent, of the firms having the thirty largest sales totals practice a preferential job inheritance rule. See "Taegiŏp koyong sesŭp ŭn pu ŭi sesŭp" (2015).
8 This incident led to the expulsion of the HHI Union from the Korean Metal Workers' Union (KMWU) under the KCTU. The HHI Union remained independent of both the KMWU and the KCTU until late December 2016, when it rejoined the KMWU.
9 For Japan, see "Plight of Irregular Workers" (2016). For a comparative study of Korea and the United States, see Chun (2009).
10 Kim's protest generated much support from the public and led to the creation of the "hope bus" throughout the country in support of the nonregular workers' struggle.
11 In 2007, Star Chemical, also called Pinetex, then bankrupt, was bought out by Starplex. During acquisition negotiations, Starplex had allegedly promised to (re)hire Star Chemicals' 800 unionized employees. Instead of hiring all of them, however,

Starplex unilaterally moved to have 228 of those workers "voluntarily retire." Twenty-eight of those 228 workers refused to go and were subsequently fired. Eleven of the twenty-eight dismissed workers, including Ch'a, then started their fight for reemployment. Ch'a came down from the chimney in July 2015, after obtaining an agreement that Starplex would rehire the eleven protesters. Three years later, in November 2018, however, two former union leaders conducted another sit-in protest on top of the same chimney, this time for 426 days, until January 11, 2019, because the company had broken its initial agreement.

12 Ha (2013). In September 2017, Ha was elected president of the Hyundai Motor Union Branch.

13 Here I have used the view expressed by Kim Yŏng-hun, former president of the KCTU (2010–12), in his discussion with Paek Nak-ch'ŏng (Paik Nak-chung), a prominent literary critique and former founding editor of *Ch'angbi*, a leading progressive quarterly in Korea.

14 My in-depth interviews with Hyundai WIA and Doosan Heavy Industries workers were conducted in July and August 2014, and with HHI workers in January and February 2015. I omitted one response from Doosan Heavy Industries mainly because the respondent started at the company in 1988, a year later than our specified timeline of 1972–87. The characteristics of the respondents are provided in appendixes 1–3. I received much help from Professor Seok-Choon Lew in arranging the in-depth interviews with the HHI workers, for which I sincerely thank him as well as for his other support for this book.

15 The question I asked was "Among working class, middle class, and upper class, to which class do you currently consider yourself to belong?"

16 The question I asked was "If our society is divided into high (H), middle high (MH), middle middle (MM), middle low (ML), and low (L) levels, to which stratum do you currently consider yourself to belong?"

17 Korean workers' average continuous employment is five years and eight months, whereas the average employment period for regular workers is seven years and three months, and two years and five months for subcontract workers (Statistics Korea Press Release 2015, 15).

18 The average monthly income for Korean workers in 2014 was ₩2,231,000: ₩2,604,000 for regular workers and ₩1,453,000 for subcontract workers (Statistics Korea Press Release 2014, 14).

19 Presumably, Korean people feel less psychological resistance to revealing their affiliated stratum than affiliated class (Hong 2005).

20 The other three workers who identified themselves as "working class" were all from the Doosan Heavy Industries and did not specify their annual income.

21 This average monthly earning of the Korean middle class was much less than what most Koreans then regarded as a middle-class monthly average income, which they considered to be ₩5.15 million, with average net assets worth ₩660 million, including a house or apartment worth ₩307 million.

22 Here "K" refers to former Kia Machine Tools workers who were now employees of Hyundai WIA, "D" refers to Daewoo Heavy Industries workers who were now

employees of Doosan Heavy Industries; and "H" refers to Hyundai Heavy Industries workers. Respondents of K and D are numbered from 1 to 19 and H from 1 to 20.

23 In the course of gathering material on these three surveys, I received invaluable help from Dr. Seung-bae Shin, who also provided his continuous help throughout this project, for which I am grateful.

24 The rate of union density dropped to 10.2 percent in 2015, although the total of union members increased to 1,938,745 from 1,905,000 in 2014, and rose again to 10.3 percent in 2016 with a total of 1,967,000 union members and a total workforce of 19,172,000. This union density ranked the lowest among OECD member countries.

CONCLUSION

1 While these words are from the manifesto of the KCTU, its counterpart, the FKTU, promotes similar ideals, specifically, "workers' rights and interests," as stated in the President's Solidarity Message. Contrary to their pledges, both union bodies have shown little evidence of changing their focus on regular workers of large firms and the public sector, to the extent of being labeled "trade unions for those regular workers." For the full content of the KCTU's manifesto, see http://kctu.org/aims; for the FKTU's Solidarity Message from President Juyoung Kim, see http://fktu.or.kr/message.

2 Korea's rank was the same in 2015–16. See the Global Competitiveness Index, 2015–2016 Rankings, http://www3.weforum.org/docs/GCR2016-2017/05FullReport/TheGlobalCompetitivenessReport2016-2017_FINAL.pdf.

3 Han'guk Kyŏngje Sinmun 2018. See especially the comparative graph.

4 The "seven-give-ups generation" evolved from the initial "three-give-ups" (samp'o) and "five-give-ups" (op'o) generations.

5 Here the current exchange rate (in January 2017) is ₩1,203 to US$1. The civic group called Promotion Committee of the Working Class Party argued that the internal cash reserves of these thirty top-ranking chaebŏls, with a total of 269 affiliated firms, were the main cause of the irregular workers' misery and youth unemployment, among other societal ills in Korea, and thus this committee was promoting a nationwide campaign to redeem the excessive internal cash reserves of these chaebŏls. For detailed background, see "Chaebŏl 'sanae poyugŭm' 754-jo" (2016).

6 This term can be best understood in the context of business relationships between vendors and clients, with buyers in a strongly favourable position and vendors often required to be more accommodating, or to compete with other contractors. In Korea, these relationships are usually referred to as Kap-Ul (buyer-vendors) relationships. In this sense, the term kapchil popularly refers to the indiscriminate bossism of an individual, firm, or organization particularly common in powerful chaebŏl corporations in dealing with SMEs and subcontractors of nonregular workers.

7 According to a team of eleven journalists, including two university professors writing for Joonang Ilbo, who jointly published a series on the power elite in Korean society in September 2005, there are 31,800 individuals who have been categorized

as power elites in various fields, including politics, economy, academia, legal circles, media, and the medical world (Kang Min-Sŏk et al. 2006).

8   Yi was first pardoned in 1997 after being sentenced to two years in prison for bribing politicians in 1996. Since May 2014, Yi has been in a coma after suffering a heart attack. For a detailed account of Samsung's systematic bribery of the power elite and associated corruption, see Kim Yŏng-ch'ŏl (2010).

9   In August 2015, Ch'oe received a presidential pardon for the second time from President Park Geun-hye after serving just two years and six months of a four-year prison sentence for misappropriating company funds.

10 Hong and Pang were each sentenced to three years imprisonment as well as being fined for tax evasion.

11 I borrow this phrase from Henry Bernstein, *Class Dynamics of Agrarian Change* (Sterling, VA: Fernwood Publishing/Kumarian Press, 2010).

12 This *undongkwŏn* force is often referred to as the 3-8-6 Generation who, by 2000, were in their thirties, studied at university in the 1980s, and were born in the 1960s. In 2018, this force is now known as "5-8-6," in which 5 indicates their age bracket of mostly in their fifties.

Bibliography

ABBREVIATIONS

FEPS   Kyŏngje che-1, Taet'ongnyŏng Pisŏsil (First Economy, Presidential Secretariat)
HPPC   87 nyŏn nodongja taet'ujaeng 20 chunyŏn kinyŏm saŏp ch'ujin wiwŏnhoe (Promotion Committee for the 20th Commemorative Projects of the Great Workers' Struggle of 1987)
KKS   Kyŏngje kwahak simŭi hoeŭi (The Economy and Science Council)
KOSTAT   T'onggyech'ŏng (Statistics Korea)
PCHTY   *Pak Chŏng-hŭi taet'ongnyŏng yŏnsŏl munjip* (President Park Chung Hee's speeches)
PS   Taet'ongnyŏng Pisŏsil (Presidential Secretariat)

ARCHIVAL AND UNPUBLISHED MATERIAL

Chunghwahak kongŏp e ttarŭn kongŏp kujo kaep'yŏnnon (On the restructuring of industry in accordance with the Declaration on Heavy and Chemical Industry Policy). January 30, 1970. N.p. The title's literal translation is "A theory on industrial restructuring based on the promulgation of heavy and chemical industrialization, January 30, 1973."

Embassy telegram 530. 1961. National Security Files. Country, Box 128, September 29, John F. Kennedy Library, Boston.

Hyŏndae chunggongŏp nodong chohap saŏp pogosŏ (Hyundai Heavy Industries Union business report). 1996.

Hyŏndae kurup nodong chohap ch'ongyŏnhap (Hyundai Group Unions; HGU). 1993–96. *Saŏp pogosŏ* (Business report).

Kia Kigong (Kia Machine Tools). 1993. *Hyŏnhwang Pogo, 1993* (Status report, 1993). Vols. 1–2.

Kisul kyoyuk chedo kaesŏnan, 1973 (Improvement scheme for skills education system, 1973). N.p.

Kwahak Kisulch'ŏ (Ministry of Science and Technology). 1968. *Changgi illyŏk sugŭp ch'ugye mit chŏngch'aek panghyang: 1967–1986* (Long-range manpower supply and demand estimation and policy direction: 1967–1986). N.p.

Kyŏngje che-1, Taet'ongnyŏng Pisŏsil (First Economy, Presidential Secretariat). 1974. *Saemaŭl kongjang silt'ae chosa pogo* (Report on the real state of New Community Factories), no. 19740716. Cited as FEPS 1974.

———. 1976a. *Chungdong chinch'ul kinŭnggong yangsŏngbi* (Training fund for skilled workers entering the Middle East), no. 19760417. Cited as FEPS 1976a.

———. 1976b. *Kunsisŏl ŭl iyonghan kinŭnggong yangsŏngbi* (The cost of technical skilled workers/craftsmen training by using military facilities), no. 19760511. Cited as FEPS 1976b.

Kyŏngje kwahak simŭi hoeŭi (The Economy and Science Council). 1970. *Kinŭnggong yangsŏng ŭl wihan chonghap taech'aek* (Comprehensive strategy for cultivating technical skilled workers: Report to the president), file no. EA0023181, PANAK. 19700226, February 26. Cited as KKS 1970.

Munhwabu (Ministry of Culture). 1992. *Kiŏp munhwa ch'ujin sarye moŭm* (A collection of corporate culture propulsion case studies). Vols. 1-2. http://contents.archives.go.kr.

"1990-nyŏn hyŏndai chunggongŏp koliat t'ujaeng, 'minju nojo undong' ŭi chajonsim ŭl kŏn t'ujaeng" (Hyundai Heavy Industries Goliat Struggle of 1990, the struggle for the pride of the "democratic labor movement"). Songkonghoe Taehakkyo Minju Charyogwan (Songkonghoe University Demos Archives). http://demos-archives.or.kr/content/309#0.

Pak Chŏng-hŭi Taet'ongnyŏng yŏnsŏl munjip, che 7 chip (President Park Chung Hee's speeches, vol. 7), 1973. Cited as PCHTY 1973.

Planning Office, Heavy and Chemical Industry Promotion Council. 1976. *Heavy and Chemical Industry.* Seoul: Government of the Republic of Korea. English text published for foreign investors. Cited as HCI 1976.

Planning Office, Heavy and Chemical Industry Promotion Council, Government of the Republic of Korea. 1976. *Heavy and Chemical Industry, 1976.* English text. Cited as Planning Office 1976.

Taet'ongnyŏng Pisŏsil (Presidential Secretariat). 1972. *Chŏngmil kongŏp kisul changhak jedo* (Scholarship system for precision manufacturing skills), no. 19720412. Cited as PS 1972.

———. 1973a. *Kongjang saemaŭl undong ŭi chŏn'gae pogo* (A report on the development of the Factory Saemaul [New Community] Movement), no. 19731912. Cited as PS 1973a.

———. 1973b. *Kŭmo konggo sich'al* (An inspection of the Kŭmo technical high school), no. 19730609. Cited as PS 1973b.

———. 1975. *Kongŏp kodŭng hakkyo chungchŏm yuksŏng kyehoek pogo* (Report on the plan for the priority rearing of technical high schools), no. 19750526. Cited as PS 1975.

———. 1977a. *Saemaŭl kongjang unyŏng silt'ae* (The real state of managing the New Community Factories), no. 19770428. Cited as PS 1977a.

———. 1977b. *Kŭmo konggo chorŏpsaeng ŭi chinhak mit kunbudae nomu hyŏnhwang* (Current state of university/college entrance and military service by the graduates of Kŭmo Technical High School), no. 19771005. Cited as PS 1977b.

SECONDARY SOURCES

Amsden, Alice H. 1989. *Asia's Next Giant: South Korea and Late Industrialization.* New York: Oxford University Press.

An Pyŏng-jik. 2002. "Kwagŏ ch'ŏngsan kwa yŏksa sŏsul: Togil kwa Han'guk ŭi pigyo" (Clearing the past and historical narration: Comparison of Germany and Korea). *Yŏksa hakpo* (History bulletin): 230–36.

An Sŭng-ch'ŏn. 2002. *Han'guk nodongja undong, t'ujaeng ŭi kirok* (Korean workers' movement, a record of struggle). Seoul: Pak Chong-ch'ŏl Ch'ulp'ansa.

Australian Broadcasting Commission. 2018. "Samsung Heir Lee Jae-yong Walks Free after Jail Term Suspended." *ABC News*, February 5.

Beeson, Mark. 2007. *Regionalism and Globalization in East Asia: Politics, Security and Economic Development.* New York: Palgrave Macmillan.

Benson, John. 2008. "The Development and Structure of Japanese Enterprise Unions." *Japan Focus* 6, no. 11 (November): 1–9.

Byun, Juna, and Linda S. Lewis, eds. 2000. *The Kwangju Uprising after Twenty Years: The Unhealed Wounds of the Victims.* Seoul: Daehae.

Ch'a Kwang-ho. 2015. "9-wŏl 12-il, hŭimang pŏsŭ ka tasi ch'ulbalhamnida" (The hope bus leaves again on September 12). *OhmyNews*, August 31. www.ohmynews.com /NWS_Web/view/at_pg.aspx?CNTN_CD=A0002140175.

Ch'ae Man-su. 1997. "P'ilyŏn e ŏlk'in ŭmmo, kŭrigo kulchŏldoen ŭisik: Kia sat'ae ŭi ponjil kwa taeŭng e taehaesŏ" (The plot that tangled of necessity, and the distorted consciousness: On the nature of the Kia situation and countermeasures). *Hyŏnjang esŏ mirae rŭl* (From the workplace to the future). Seoul: Policy Institute of Korean Labor Theory. http://kilsp.jinbo.net/publish/97/9708-02.htm.

"Chaebŏl 'sanae poyugŭm' 754-jo . . . kiŏpdŭl sahoejŏk ch'aengmu chyŏya" (Chaebŏls' 740 billion won 'internal reserves' . . . corporations must take charge of their social obligations). 2016. *Hankyoreh Sinmun*, June 2. www.hani.co.kr/arti/economy /economy_general/746569.html.

Chang, Dae-Oup. 2002. "Korean Labor Relations in Transition: Authoritarian Flexibility?" *Labor, Capital and Society* 35, no. 1: 10–40.

Chang, Ha-Joon. 1998. "Korea: The Misunderstood Crisis." *World Development* 26, no. 8: 1555–61.

———. 1999. "The Economic Theory of the Developmental State." In *The Developmental State*, ed. Meredith Woo-Cumings, 182–99. Ithaca, NY: Cornell University Press.

———. 2002. *Kicking Away the Ladder: Development Strategy in Historical Perspective.* London: Anthem.

———. 2007. *Bad Samaritans: The Myth of Free Trade and Secret.* London: Bloomsbury Press.

Chang, Ha-Joon, and Peter Evans. 2005. "The Role of Institutions in Economic Change." In *Reimagining Growth: Towards a Renewal of Development Theory*, ed. Gary A. Dymski and Silvana De Paula, 99–129. London: Zed Press.

Chang, Kyung-sup. 2007. "The End of Developmental Citizenship? Restructuring Social Displacement in Post-Crisis South Korea." *Economic and Political Weekly* (December): 67–72.

———. 2010. *South Korea under Compressed Modernity: Familial Political Economy in Transition*. Abingdon: Routledge.

Chibber, Vivek. 2014. "The Developmental State in Retrospect and Prospect: Lessons from India and South Korea." In *The End of the Developmental State,* ed. Michelle Williams, 30–54. London: Routledge.

Cho, Joonmo, and Jaeseong Lee. 2015. "Persistence of the Gender Gap and Low Employment of Female Workers in Stratified Labor Market: Evidence from South Korea." *Sustainability* 7, no. 9: 12425–51.

Cho Hwang-hŭi, Yi Ŭn-kyŏng, Yi Ch'un-kŭn, and Kim Sŏn-u. 2002. *Han'guk ŭi kwahak kisul illyŏk chŏngch'aek* (Korea's science-technology developmental strategy). Seoul: STEPI, Kwahak Kisul Chŏngch'áek Yŏn'guwŏn.

Cho Hyŏng-je. 1999. "Hyŏndae chadongch'a ŭi koyong chojŏng: 'Kiŏmnae nosa kwan'gye rŭl chungsim ŭiro'" (Hyundai Motor's employment adjustment: Focused on the labor-management relationship within a company). *Sanŏp nodong yŏn'gu* (A study of industrial labor) 5, no. 1: 63–95.

Cho Kye-wan. 2011. "Munŭnghan chabon, t'ŭkkwŏnhwahan nodong" (Incapable capital, privileged labor). *Le Monde Diplomatique*. www.ilemonde.com/news/article View.html?idxno=1303.

———. 2012. *Uri sidae nodongŭi saengae* (The life of labor in our time). Seoul: Aelp'i.

Cho Sŏng-jae. 1998. "Kia ch'ŏri wa chadongch'a sanŏp ŭi kujo chojŏng" (Kia deal and restructuring of the motor industry). *Tonghyang kwa chŏnmang* (Trend and prospect), no. 39: 74–103.

———. 2006. "Chadongch'a sanŏp sanae hach'ŏng silt'ae wa kaesŏn panghyang: H-sa sarye rŭl chungsim ŭro" (The reality of in-house contractors in the motor industry and its improvement direction: Focused on H company). *Minjung sahoe wa chŏngch'aek yŏn'gu* (A study of mass society and its policy), no. 10: 151–83.

Cho Yŏng-rae. 2001. *Chŏn T'ai-il p'yŏngjŏn* (A Chŏn T'ae-il biography). Seoul: Tolpegae. Its English translation, titled *A Single Spark: The Biography of Chun Tai-il,* was published in 2003.

Ch'oe Chang-jip. 1992. "Saeroun nodong undong ŭi panghyang mosaek ŭl wihayŏ" (For the sake of direction for a new labor movement). *Sahoe P'yŏngnon* (Social critique) (June): 232–46.

———, ed. 2005. *Wigi ŭi nodong: Han'guk minjujuŭi chwiyakhan sahoe kyŏngjejŏk kiban* (Labor in crisis: The weakness of the socioeconomic base of Korean democracy). Seoul: Humanit'as.

Ch'oe Chong-sŏk. 2014. "Chŏnch'e kŭlloja ŭi 7.4% (nojo innŭn tae kiŏp chŏnggyujik) ka nodong sijang yanggŭk hwa simhwa sik'iyŏ" (7.4 percent of the total number of workers [who are regular workers of large firms with trade unions] deepen labor market segmentation). *Chosun Ilbo*, November 28. http://news.chosun.com/site/data/html_dir/2014/11/28/2014112800280.html.

Ch'oe Yŏng-hwan, Na To-un, and Chŏng Yun. 2010. "Chŏn kungmin kwahakhwa undong ŭi chungch'u" (The pivot of the Pan-National Scientization Movement). In *Kwahak taet'ongnyŏng Pak Chŏng-hŭi wa lidŏsip* (Science, President Park Chung Hee, and [his] leadership), ed. Hong Ji-ŭn and Pak Pyŏng-gwan, 428–47. Seoul: MSD Midiŏ.

Chŏng Chang-yŏl. 2013. "Taehan min'guk mandŭn 'konggosaeng' 77manmyŏng ch'ujŏkki (A tracking of 770,000 'technical high school students' who have built the Republic of Korea). *Chugan chosŏn* (Weekly Chosun), no. 2282, November 18–24. http://weekly.chosun.com/client/news/viw.asp?ctcd=C08&nNewsNumb =002283100000.

Chŏng Chu-yŏng. 1998. *I ttang e t'aeŏnasŏ: Na ŭi saraon iyagi* (Born in this land: My life story). Seoul: Sol.

Chŏng I-hwan. 1992. "Chejoŏp naebu nodong sijang ŭi pyŏnhwa wa nosa kwan'gye" (Change and the labor-management relationship in the labor market within the manufacturing sector). PhD diss., Seoul National University.

Chŏng Si-a. 2012. "NL-PD 30nyŏn chŏnchaeng" (A 30-year NL-PD war). *Chugan chosŏn* (Weekly Choson), no. 2205, http://weekly.chosun.com/client/news/viw.asp ?nNewsNumb=002205100002&ctcd=C01.

Chŏng Un-yŏng. 1997. "Kia Hyŏnsang" (Kia phenomenon). *Hankyoreh Sinmun*, August 5.

"Ch'ŏngnyŏn ilchari mangnŭn chujŏk ŭn kangsŏng nojo (The main adversary that prevents young people's employment is militant trade unions). 2015. *Maeil Kyŏngje/MK News*, August 26. http://news.mk.co.kr/newsRead.php?year=2015&no =819123.

Chu Tae-hwan. 2017. "Mun chŏngbu 3 kaewŏl 'wŏnjo chwap'a' Chu Tae-hwan ŭi ssŭn sori" (The Moon [Jae-in] government's three months—"original Left" Chu Tae-hwan's bitter comments). *Weekly Chosun*, August 13.

Chun, Jennifer Jihye. 2009. *Organizing at the Margins: The Symbolic Politics of Labor in South Korea and the United States*. Ithaca, NY: Cornell University Press.

Clark, Donald. 1988. *The Kwangju Uprising: Shadows over the Regime in South Korea*. Boulder, CO: Westview Press.

Cotton, James, and Kim Hyung-A Van Leest. 1996. "The New Rich and the New Middle Class in South Korea." In *New Rich in Asia*, ed. Richard Robinson and David S. Goodman, 185–203. London: Routledge.

Crotty, James, and Kang-Kook Lee. 2002. "A Political-Economic Analysis of the Failure of Neoliberal Restructuring in Post-Crisis Korea." https://pdfs.semanticscholar.org /85f7/7f4ad8bc476fc3e30e539776e8f9c6bdd237.pdf.

Dayo, Frederic. 1989. *Beneath the Miracle: Labor Subordination in the New Asian Industrialism*. Berkeley: University of California Press.

Di Giovanni, Julian, and Andri A. Levchenko. 2012. "Country Size, International Trade, and Aggregate Fluctuations in Granular Economies." *Journal of Political Economy* 120, no. 6 (December): 1083–1132.

Eckert, Carter. 2016. *Park Chung Hee and Modern Korea: The Roots of Militarism, 1866–1945*. Cambridge, MA: Harvard University Press.

87 nyŏn nodongja taet'ujaeng 20 chunyŏn kinyŏm saŏp ch'ujin wiwŏnhoe (Promotion Committee for the 20th Commemorative Projects of the Great Workers' Struggle of 1987). 2007. *Koliat ŭn marhanda, 1987–2007* (The Goliat speaks, 1987–2007). Ulsan: Taeil Insoe. Cited as HPPC 2007.

Evans, Peter. 1995. *Embedded Autonomy: States and Industrial Transformation.* Princeton, NJ: Princeton University Press.

Goodman, David S., and Richard Robinson, eds. 1996. *New Rich in Asia: Mobile Phones, McDonald's, and Middle-Class Revolution.* London: Routledge.

Gray, Kevin. 2008. *Korean Workers and Neoliberal Globalization.* London: Routledge.

Green, Andy. 1999. "East Asian Skill Formation System and the Challenge of Globalization." *Journal of Education and Work* 12, no. 3: 253–79.

Green, F., D. James, D. Ashton, and J. Sung. 1999. "Post-school Education and Training Policy in Developmental States: The Cases of Taiwan and South Korea." *Journal of Education and Work* 14, no. 3: 301–15.

Ha Pu-yŏng. 2013. "Hyŏndaech'a chŏnggyujik nojo kanbu ŭi t'ongryŏlhan pansŏngmun" (A pointed letter of apology by a representative of Hyundai Motor regular workers' union). *Hankyoreh Sinmun*, March 29. www.hani.co.kr/arti/society/labor/580360.html.

Hacker, Jacob S., and Paul Pierson. 2010. *Winner-Take-All Politics: How Washington Made the Rich Richer—and Turned Its Back on the Middle Class.* New York: Simon & Schuster.

Halper, Stephan A. 2010. *The Beijing Consensus: How China's Authoritarian Model Will Dominate the Twenty-First Century.* New York: Basic Books.

Han'guk Chosŏn Kongŏp Hyŏphoe. 1994. *Chosŏn charyojip* (A shipbuilding sources collection). N.p.

Han'guk Kidokkyo Sahoe Munje Yŏn'guwŏn (Korea Institute of Christian Social Issues). 1989. *Taegu, Ulsan chiyŏk silt'ae wa nodong undong* (The reality of the Taegu-Ulsan and Ulsan region). Seoul: Minjungsa.

Han'guk Kyŏngje Sinmun. 2018. "Yangdae noch'ong chohabwŏn Ilnyŏnsae 8manmyŏng . . . taegiŏp konggong pumun chŏnggyujik man paebullyŏ" (Union membership of both the two umbrella labor organizations [the FKTU and KCTU] up 80,000 within one year . . . only regular workers of large firms and the public sector spoiled themselves). *Mobile Hangyŏng*, April 20. http://plus.hankyung.com/apps/newsinside.view?aid=2018041982141&category=NEWSPAPER&sns=y.

Han'guk Kyŏngje 60onyŏnsa P'yŏnch'an Wiwŏnhoe. 2010. *Han'guk kyŏngje 60onyŏnsa, II* (A sixty-year history of the Korean economy, vol. 2). Seoul: Han'guk Kaebal Yŏn'guwŏn.

Han'guk Nodong Yŏn'guwŏn (Korea Labor Institute; KLI). 2000. *Han'guk ŭi nodongbŏp kaejŏng kwa nosa kwan'gye* (The revision of labor law and the labor-management relationship in Korea). N.p.

———. 2007. "2007nyŏndo nosa kwangye silt'ae punsŏk mit p'yŏngga: Sanae hach'ŏng nosa kwangye rŭl chungsim ŭro" (An analysis of the reality and assessment of the labor-management relationship in 2007: Focused on the labor-management relations of in-house subcontractors). Seoul: Nodongbu (Ministry of Labor).

Han'guk Sahoe Yŏn'guso (Institute of Korean Society). 1989. *Han'guk sahoe nodongja yŏn'gu II* (A study of workers in Korean society, vol. 2). Seoul: Paeksan Sŏdang.

Han'guk Ŭnhaeng (Bank of Korea). 2010. *6onyŏnsa* (A sixty-year history). N.p.

Harlan, Chico. 2012. "In S. Korea, the Republic of Samsung." *Washington Post*, December 9.

Hart-Landsburg, Martin. 1993. *The Rush to Development: Economic Change and Political Struggle in South Korea*. New York: Monthly Review Press.

Harvey, David. 2005. *A Brief History of Neoliberalism*. New York: Oxford University Press.

Hŏ Hwan-ju. 2016a. "Hyŏndae chunggongŏp, sŭp'ai simŏ nojo kamsihaetta" (Hyundai Heavy Industries, surveilled its workers by planting spies). *Pressian*, March 18. www.pressian.com/news/article.html?no=134197.

———. 2016b. "Hyŏndae chunggongŏp 'ŏyongnojo' changgi tokjae ŭi pimil ŭn" (The secret of the Hyundai Heavy Industries "pro-company" union's long-term dictatorship). *Pressian*, March 21. www.pressian.com/news/article.html?no=134296.

Hobsbawm, Eric. 1964. *Labouring Men: Studies in the History of Labour*. London: Weidenfeld and Nicolson.

Hong Tu-sŭng. 2005. *Han'guk ŭi chungsangch'ŭng* (The Korean middle stratum). Seoul: Seoul National University Press.

Hundt, D. 2005. "A Legitimate Paradox: Neo-Liberal Reform and the Return of the State in Post-Crisis South Korea." *Journal of Development Strategies* 41, no. 2 (February): 242–60.

Hyundae Chunggongŏp Nodongjohap (Hyundai Heavy Industries Union). 1991. *Taphara, Chŏnsegye nodongja* (Answer, workers of the world!). Ulsan: Nodongja Munhwa Yesul Undong Yŏnhap Sahoe Sajin Yŏn'guso.

Ik'onomi Insait'ŭ (Economy Insight). 2013. "Chaebŏl chudo sin chŏnggyŏng yuch'ak, Han'guk kyŏngje ŭi kŏllimdol" (Chaebŏl-led new political-business collusion: The obstacle of Korean economy). *Economy Insight*, May 1. www.economyinsight.co.kr/news/articleView.html?idxno=1793.

Im Chihyŏn and Kim Yongwu, eds. 2005. *Taechungdokchae 2* (A popular dictatorship, vol. 2). Seoul: Ch'aek saesang.

Im Yŏng-il. 1998. *Han'guk nodong undong kwa kyegŭp chŏngch'i, 1987–1995: Pyŏnhwa rŭl wihan t'ujaeng, hyŏpsang ŭl wihan t'ujaeng* (The Korean labor movement and class politics, 1987–1995: Struggle for change, struggle for negotiation). Masan: Kyungnam University Press.

Jeon, Jong-hwi. 2014. "More than 2 million in S. Korea living as subcontractor workers." *Hankyoreh Sinmun*, September 29. http://english.hani.co.kr/arti/english_edition/e_national/657350.html.

Jeong, Jooyeon. 2007. *Industrial Relations in Korea: Diversity and Dynamism of Korean Enterprise Unions from a Comparative Perspective*. London: Routledge.

Jeong, Seong-jin. 1997. "The Social Structure of Accumulation in South Korea: Upgrading or Crumbling?" *Review of Radical Political Economics* 29, no. 4: 92–112.

Johnson, Chalmers. 1982. *MITI and the Japanese Miracle: The Growth of Industrial Policy, 1925–1975*. Stanford, CA: Stanford University Press.
——. 1987. "Political Institutions and Economic Performance: The Government-Business Relationship in Japan, South Korea, and Taiwan." In *The Political Economy of the New Asian Industrialism*, ed. Frederic C. Deyo, 136–64. Ithaca, NY: Cornell University Press.
——. 1989. "South Korean Democratization: The Role of Economic Development." *Pacific Review* 2, no. 1: 1–10.
Kang, David. 2002. *Crony Capitalism: Corruption and Development in South Korea and the Philippines*. Cambridge: Cambridge University Press.
Kang, Myung-Koo. 2011. "Compressed Modernization and the Formation of Developmental Mentalité." In *Reassessing the Park Chung Hee Era, 1961–1979*, ed. Hyung-A Kim and C. W. Sorensen, 166–86. Seattle: Center for Korea Studies at the University of Washington.
Kang Chun-Man. 2013. *Kapkwa ŭlŭi nara: Kapŭl kwan'gye nŭn Taehanmin'gukŭl ŏttŏkke chibaehaewatnŭn'ga* (The country of Kap and Ŭl: How has the kapŭl relationship dominated Korea?). Seoul: Inmulkwa sasangsa.
Kang Min-sŏk, Kim Sŏng-t'ak, Min Tong-gi, Pak Su-ryŏn, Yang Yŏng-yu, Yi Kyu-yŏn, Im Mi-jin, Chŏng Sŏn-gu, Chŏng Hyo-sik, Kim Ki-hun, and Chang Tŏk-chin. 2006. *Taehanmin'guk p'awŏ ellit'ŭ: Han'guk ŭi umjiginŭn ellit'ŭ, kŭdŭl ŭn nuguin'ga* (Korean power elite: Who are those elites who move Korea). Seoul: Hwangŭm Nach'imban.
Kang Sŏk-jae. 2002. "Chosŏn sanŏp taegiŏp ŭi chagŏpchang ch'eje wa nosa kwan'gye ŭi pyŏnhwa" (The change in the workplace system and labor-management relationship in large firms in the shipbuilding industry). PhD diss., Yonsei University.
Kang Yŏng-Hae, Yoon J. H., Lee H. S. and Kim N. K. 2005. *Kogyo p'yŏngjunhwa chŏngchaekŭi chŏkhapsŏng yŏn'gu (II)* (A study of the compatibility of high school equalization policy [II]), Seoul: Korean Educational Development Institute.
Kim, Choong-soon. 1996. *The Culture of Korean Industry: An Ethnography of Poongsan Corporation*. Tucson: University of Arizona Press.
Kim, Dae-Jung. 1985. *Mass Participatory Economy: A Democratic Alternative for Korea*. Cambridge, MA: Harvard University Press.
Kim, Hyung-A. 2004. *Korea's Development under Park Chung Hee: Rapid Industrialization, 1961–79*. London: RoutledgeCurzon.
——. 2011. "Heavy and Chemical Industrialization, 1973–1979: South Korea's Homeland Security Measure." In *Reassessing the Park Chung Hee Era, 1961–1979: Development, Political Thought, Democracy and Cultural Influence*, ed. Hyung-A Kim and C. W. Sorensen, 20–42. Seattle: Center for Korea Studies at the University of Washington,
——. 2013. "Industrial Warriors: South Korea's First Generation of Industrial Workers in Post-Developmental Korea." *Asian Studies Review*, no. 4: 577–95.
——. 2015. "South Korea's Deepening Youth Unemployment Crisis." *Asian Currents*, August 25. http://asaablog.tumblr.com/post/127600865946/south-koreas-deepening-youth-unemployment-crisis.

———. 2016. "President Roh Moo-Hyun's Last Interview and the Roh Moo-hyun Phenomenon in South Korea." *Journal of Contemporary Asia*, December 16. www.tandfonline.com/eprint/SJiTNnAwg8rXgJIevv5j/full.

Kim, Jong-il, and J. Lawrence. 1994. "The Sources of Economic Growth of the East Asian Newly Industrialized Countries." *Journal of the Japanese and International Economies* 8: 235–71.

Kim, Seung-Kyung. 1997. *Class Struggle or Family Struggle?* Cambridge: Cambridge University Press.

Kim, Sun-Hyuk. 2000. *Politics of Korean Democratization in Korea: The Role of Civil Society*, Pittsburgh: University of Pittsburgh Press.

Kim Chin-gyun. 1978. "Illyŏk kaebal" (Human resource development). In *Han'guk sahoe: In'gu wa kaebal (II)* (Korean society: Population and development, 2), 389–450. Seoul: Sŏul Taehakkyo Sahoe Kwahak Taehak In'gu mit Palchŏn Yŏn'guso.

———. 2008. "87nyŏn ihu minju nojo undong ŭi kujo wa t'ŭkching: 'Chŏn'guk nodongjohap hyŏbŭihoe ŭi chŏn'gae kwajŏng kwa chuyo hwaltong ŭl chungsim ŭro" (The structure and character of the democratic labor movement after 1987: Focused on the development process and major activities of the National Council of Trade Unions). In *Minjunojo undong 20-nyŏn* (Twenty years of the democratic labor movement), ed. Cho Ton-mun and Yi Su-bong, 17–85. Seoul: Humanit'as.

Kim Ch'ŏl-ha. 2015. "Minju noch'ong ŭi hyŏksin i chŏlsilhada" (The Korean Confederation of Trade Unions desperately needs reform). *Chinbo nodongjahoe* (Progressive Workers' Association). http://ruwaf.net/xe/index.php?document _srl=1204&mid=main.

Kim Chŏng-ho. 2015. *Kkŭnnaji anŭn chŏhang: T'ongil-S&T chungkongŏp nojo undong 30-nyŏnsa, 1985–2015* (Unfinished struggle: A thirty-year history of the T'ongil-S&T heavy industry, 1985–2015). Seoul: Hannae.

Kim Chu-a and Mun Hyŏng-gu. 2004. "Hyŏndae chunggongŏp hach'ŏngŏpch'e nodongja Pak Il-su ssi punsin (Self-immolation of Mr. Pak Il-su, a subcontract worker of Hyundai Heavy Industries). *Minjungui sori* (Workers' voice), February 14. www.vop.co.kr/A00000008229.html.

Kim Chun. 2005. "Irŏbŏrin kongdongch'e? Ulsan tonggu chiyŏk nodongja chugŏ kongdongch'e ŭi hyŏngsŏng kwa haech'e" (Lost community? The formation and dismantling of the workers' community at the eastern district, Ulsan). *Kyŏngje wa Sahoe* (Economy and society), no. 68 (Winter): 71–106.

Kim Ch'un-su. 2003. "1960-70-nyŏndae kukka ŭi yŏsŏng paeje chŏllyak: Kisul kyoyuk hullyŏn ŭl chungsim ŭro" (The state's exclusion of females strategy during the 1960s and '70s: Focused on technical education and skills training). *Yŏksa Yŏn'gu* (A study of history), no. 12: 69–107.

Kim Ki-ch'ŏl. 2014. "Hyŏndaejung mubun'gyu 20nyŏn nojo nŭn hanbŏndo yangbohaji annatta" (Hyundai Heavy Industries Union did not give way even once during its no-strike [deal] for twenty years). *Maeil Kyŏngje*, November 20.

Kim Ki-ha. 2011. *Yŏlchŏng ŭi ondol ŭl nop'yŏra* (Increase the heat of passion). Seoul: Ministry of Employment and Labor.

Kim Ki-wŏn. 2001. "Chaebŏl ch'eje ŭi palchŏn kwa mosun" (The development and contradiction of the *chaebŏl* system). *Tonghyangga Chŏnmang* (Trends and perspectives), no. 50: 200–23.

———. 2002. "Han'guk chadongch'a sanŏp ŭi kujo chojŏng ŭl tullŏssan chaengchŏm" (Issues surrounding the restructuring of the Korean motor industry). *Sanŏp nodong yŏn'gu* (A study of industrial labor) 8, no. 1: 1–37.

Kim Sang-jo, Yu Chong-il, and Hong Chong-hak. 2007. *Han'guk kyŏngje saep'an tchagi* (Making a new Korean economy framework). Seoul: Middle House.

Kim Se-gyun. 2002. "Han'guk ŭi 'minju' nodong undong: P'yŏngga wa chŏnmang" (The Korean "democratic" labor movement: Critique and prospect). *Chinbo P'yŏngnon* (Radical review), no. 13: 11–53.

Kim Tong-ch'un. 2015. *Taehan Min'guk ŭn wae, 1945–2015* (Why the Republic of Korea? 1945–2015). Seoul: Sagyejŏl.

Kim Wŏn. 2007. "Han'guk ŭi nodongja munhwa, panbok pyŏnjudoenŭn wigidŭl" (The Korean working class culture: Crises that repeat and vary). *Chinbo P'yŏngnon* (Progressive critique), no. 32 (Summer): 85–114.

———. 2011. *Itch'yŏjin kŏtdŭl e taehan kiŏk* (Memories of forgotten things), Seoul: Imaejin.

Kim Yŏng-bae. 2007. "T'ŭkchip: Ch'amyŏ chŏngbu wa Samsŏng ŭi kkŭnjŏk-kkŭnjŏkhan 5-nyŏn" (Special edition: The sticky five years of the participatory government and Samsung). *Hankyoreh 21*, November 29. http://legacy.h21.hani.co.kr/section-021106000/2007/11/021106000200711290687041.html.

Kim Yŏng-ch'ŏl. 2010. *Samsŏng ŭl saenggakhanda* (Recalling Samsung). Seoul: Sahoe P'yŏngnon.

Kim Yun-t'ae. 2002. *Han'guk injŏk chawŏn kaebal chŏngch'aek ŭi punsŏk mit p'yŏngga, 1962–2002* (An analysis and assessment of Korea's human resource development policy, 1962–2002). Seoul: Han'guk Chigŏp Nŭngnyŏk Kaebarwŏn.

Kim Yun-t'ae, Roh J. H., Kang M. S., Chung J. H., and Kang S. G. 1978. "Kodŭnghakkyo Pyŏngjunhwa Chŏngchaekŭi Pyŏngkkayŏn'gu" (Assessment study of the high school equalization policy). Seoul: Korean Educational Development Institute.

Kim Yu-sŏn. 2016a. "Pak Kŭn-hye chŏngbu nodong kaeak, tto hana ŭi '*chaebŏl* p'ŏjugi'" (Park Geun-hye government's labor reform another reckless favor for *chaebŏls*). *Pressian*, February 24. www.pressian.com/news/article/?no=133430#09To.

———. 2016b. "Pijŏnggyujik kyumo wa silt'ae: T'onggyech'ŏng kyŏngje hwaltong in'gu chosa puga chosa (2016.8) kyŏlkwa" (The size and real condition of nonregular [workers'] positions: Outcome of the supplementary census survey of economic activity by KOSTAT [August 2016]). www.klsi.org.

Kirk, Donald. 1994. *Korean Dynasty: Hyundai and Chung Ju Yung*. New York: M. E. Sharp.

Kohli, Atul. 2004. *State-Directed Development: Political Power and Industrialization in the Global Periphery*. Cambridge: Cambridge University Press.

Kong, Tat Yan. 2000. *The Politics of Economic Reform in South Korea: A Fragile Reform*. London: Routledge.

Koo, Hagen. 2001. *Korean Workers: The Culture and Politics of Class Formation*. Ithaca, NY: Cornell University Press.

Koyong Nodongbu (Ministry of Employment and Labor). 1993. *Kigob imkum pogosŏl* (Report on occupational wages survey). N.p.: Koyong Nodongbu.

"Kukka kyŏngjaengryŏk, kŭmyung nodong kaehyŏk ŭro toesallyŏya" (National competitiveness should be revived through financial and labor reform). 2015. *Digit'ŏl T'aimsŭ* (Digital times), September 30.

Kukka T'onggye Pot'ol (KOSIS). 2017. *Yŏndobyŏl nodong chohap chojik hyŏnhwang* (The current organizational state of year-on-year labor unions in Korea). http://kosis.kr/statHtml/statHtml.do?orgId=118&tblId=TX_11824_A009.

Kwon, Peter-Banseok. 2016. "The Anatomy of *Chaju Kukpang*: Military-Civilian Convergence in the Development of the South Korean Defense Industry under Park Chung Hee, 1968–1979." PhD diss., Harvard University, 2016.

Kwŏn Yong-mok. 1988. *Hyŏndae kurup nodong undongsa (1)-(4), Saebyŏk* (The history of the labor movement at Hyundai group, (1)-(4), the dawn). Seoul: Seokt'ap.

Lee, Kyung-Sung. 2011. *The Korean Financial Crisis of 1997: Onset, Turnaround, and Thereafter*. Washington, DC: World Bank and Korean Development Institute.

Lee, Nam-Hee. 2005. "Representing the Worker: The Worker-Intellectual Alliance of the 1980s in South Korea." *Journal of Asian Studies* 64, no. 4 (November): 911–37.

———. 2007. *The Making of Minjung: Democracy and the Politics of Representation in South Korea*. Ithaca, NY: Cornell University Press.

Lee, Wonduck, and Joohee Lee. 2004. "Will the Model of Uncoordinated Decentralization Persist? Changes in Korean Industrial Relations after the Financial Crisis." In *The New Structure of Labor Relations*, ed. H. Katz, 143–65. Ithaca, NY: Cornell University Press.

Lee, Yoon-Kyung. 2011. *Militants or Partisans: Labor Unions and Democratic Politics in Korea and Taiwan*. Stanford, CA: Stanford University Press.

Leftwich, Adrian. 2008. "Developmental States, Effective States and Poverty Reduction: The Primacy of Politics." United Nations Research Institute for Social Development (UNRISD). www.unrisd.org/80256B3C005BCCF9/search/EE2D4DF653F6077BC125 7A5D004C7E5E.

Lew, Seok-choon. 2013. *The Korean Economic Developmental Path: Confucian Tradition, Affective Network*. New York: Palgrave Macmillan.

Lim, Hyun-chin, and Jin-Ho Jang. 2006. "Neo-liberalism in Post-crisis South Korea: Social Conditions and Outcomes." *Journal of Contemporary Asia* 36, no. 4: 442–63.

Markusen, Ann, and Sam-ok Park. 1993. "The State as Industrial Locator and District Builder: The Case of Changwon, South Korea." *Economic Geography* 69, no. 2: 157–81.

McGregor, James. 2012. *No Ancient Wisdom, No Followers: The Challenges of Chinese Authoritarian Capitalism*. Burlington, VT: Prospecta Press.

Migdal, Joel S. 1988. *Strong Societies and Weak States: State-Society Relations and State Capabilities in the Third World*. Princeton, NJ: Princeton University Press.

Moon, Seungsook. 2005. *Militarized Modernity and Gendered Citizenship in South Korea*. Durham, NC: Duke University Press.

Mun Sŏng-hyŏn. 2010. *Hŭimang ŭn tangsin kyŏt e issŭmnida* (Hope is near you). Seoul: Tosŏch'ulp'an Samuban.

Mun'gyobu (Ministry of Education). 1977. *Choguk kŭndaehwa ŭi kisu: Kongŏp kodŭng hakkyo kinŭngsa yangsŏng* (The flagbearers of the national fatherland's modernization: Skills training at technical high schools). N.p.

———. 1979. *Mun'gyo t'onggye yŏnbo* (Annual statistics report). N.p.

———. 1980. *Han'guk ŭi kongŏp kyoyuk: Choguk kŭndaehwa ŭi kisu* (Korea's industry education: The flagbearers of the national fatherland's modernization). N.p.

———. 1999. *Mun'gyo t'onggye yŏnbo* (Annual statistics report, 1969–89). Seoul: Konghwa Ch'ulp'ansa.

Nam, Hwa-Sook. 2009. *Building Ships, Building a Nation: Korea's Democratic Unionism under Park Chung Hee*. Seattle: University of Washington Press.

Nam, Il-chong, Yeoung-jae Kang, and Joon-kyung Kim. 1999. "Corporate Governance in Korea: A Comparative Perspective." Presented at the conference "Corporate Governance in Asia: A Comparative Perspective," Organization for Economic Cooperation and Development (OECD) and the Korea Development Institute, Seoul, March 3–5. https://www.oecd.org/corporate/ca/corporategovernance principles/1931556.pdf.

Neary, Michael. 2000. "Hyundai Motors 1998–1999: The Anatomy of a Strike." *Capital and Class* 70: 1–7.

No Chung-gi. 2011. "Han'guk minjuhwa ŭi sŏnggwa wa han'gye" (The outcome and limitations of Korean democracy). *Kiŏk kwa chŏnmang* (Memories and perspective), no. 22 (Summer): 37–62.

Nodongbu (Ministry of Labor). 1992. *Chigŏp hullyŏn saŏp hyŏnhwang* (Current state of vocational training), no. 8. N.p.

Nosajŏng Wiwŏnhoe (Tripartite Committee). 2003. *Nosajŏng wiwŏnhoe 5nyŏn paeksŏ* (The five-year white paper of the Tripartite Committee). Seoul, N.p.

O Wŏn-ch'ŏl. 1995. *Han'gukhyŏng kyŏngje kŏnsŏl: Enjiniŏring ŏp'ŭroch'i* (Korean model of economic construction: Engineering approach). Vol. 1. Seoul: Kia Kyŏngje Yŏn'guso.

———. 2006. *Pak Chŏng-hŭi nŭn ŏttŏk'e kyŏngje kangguk ŭl mandŭrŏnna* (How did Park Chung Hee build economic power?). Seoul: Tongsŏ Munhwasa.

Organization for Economic Cooperation and Development (OECD). 2014. *OECD Economic Surveys: Korea 2014*. https://www.oecd.org/eco/surveys/Overview_Korea _2014.pdf.

———. 2016. *OECD Economic Surveys: Korea 2016*. https://www.oecd.org/eco/surveys /Korea-2016-OECD-economic-survey-overview.pdf.

Paek, Chong-chon. 1985. "Military Education System and National Development: The Case of the Republic of Korea (ROK) Army." *Korea Observer* 14 (Winter): 400–31.

Paek Nak-ch'ŏng. 2015. *Paek Nakch'ŏng i taejŏnhwan ŭi kil ŭl mutta* (Paek Nak-chung asks the way for a great transition). Seoul: Ch'angbi.

Pak Chŏm-gyu. 2014. "Pijŏnggyujik oemyŏnhal ttae chŏnggyujik nojo muryŏkhwa hogŭn t'arak" (When irregular workers are being dismissed, regular workers' unions become either paralyzed or corrupt). *Redian*, January 28. www.redian.org /archive/66263.

Pak Chun-sik. 1993. "Kyŏngyŏng hamnihwa wa chagŏpchang ch'eje ŭi pyŏnhwa: D chosŏn ŭl chungsim ŭro" (Economic rationalization and change in the workplace system: Focused on D shipbuilding [company]). *Kyŏngje wa sahoe* (Economy and society), Autumn: 191–223.

Pak Hyŏng-jun. 2016. "Kyŏngje ga sŏngchang halsurok chasal ŭn nŭrlŏnanda" (The more the economy grows, the more suicide increases). *Pressian*, January 27. www.pressian.com/news/article.html?no=132857.

Pak Hyŏn-jung. 2003. *T'onggyero pon chungdŭng kyoyuk* (Secondary education viewed through statistics). Seoul: Korean Educational Development Institute.

Pak Sang-ŏn. 1992. "Han'guk taegiŏp e issŏsŏ insa, nomu kwalli chŏllyak ŭi yŏksajŏk pyŏnhwa e kwanhan yŏn'gu: 1970–1990" (A study of historical change in the personnel and labor management strategy of large firms in Korea). PhD diss., Yonsei University.

Pak Sŭng-ok. 1992. "Han'guk nodong undong, kwayŏn wigiin'ga?" (Korea's labor movement, is it really in crisis?). *Ch'angjak gwa pip'yŏng* (Creation and criticism), Summer: 214–46.

Pak Tong-gyu. 1994. "Nosa munje ŭi ponjil kwa ch'ŏbang: Taewu chosŏn saŏp pyŏnhwa ch'ujin sarye" (The nature and prescription of the labor-management problem: A case study of the change of the Daewoo shipbuilding business). *Taehan chosŏn hakhoeji* (Journal of the Korean Shipbuilding Association) 31, no. 1: 7–11.

Pak Yŏng-gu. 2012. *Han'guk ŭi chunghwahak kongŏphwa: Kwajŏng kwa naeyong (II)* (Korea's heavy and chemical industrialization: Its process and contents, II). Seoul: Haenam.

Park, Chung Hee. 1962. *Our Nation's Path: Ideology of Social Reconstruction*. 2d ed. Seoul: Hollym Corporation.

———. 1979. *Saemaul: Korea's New Community Movement*. Seoul: Korea Textbook.

Park, Hyeng-Joon. 2015. "Korea's Post-1997 Restructuring: An Analysis of Capital as Power." *Review of Radical Political Economics* 48, no. 2: 287–309.

Park, Sang-young. 1999. "Crafting and Dismantling the Egalitarian Social Contract: The Changing State-Society Relations in Korea's Educational Policymaking." PhD diss., University of Hawaii.

———. 2010. "Crafting and Dismantling the Egalitarian Social Contract: The Changing State-Society Relations in Globalizing Korea." *Pacific Review* 23, no. 5 (November): 579–601.

Pempel, T. J. 1999. *The Politics of the Asian Economic Crisis*. Ithaca, NY: Cornell University Press.

Pham, Peter. 2018. "What Is South Korea's Secret Weapon?" *Forbes*, May 31. https://www.forbes.com/sites/peterpham/2018/05/31/what-is-south-koreas-secret-weapon/#784b03686b2f.

Pham, Sherisse. 2017. "South Korea's Long History of Light Sentences for Business Leaders." *CNN*, January 17. https://money.cnn.com/2017/01/17/investing/south-korea-chaebol-culture-corruption/index.html.

"Plight of Irregular Workers." 2016. *Japan Times*, January 5. https://www.japantimes.co.jp/opinion/2016/01/05/editorials/plight-of-irregular-workers/#.XaasLimP4uQ.

Premack. Rachel. 2017. "South Korea's Conglomerates." *Sage Business Researcher*, August 21. http://businessresearcher.sagepub.com/sbr-1863-103804-2830718/20170821/south-koreas-conglomerates.

Ramo, J. Cooper. 2004. *The Beijing Consensus*. London: Foreign Policy Centre.

Reich, Robert B. 2007. *Supercapitalism: The Transformation of Business, Democracy and Everyday Life*. New York: Vintage Books.

Rhyu, Sang-young, and Seok-jin Lew. 2011. "Pohang Iron and Steel Company." In *The Park Chung Hee Era: The Transformation of South Korea*, ed. Byung-Kook Kim and Ezra F. Vogel, 322–44. Cambridge, MA: Harvard University Press.

Rowan, Bernard. 2018. "Of Accumulated Evils and Foolishness." *Korea Times*, January 16. http://m.koreatimes.co.kr/pages/article.asp?newsIdx=242467.

Ryu, D., and H. Ahn. 2010. "The Development of Neoliberalism and Its Alternative in Korea." *Review of Social Economy* 35: 237–82.

Sahoe Chŏnghwa Wiwŏnhoe (Committee for Social Purification). 1986. *Sahoe Chŏngwha Undongsa* (The history of the social purification movement). Seoul: Sahoe Chŏnghwa Wiwŏnhoe.

Salmon, Andrew. 2018. "Former President Park Now Facing 33 Years in Jail." *Asia Times*, August 24. www.atimes.com/article/korean-ex-president-now-facing-33-years-in-jail/.

Selwyn, Benjamin. 2016. "Elite Development Theory: A Labour-Centered Critique." *Third World Quarterly* 37, no. 5: 781–99.

Shin, Jang-sup, and Ha-joon Chang. 2003. *Restructuring Korean Inc*. New York: RoutledgeCurzon.

Shin, Kwang-Yeong. 2013. "Economic Crisis, Neoliberal Reforms, and the Rise of Precarious Work in South Korea." *American Behavioral Scientist* 57: 335–53.

Shin, Kyong-ho, and Paul S. Ciccantell. 2009. "The Steel and Shipbuilding Industries of South Korea: Rising East Asia and Globalization." *Journal of World-Systems Research* 15, no. 2: 167–92. http://jwsr.pitt.edu/ojs/index.php/jwsr/article/view/316.

Shin Kwang-yŏng. 2004. *Han'guk ŭi kyegŭp kwa pulp'yŏngdŭng* (Class and inequality in Korea). Seoul: Ulyu Munhwasa.

Shin Pyŏng-hyŏn and Kim To-gŭn. 1993. "Chabon hamnihwa undong ŭi sin kyŏnghyang: Kiŏp munhwa chŏllyak ŭl chungsim ŭro" (A new trend of capital rationalization: Focused on corporate culture strategy). *Tonghyang kwa chŏnmang* (Trend and prospect): 176–207.

Shin Wŏn-ch'ŏl. 2001. "Kiŏp naebu nodong sijang ŭi hyŏngsŏng kwa chŏn'gae: Han'guk chosŏn sanŏp e kwanhan sarye yŏn'gu" (The formation and development of the labor market within business: A case study of Korea's shipbuilding industry). PhD diss., Seoul National University.

Silver, Beverly J. 2003. *Forces of Labor: Workers' Movements and Globalization since 1870*. Cambridge: Cambridge University Press.

"Som pangmangi ch'ŏbŏl . . . ch'oejŏ imgŭm to moppannŭn kŭlloja 300manmyŏng" (Light punishment . . . three million workers who do not receive even the minimum wage). 2016. *Yonhap News*, August 16. https://www.yna.co.kr/view/AKR20160815068800002.

Standing, Guy. 2013. "Job Security Is a Thing of the Past: So Millions Need a Better Welfare System." *Guardian*, May 22. https://www.theguardian.com/commentisfree/2013/may/21/job-security-welfare-flexible-labour-precariat.

Statistics Korea Press Release. 2015. http://kostat.go.kr/portal/eng/index.action.

Stubbs, Richard. 2009. "What Ever Happened to the East Asian Developmental States? The Unfolding Debate." *Pacific Review* 22, no. 1: 1–22.

Suh, Doowon. 2009. *Political Protest and Labor Solidarity in Korea: White-Collar Labor Movements after Democratization (1987–1995)*. London: Routledge.

Sun, Hak Tae. 2002. *The Political Economy of Democratic Consolidation: Dynamic Labor Politics in South Korea*. Kwangju: Chŏnnam National University Press.

"Taegiŏp koyong sesŭp ŭn pu ŭi sesŭp . . . muryŏkkam nŭkkinda" (The employment inheritance of large firms is inheritance of wealth . . . feeling a sense of helplessness). 2015. *Chungang Ilbo*, June 25. https://news.joins.com/article/18102638.

Tilly, Charles. 1990. *Coercion, Capital, and European States, A.D. 990–1992*. Cambridge, MA: Harvard University Press.

T'onggyech'ŏng (KOSTAT). 2014. "Kŭllo hyŏngt'aebyŏl puga chosa kyŏlkwa: 2014nyŏn 8-wŏl kyŏngje hwaltong in'gu chosa" (Supplementary results of the economically active population survey by employment type in August 2014). Press release, October 28. http://kostat.go.kr/portal/eng/pressReleases/5/5/index.board.

———. 2016. "2016nyŏn 8wŏl kyŏngje hwaltong in'gu chosa: Kŭllo hyŏngt'ae pyŏl puga chosa kyŏlkwa" (Supplementary results of the economically active population survey by employment type in August 2016). http://blog.naver.com/PostView.nhn?blogId=puremassage&logNo=220854021193&widgetTypeCall=true.

Van Leest, Hyung-A Kim. 1992. "The Impact of Concepts of *Minjung* on Thought and Culture in Korea during the Period of Authoritarian Politics (1948–1987)." MA thesis, Australian National University.

Vartiainen, Juhana. 1999. "The Economics of Successful State Intervention in Industrial Transformation." In *The Developmental State*, ed. Meredith Woo-Cummings, 200–34. Ithaca, NY: Cornell University Press.

Vu, T. 2007. "State Formation and the Origins of Developmental States in South Korea and Indonesia." *Studies in Comparative International Development* 41, no. 4: 27–56.

Wade, Robert. 1990. *Governing the Market: Economic Theory and the Role of Government in East Asian Industrialization*. Princeton, NJ: Princeton University Press.

Watanabe, Hiroaki Richard. 2017. "Labour Market Dualism and Diversification in Japan." *British Journal of Industrial Relations* 56, no. 3: 579–602.

Weakliem, David L., and Julia Adams. 2011. "What Do We Mean by 'Class Politics'?" *Politics and Society* 39, no. 4: 475–95.

Williams, Michelle. 2014. "Rethinking the Developmental State in the Twenty-First Century." In *The End of the Developmental State?*, ed. Michelle Williams, 1–29. London: Routledge.

Woo-Cumings, Meredith, ed. 1999. *The Developmental State*. Ithaca, NY: Cornell University Press.

———. 2003. "South Korean Anti-Americanism." Japan Policy Research Institute Working Paper 93 (July). www.jpri.org/publications/workingpapers/wp93.html.

World Bank. 1993. *The East Asian Miracle: Economic Growth and Public Policy.* New York: Oxford University Press.

Wright, Eric Olin. 2000. "Working Class Power: Capitalist-Class Interests and Class Compromise." *American Journal of Sociology*, no. 4 (January): 957–1002.

XinhwaNet. 2018. "S. Korea's Youth Jobless Rate Hits Record High, with Those Unemployed Topping 1 Mln." *XinhwaNet*, January 10. www.xinhuanet.com/english/2018-01/10/c_136885298.htm.

Yang Mun-sŏk. 2006. "No Muhyŏn chŏnggwŏn, ŏttŏk'e kwŏllyŏk ŭl Samsŏng e nŏmgyŏnna" (The Roh Moo-hyun government, how did it hand over its power to Samsung?). *Taejabo*, August 4. http://jabo.co.kr/sub_read.html?uid=16601.

Yi Chu-yŏng. 2015. "Chaebŏl chumŏni man kadŭkch'aeun sanae poyugŭm (Internal reserves of firms that filled the chaebŏls' pockets). *Kyŏnghyang sinmun*, September 23. http://biz.khan.co.kr/khan_art_view.html?artid=201509230600015&code=920100.

Yi Ho-ch'ang, Kim To-gŭn, Kim Sŏng-gyu, Wŏn In-sŏng, Pak Hae-gwang, and Kang Sŏk-chae. 2012. *Ilbonchŏk saengsan pangsik kwa chagŏpchang ch'eje* (The Japanese-style production mode and its workplace system). Seoul: Chungwŏn Munhwa.

Yi Kab-yong. 2009. *Kil ŭn pokchaphaji ant'a: Koliat chŏnsa Yi Kab-yong ŭi nodong iyagi* (The road is not complex: Goliat warrior Yi Kap-yong's labor story). Seoul: Ch'ŏlsu wa Yŏnghŭi.

Yi Kang-guk. 2004. "Chabon chayuhwa wa kyŏngje sŏngjang kŭrigo wigi: Han'guk ŭi kyŏnghŏm ŭl chungsim ŭro" (Liberalization of capital transactions, economic growth, and crisis: Focused on the Korean experience). In *Han'guk kyŏngjega sarajinda* (The Korean economy is evaporating), ed. Yi Ch'an-gun, 52–57. Seoul: 21st Century Books.

Yi Nam-sin. 2017. "Pijŏnggyujik 1000 man sidae! Imgŭm kyŏkch'a nŭn 15nyŏn man e tubae!" (The era of 10 million irregular workers! A doubling of the wage gap in fifteen years!). *Pressian*, August 14. www.pressian.com/news/article/?no=165544#09To.

Yi Pyŏng-hun. 2004. "Wansŏngch'a sanae hyŏmnyŏk ŏpch'e ŭi koyong kwan'gye" (The employment relationship of motor companies' in-house subcontractors). In *Chadongch'a sanŏp ŭi togŭp kujo wa koyong kwan'gye ŭi kyech'ungsŏng* (The contract structure and employment relationship in the motor industry), ed. Cho Sŏng-je, 93–112. Seoul: Korea Labor Institute.

Yi Sang-ch'ŏl. 1991. "Han'guk nodong undong ŭi chiyŏkchŏk t'ŭksŏng, 1987–1990: P'ohang, Ulsan, Masan, Ch'angwŏn chiyŏk ŭi pigyo" (The regional characteristics of the labor movement in Korea, 1987–1990: A comparative study of P'ohang, Ulsan, Masan and Ch'angwŏn). PhD diss., Seoul National University.

Yi Sŏng-ch'ŏl. 1994. "Han'guk ŭi sung'ryŏn hyŏngsŏng kwa nodong gwajŏng ŭi sŏnggyŏk" (The characteristics of skills formation and labor processes in Korea). *Chiyok sahoe yon'gu* (A study of regional community) 2: 157–85.

Yi Wŏn-bo. 2005. *Han'guk nodong undongsa: paengnyŏn ŭi kirok* (A history of the Korean labor movement: A record of one hundred years). Seoul: Han'guk Nodong Sahoe Yŏn'guso.

Yi Yŏng-kyŏng. 2013. "Han'guk. Minju yangdae noch'ong enŭn hyŏnjang chach'e ka chugŏ itta" (Korea: The on-site itself is dead in the both the democratic KCTU and the FKTU). *Kyŏnghyang Sinmun*, May 1. http://news.khan.co.kr/kh_news/khan_art_view.html?artid=201305012225555&code=940702.

Yi Yŏng-mi. 2009. "1970nyŏndae kwahak kisul ŭi 'munhwajŏk tongwŏn': Saemaŭl kisul pongsadan saŏp ŭi chŏn'gae wa sŏnggyŏk" (A 'cultural mobilization' of science and technology during the 1970s: The development and character of the New Community Movement project's technology service force). MA thesis, Seoul National University.

Yoon, Seok-man. 2011. "POSCO: Building an Institution." In *Reassessing the Park Chung Hee Era, 1961–1979: Development, Political Thought, Democracy and Cultural Influence*, ed. Hyung-A Kim and C. W. Sorensen, 43–65. Seattle: Center for Korea Studies at the University of Washington.

Young, Alwyn. 1994. "Lessons from the East Asian NICs: A Contrarian View." *European Economic Review* 38: 964–73.

Yu Chong-yŏng. 1983. "3.15 Masan ŭigŏ ŭi paegyŏng kwa kyŏnggwa" (The background and progress of the March 15 democratic protests). *Masan Munhwa* (Masan culture) 2: 65–97.

Yu Hyŏng-gŭn. 2012. "Han'guk nodong kyegŭp ŭi hyŏngsŏng kwa pyŏnhyŏng: Ulsan chiyŏk taegiŏp nodongja rŭl chungsim ŭro, 1987–2010" (Working class formation and its transformation in South Korea: Focused on workers of large firms in the Ulsan area, 1987–2010). PhD diss., Seoul National University.

Yu Kwang-ho. 2013. "1970-80nyŏndae yangsŏngdoen chunghwahak kongŏp pumun kinŭnggong ŭi kyech'ŭng idong e kwanhan saengaesajŏk yŏn'gu" (A study of the life history of the mobility of the social stratum of skilled workers trained in the heavy and chemical industry during the 1970s and 1980s). PhD diss., Yonsei University.

Yu Kyŏng-sun. 2010. "Tto tasi p'aebae rŭl panpokhalkŏn'ga" (Will [we] repeat the failure again). *Kŭmsok nodongja* (Metal workers), August 9. www.ilabor.org/news/articleView.html?idxno=914.

Index

A

activism (unions). *See* militancy (unions)
Agency for National Security Planning, 91
An Sŭng-ch'ŏn (president, Korean Workers' Labor Movement Solidarity), 87–88
Anam Industry (Vision 92 campaign), 72
Asian Development Bank, 36
Asian financial crisis (1997–98), 3, 5, 80, 91–114, 126, 129, 152, 153; bankruptcy, 92–100, 132; business restructuring, 92–100; "consciousness reform," 71; fluctuations in employment, 93–94; International Monetary Fund, 92–93, 100, 113, 132, 146–47; unemployment, 63, 90, 91, 93–94, 96–97, 98, 100, 101, 105, 107, 109, 128, 148; workers' response, 92–100, 131, 132, 134, 135. *See also* postcrisis/postrestructuring
automobile industry, 3, 16, 61, 90, 94, 120. *See also* Hyundai Motor; Kia Motors

B

Bank for International Settlements, 92
Bank of Korea, 126
bankruptcy, 92–100, 132
"Beijing consensus," 14
Blue House (Ch'ŏngwadae), 17, 22

bossism (*kapchil*), 145, 148
bread-and-butter unionism. *See* economic unionism (HCI workers)

C

capitalism, 111; "capitalist developmental state" (CDS), 15; "Chinese authoritarian capitalism," 14; "crony capitalism," 14, 109, 110, 141. *See also chaebŏls* (family-owned conglomerates); neoliberalism
"capitalist developmental state" (CDS), 15
Catholic Women's Association, 47
CCM. *See* Corporate Culture Movement (CCM)
CDS. *See* capitalist developmental state (CDS)
Central Faction (Chungangp'a) (KCTU), 106
Ch'a Kwang-ho (aerial protest), 127
Ch'adolhoe (White Pebble club), 50, 63
chaebŏl republic, 110, 113, 115, 145, 153
"*chaebŏl*-centered developmentalism", 14
chaebŏl-led accumulation, 107, 108–14, 141; *chaebŏl* republic, 110, 113, 115, 145, 153; changed power relations, 112–13; concentration of net profit, 108; in postrestructuring Korea, 5, 6, 107, 110–12, 144, 147, 148, 149, 152–53; nonregular workers, 111. *See also* developmental state (DS)

195

chaebŏls (family-owned conglomerates), 4, 5–6, 16, 72, 90, 102, 107–14, 128, 144–49, 153–54; bossism (*kapchil*), 145, 148; cash reserves, 144–45; *chaebŏl* republic, 110, 113, 115, 145, 153; *chaebŏl* training, 109; "*chaebŏl*-centred developmentalism," 14; collaboration with HCI workers, 147–48, 149; in-plant training, 8, 30, 32, 36–37, 62, 129; media *chaebŏls*, 146; subsidies-as-contracts system, 7, 40, 108–9, 145; top-ranking, 112, 113, 141, 144–45, 146, 152, 153; unions, 87, 97, 98, 103, 126–27. See also Corporate Culture Movement (CCM); corruption (*chaebŏls*); graduates (technical high schools); industrial cities; labor aristocracy (*nodong kwijok*); Tripartite Commission; *and entries at Daewoo; Hanjin; Hyundai; Kia; Samsung; Ssangyong; Hanhwa Group; LG; Lotte; SK Group*

chaju kukpang (self-reliant national defense), 8–9, 21, 25

Ch'angwŏn, 37, 40, 42, 46, 58, 80–81, 85, 134, 137, 138; Catholic Women's Association, 47–48; company housing, 43–44, 45, 71; small club (*somoim*)/small-group activities, 47–48, 49, 50, 62, 71, 75, 82

Ch'angwŏn Industrial Park (CIP), 81; HCI workers, 42–43, 45, 46–48, 50, 134, 138, 150; T'ongil Corporation workers' strike (1985), 49–51, 64. See also Masan; Ulsan

chemical industry. See heavy and chemical industrialization (HCI)

chigŏp sesŭp (job inheritance), 4, 115, 124, 147

chikkong. See factory workers (*chikkong*)

ch'ilp'o sedae ("seven-give-ups generation"), 144, 148

China, 68; "Beijing consensus," 14; "China model," 14; "Chinese authoritarian capitalism," 14; developmental state model, 14

"Chinese authoritarian capitalism," 14

ch'ŏbapt'ong ("iron rice bowls"), 18, 133

Ch'oe T'ae-wŏn (CEO, SK Group), 146

choguk kŭndaehwa ŭi kisu ("flag-bearers of modernization of the fatherland"), 34, 40

Chŏn T'ae-il (self-immolation), 49, 63, 125

Chŏng Chu-yŏng (chairman, Hyundai Group), 39, 53, 56, 96

Chŏng Kap-tŭk (president, HMU), 61, 119

Chŏng Mong-ku (CEO, Hyundai Motor), 146

chŏnggyujik (regular workers). See regular workers (*chŏnggyujik*)

Chŏnguk Konggong Unsu Nodongjohap (Transportation Workers' Union), 106

Chon'guk Kŭmsok Nodongjohap (Korean Metal Workers' Union), 106

Ch'ŏngwadae (Blue House), 17, 22

Chŏnnodae (Congress of National Trade Union Representatives), 103, 104

Chŏnnohyŏp. See National Council of Trade Unions (NCTU)

Chŏnp'yŏng (National Council of Korean Labor Unions), 48

Chosun Ilbo (newspaper), 81, 146

Christian Academy, 49

Chun Doo-hwan regime (1980–87), 8, 12, 28, 37, 104, 148; draconian labor laws, 40, 41–42, 48–49, 52

Chungangp'a (Central Faction) (KCTU), 106

church organizations, 42; Catholic Women's Association, 47; Christian Academy, 49; Urban Industrial Mission, 49; Young Catholic Workers' Organization, 49; Young Men's Christian Association, 62

CIP. See Ch'angwŏn Industrial Park (CIP)

Citizens' Coalition for Economic Justice, 111

CMCU. *See* Council of Masan and Ch'angwŏn Unions (CMCU; Mach'ang Noryŏn)
collective bargaining, 6, 62, 67, 89, 116, 118, 120, 122, 124, 147, 151, 153
company spirit (*kiŏp chŏngsin*), 78, 79
Congress of National Trade Union Representatives (Chŏnnodae), 103, 104
"consciousness reform" (*ŭisik kaehyŏk*), 71
construction industry, 32, 36, 90. *See also* Hanjin Heavy Industries and Construction; Hyundai Construction
co-op system (*ture hwaltong*), 78, 79
Corporate Culture Movement (CCM), 4, 5, 24, 66, 67–90, 143, 153; campaigns, 71–72, 73, 82; company spirit, 78, 79; as counterrevolution, 69, 74–80, 90, 111; Daewoo Heavy Industries, 71–72, 79, 83; four main program areas (table 3.1), 73; Hope Movement (Daewoo), 71–72, 79, 83; labor flexibility, 69, 71, 74, 75, 77, 78, 80–86, 90, 111, 115, 118, 147, 152, 154; launch (1992), 74; "management rationalization," 69; neoliberal strategy, 68–69, 75, 88, 90, 111, 118; new management strategy (*sin kyŏngyŏng chŏllyak*), 68, 69–74, 81, 87, 88, 104, 118; no-strike agreements, 79, 86, 94, 98–99, 132; "Organizational Innovation and Culture Management" symposium, 72, 74; POSCO, 69–71, 74, 75, 78, 79, 83; public relations, 72, 73, 82; Samsung Group, 68, 74–75, 78, 79, 83, 95; special events/social activities, 72, 73, 78, 83, 89; training/education, 72, 73, 77, 78, 82, 83; and union militancy, 67, 68, 69, 79, 80, 89, 90; Vision 92 campaign (Anam Industry), 72; worker surveillance, 80, 85–86, 99–100. *See also* labor aristocracy (*nodong kwijok*)
corruption (*chaebŏls*), 92, 113, 146; Park Geun-hye, 113, 146; presidential pardons, 145–46

Council of Daewoo Group Unions (Daenohyŏp), 103, 104
Council of Hyundai Group Unions (Hyondae Kurup Nodongjohap Hyŏbŭihoe or Hŏynch'ongnyŏn), 52, 103, 104, 105; Kwŏn Yong-mok, 48, 52
Council of Masan and Ch'angwŏn Unions (CMCU; Mach'ang Noryŏn), 64; withdrawal of KMTU, 18, 80–86
Council of National Labor Movement Organizations (Nounhyŏp), 64
Council of Unions of the Daewoo Group (Daenohyŏp), 103, 104
counterrevolution. *See* Corporate Culture Movement (CCM)
craftsmen. *See* skilled workers (*kinŭngsa*)
"crony capitalism," 14, 109, 141

D

DACOM, 74
Daelim Industrial Co. Ltd, 31
Daenohyŏp (Council of Unions of the Daewoo Group), 103, 104
Daewoo Auto Company, 96; Auto strike 1985, 10, 49–50, 51
Daewoo Heavy Industries, 19, 56, 68, 75, 128, 129, 131, 134; Hope Movement, 71–72, 79, 83; labor flexibility, 77–78; Pak Sam-hun (self-immolation), 87. *See also* Doosan Heavy Industries
Daewoo Heavy Industries Union, 87; "absence" strike, 87
defense firms (*pangwi sanŏp*), 8, 33, 47, 50, 58. *See also* special soldiers (*t'ŭngnyebyŏng*)
defense industry (*pangsan ŏpch'e*), 12, 13, 21–22, 27, 30, 33, 37, 47, 49–51, 58, 71; Five-Year Military Modernization Plan (1971–76), 25; Kuro Industrial Park, 50, 51; Lightning Operation, 25; self-reliant national defense, 8–9, 21, 25. *See also* Ch'angwŏn Industrial Park

democratic (*minju*) labor unions, 4, 53, 87, 134, 153
Democratic Justice Party (DJP), 68
Democratic Labor Party, 64, 106
democratic labor union movement, 24, 41, 42, 43, 52, 60, 61, 62, 64, 70, 81, 87, 88, 102, 106, 107, 120, 142, 148; collective bargaining, 6, 62, 67, 89, 116, 118, 120, 122, 124, 147, 151, 153; female workers, 12, 49, 53, 54, 58–59; power struggle, 87–88. *See also* militancy (unions); *minjung* democracy movement
developmental state (DS), 13–17; Chinese model, 14; Marxist modernization model, 5, 11, 13, 17, 58; reductionist/essentialist approach, 9; statist political economy model, 5, 9, 13, 109; theory of, 13–15. *See also* East Asian developmental state; Korean developmental state; skilled workers (*kinŭngsa*)
"developmentalist mentalité," 14, 109, 111
disguised workers (*wijang ch'wiŏpcha*), 49, 58, 59, 62; worker-intellectual partnership. *See* worker-intellectual partnership (HCI)
DJP. *See* Democratic Justice Party (DJP)
Doosan Heavy Industries, 19, 88, 112, 124. *See also* Daewoo Heavy Industries; labor aristocracy (HCI workers' interviews)
"dragon from a stream" (*kaech'ŏne yong*), 28, 34, 64
DS. *See* developmental state (DS)
dual labor-market system, 102, 122, 127, 139, 142–43, 154; SMEs, 115, 116, 119, 128, 153. *See also* labor aristocracy (*nodong kwijok*); rise of HCI workers; nonregular workers (*pijŏnggyujik*)

E

East Asian developmental state, 14–16, 19, 109; review of literature, 9–13; role of skilled workers, 13–17

East Asian economic miracle, 13, 14, 15; Korea, 3, 37, 40
economic development theories: Marxist modernization model, 5, 11, 13, 17, 58; statist political economy model, 5, 9, 13, 109
economic unionism (HCI workers), 89–90, 102–3, 116, 144, 145, 148, 151, 153
economy (Korea), 3, 37, 40; boom years, 42, 68, 97; "economy-first" national psyche, 111, 150; GDP, 3, 108, 110, 112, 145, 153, 154; state-led accumulation, 5, 107, 108–10, 111, 113, 144, 148, 152; winner-take-all, 111, 145, 154; world ranking, 3, 152. *See also* Asian financial crisis (1997–98); *chaebŏl*-led accumulation; Korean developmental state; postcrisis/postrestructuring
Economy and Science Council (MST), 26
education and training (Park state), 7–9; "dragon from a stream," 28, 34, 64; "education fever," 28; High School Equalization Policy (1974), 7, 28; Improvement Plan for Korea's Technological Education System (1973), 28–29; industry-education co-op system (*sanhak hyŏptong*), 31; institutions by type/entry age/school year, 161; Middle School Equalization Policy (1968), 7, 28; National Technical Qualification Act (1973), 7, 29; National Technical Qualification System (1973), 7, 29; National Technical Qualification Test, 8, 30, 31, 34; Plan for the Priority Promotion of Technical High Schools (1975), 28–29; subsidies-as-contracts, 7–8, 12, 25, 29, 30, 34, 36, 40, 109, 149; Technical High School Characterization Policy, 30–35; Vocational Training Act (1967), 36. *See also* reciprocal social

contract; science and technology
manpower; technical high schools;
vocational training
"education fever" (*kyoyungyŏl*), 28
electronics industry, 16, 32, 34, 35, 36
elite technical high schools, 29, 30–35;
 Kŭmo Technical High School, 32–34
EM Korea, 17; Yu Han-sik (CEO), 17–18,
 83, 84, 96
employment: before/after 1997 crisis
 (table 4.1), 93; job inheritance (*chigŏp sesŭp*), 4, 115, 124, 147. *See also*
 graduates (technical high schools);
 industrial cities; rise of HCI workers;
 unemployment
employment inheritance. *See* job
 inheritance (*chigŏp sesŭp*)
engineers/scientists (*kwahak kisulcha*), 6,
 8, 21, 22, 23, 26, 163
experimental technical high schools
 (*sibŏm konggo*), 30, 31, 32, 34, 39

F

Factory New Community Movement
 (Kongjang Saemaŭl Undong), 12, 23;
 community circle-activity, 24. *See also*
 New Community Movement (Saemaŭl
 Undong)
factory workers (*chikkong*), 19, 59, 60, 62,
 64, 134, 136, 151. *See also* female
 workers (light industries); HCI
 workers; skilled workers (*kinŭngsa*)
Federation of Korean Trade Unions
 (FKTU), 48, 54, 91, 100, 106, 107, 128,
 143–44; loss of public support, 144;
 youth unemployment, 128, 144. *See
 also* Tripartite Commission
female workers (light industries), 10, 19,
 24, 103; and democratic labor union
 movement, 12, 49, 53, 54, 58–59;
 education levels, 6, 34–35, 47, 58;
 employed in Masan, 47, 49, 58–59; Kim
 Chin-suk (aerial protest), 61–62, 127;

nonregular workers, 97, 126, 142, 154;
 Seoul-Kyŏngin area, 49, 58, 62
Five-Year Economic Development Plans
 (FYEDP): 1962–66 (1st), 35, 44–46;
 1967–71 (2nd), 25–26, 38; 1972–76 (3rd),
 26, 34, 37, 38, 129; 1977–81 (4th), 27, 34,
 37, 38; 1982–86 (5th), 38; 1987–91 (6th),
 38; vocational training institutes
 (table 1.3), 38
Five-Year Military Modernization Plan
 (1971–76), 25
Five-Year Technology Advancement Plan
 (1972–76), 25
FKTU. *See* Federation of Korean Trade
 Unions (FKTU)
"flag-bearers of modernization of the
 fatherland" (*choguk kŭndaehwa ŭi
 kisu*), 34, 40
Foreign Capital Inducement Law (1966),
 46
foreign firms/foreign investment, 46, 92,
 94, 96, 108, 110
freedom community (*haebang
 kongdongch'e*), 44, 52–53
FYEDP. *See* Five-Year Economic
 Development Plans (FYEDP)

G

GDP (Korea), 3, 108, 110, 112, 145, 153, 154
generals-turned-presidents. *See* Chun
 Doo-hwan regime (1980–87); Park
 Chung Hee (President, 1963–79); Park
 state (1963–79); Roh Tae-woo regime
 (1988–92)
global financial crisis (2008), 3, 123
GM Daewoo: nonregular workers' union,
 125
GNP (Korea), 34, 92
Goliat Struggle (HHIU) (1990), 54–57, 63,
 65, 105; divide-and-rule policy (HHI),
 56–57; May Struggle (1991), 56–57, 58.
 See also worker-intellectual
 partnership (HCI)

Goliat warriors (HHIU), 4, 5, 24, 41–66, 149, 150–52; mainstream rank-and-file HCI workers, 62–63, 64–65; rank-and-file workers, 61–62, 63, 66; three types of, 61–65. *See also* industrial cities; militancy (unions); labor union movements (1945–87); students-turned-workers (*hakch'ul*); worker-intellectual partnership (HCI)
graduates (technical high schools), 8, 18, 22, 26, 32–35, 46, 62, 102, 109, 129; 1969–87 (table 1.2), 35; female, 34–35
Great Workers' Struggle (GWS) 1987, 4, 5, 10, 12, 13, 18, 24, 40, 42–45, 60–65, 67, 68, 82, 102, 117, 134, 135, 153; Hyundai Engine Union, 48, 51–52; Hyundai industrial warriors, 44–46, 51–53. *See also* Goliat Struggle (HHIU) (1990); worker-intellectual partnership (HCI)

H

haebang kongdongch'e (freedom community), 44, 52–53
hakch'ul (students-turned-workers). *See* students-turned-workers (*hakch'ul*)
Halla Heavy Industry: bankruptcy, 92, 93; union, 85
Hanbo bankruptcy, 92, 93
Han'guk Noc'ong. *See* Federation of Korean Trade Unions (FKTU)
Han'guk Nodongja Undong Yŏndae. *See* Korean Workers' Labor Movement Solidarity (Han'guk Nodongja Undong Yŏndae)
Han'gyoreh sinmun (newspaper), 95
Hanhwa Group, 112; Kim Sŭng-yŏn (CEO), 146
Hanjin Heavy Industries, 11, 85, 87
Hanjin Heavy Industries and Construction, 62, 127
Hanjin Heavy Industry Union, 87; Pak Ch'ang-su (president), 56

HCI. *See* heavy and chemical industrialization (HCI)
HCI project (Park state), 5, 8, 12, 16; Blue House, 17, 22; commitment by HCI workers, 6, 61; Industrial Corps, 9, 22; master plan, 17, 21–22; National Scientization Movement, 21, 23; Second Economic Secretariat, 17. *See also* defense industry (*pangsan ŏpch'e*); education and training (Park state); Five-Year Economic Development Plans; industrial warriors (*sanŏp chŏnsa*); special soldiers (*t'ŭngnyebyŏng*)
HCI workers, 6–7, 12–13, 16–17, 20; change in lifestyle, 88–90; Ch'angwŏn Industrial Park (CIP), 42, 46, 47–48, 50, 150; collaboration with *chaebŏl*s, 147–48, 149; compared to rest of labor force, 4, 5, 10, 142, 149, 154; deployment to Middle East, 31, 36, 37–38, 39; economic unionism, 89–90, 102–3, 116, 144, 145, 148, 151, 153; Hyundai workers (Ulsan), 44–46, 47; as shareholders, 122, 123, 124; social closure, 90, 91–92, 97, 98, 102–7, 114, 116, 124, 126–27, 135, 139, 142, 147, 153; social isolation, 128, 134, 142, 144–48; sources/data collection/surveys/interviews, 17–19; view of labor unions, 134–41. *See also* Corporate Culture Movement (CCM); democratic labor union movement; education and training (Park state); Goliat warriors (HHIU); Great Workers' Struggle (GWS) 1987; industrial warriors (*sanŏp chŏnsa*); labor aristocracy (*nodong kwijok*); labor flexibility; militancy (unions); rise of HCI workers; special soldiers (*t'ŭngnyebyŏng*); unions; worker-intellectual partnership (HCI)
heavy and chemical industrialization (HCI), 3, 20, 25, 27, 45, 72, 80, 109, 149; National Scientization Movement, 21,

23. See also HCI project (Park state); HCI workers; industrial cities; industrial warriors (sanŏp chŏnsa)
HHI. See Hyundai Heavy Industries (HHI)
HHUI. See Hyundai Heavy Industries Union (HHIU)
High School Equalization Policy (HSEP) (1974), 7, 28
HMU. See Hyundai Motor Union (HMU)
Homeland Guards (Hyangt'o Yebigun), 22
Hope Movement (Daewoo), 71–72, 79, 83
HSEP. See High School Equalization Policy (HSEP)
Hyangt'o Yebigun (Homeland Guards), 22
Hyomun-Yŏnam Industrial Complex, 116–17; average monthly salaries (table 5.1), 117
Hyondae Kurup Nodongjohap Hyŏbŭihoe (Council of Hyundai Group Unions), 52, 103, 104, 105
hyŏnjangp'a (On-Site Faction) (KCTU), 105, 106
Hyundai Construction, 31, 113
Hyundai Engine, 51
Hyundai Engine Union (Kwŏn Yong-mok), 48, 52
Hyundai Group, 44, 45, 51–53, 83, 103–5, 132; Chŏng Chu-yŏng (chairman), 39, 53, 56, 96; Corporate Culture Movement, 68, 69, 79
Hyundai Heavy Industries (HHI), 3, 19, 61, 63, 69, 112, 124, 130, 134; casualization of labor, 75–77; Ch'oe Kil-sŏn (CEO), 45; co-op system, 78, 79; dormitories (Kwakchŏngwan, Man Sedae, Ojwabul, Samjŏngwan), 44, 45, 52; freedom community (haebang kongdongch'e), 44, 52–53; no-strike/no restructuring agreement, 86, 94, 98–100, 129, 132; Pak Il-su (self-immolation), 125; regular/nonregular workers, 117–18; in Ulsan, 44–46, 52; worker surveillance, 99–100. See also labor aristocracy (HCI workers' interviews)
Hyundai Heavy Industries Union (HHIU), 52–56, 63, 86, 125; divide-and-rule policy (HHI), 56–57; militant democracy faction (minjup'a), 56; no-strike/no restructuring agreement, 86, 94, 98–100, 129, 132; regular/nonregular workers, 117–18; shipbuilding strikes (1974, 1988), 45, 53, 56, 59–60, 151; Sŏ T'ae-su (president), 60; Yi Yŏng-hyŏn (president), 55. See also Goliat Struggle (HHIU); Goliat warriors (HHIU); Yi Kab-yong (Goliat warrior)
Hyundai Hysco: nonregular workers' union, 125
Hyundai Industrial Complex, 116; average monthly salaries (table 5.1), 117
Hyundai Motor Group, 18
Hyundai Motor Union (HMU), 87–88, 122; Chŏng Kap-tŭk (president), 61, 119; Full Employment Guarantee agreement, 115, 118–20; Ha Pu-yŏng (vice president), 127–28; Hyundai Motor restructure, 96–98; Kim Kwang-sik (president), 97, 98; moderate/pragmatist faction (sillip'a), 56; thirty-six-day strike (1998), 96–97, 105, 118; wage negotiation 2001–10 (table 5.3), 123; Yang Pong-su (self-immolation), 87; Yi Sang-bŏm (president), 55, 61. See also Tripartite Commission
Hyundai Motor, 3, 87, 112, 113, 116, 118, 119, 127, 129, 145; average monthly wage, 123–24; casualization of labor, 75–77; Chŏng Mong-ku (CEO), 96, 97, 146; layoffs, 96–97, 98; nonregular workers' union, 125; restructuring, 94, 96–98; in Ulsan, 44–46. See also Hyundai-Kia Motors
Hyundai Synthetic Timber Company, 118

Hyundai WIA, 17, 19, 96, 124. *See also* Kia Machine Tools (KMT); labor aristocracy (HCI workers' interviews)
Hyundai-Kia Motors, 127

I

IMF. *See* International Monetary Fund (IMF)
Improvement Plan for Korea's Technological Education System (1973), 28–29
income. *See* wages/income
industrial cities, 40, 47, 57; company housing, 43–44, 45, 71; employment, 42, 44; industrial warriors, 42, 43, 44, 48, 49, 50, 51, 52, 55, 61, 65; Kŏje, 50; Kyungju, 50; M P'ohang, 71; rise of, 43–44. *See also* Ch'angwŏn; Ch'angwŏn Industrial Park (CIP); Hyomun-Yŏnam Industrial Complex; Hyundai Industrial Complex; Masan; Petrochemical Industrial Complex; Ulsan
Industrial Corps (Sanŏp Kundan), 22
industrial warrior consciousness, 22, 24, 33, 37, 39, 43, 44, 47, 65, 83
industrial warriors (*sanŏp chŏnsa/sanŏp yŏkkun*), 4, 5, 8, 13, 20–40, 52, 61, 86, 90, 149–50; concept of, 20–25; "flag-bearers of modernization of the fatherland," 34, 40; industrial warrior consciousness, 22, 24, 33, 37, 39, 43, 44, 47, 65, 83. *See also* Great Workers' Struggle (GWS) 1987; industrial cities; science and technology manpower; technical high schools; vocational training
industry-education co-op system (*sanhak hyŏptong*), 31
in-house subcontractor workers. *See* subcontract workers
intellectuals. *See minjung* intellectuals
International Bank for Reconstruction and Development, 36

International Monetary Fund (IMF), 92–93, 100, 113, 132, 147
interviews/surveys. *See* labor aristocracy (HCI workers' interviews); unions (HCI workers' surveys)
"iron rice bowls" (*ch'ŏbapt'ong*), 18, 133

J

Japan, 13, 35, 36, 46, 77, 82, 126, 127; corporate culture, 69, 70, 72, 73, 74, 75, 78, 79, 86, 90, 111, 147; Korean liberation from (1945), 51; management system, 69, 70, 71
Jinro bankruptcy, 92, 93
job inheritance (*chigŏp sesŭp*), 4, 115, 124, 147
job insecurity, 4, 81, 94; nonregular workers, 18, 126, 154
JoongAng Ilbo (newspaper), 146

K

kaech'ŏne yong ("dragon from a stream"), 28, 34, 64
Kang Kyŏng-dae (student), 56
Kang Kyŏng-sik (Deputy PM), 95
kangsŏng nojo (militant union), 18, 89
kapchil (bossism), 145, 148
KCTU. *See* Korean Confederation of Trade Unions (KCTU)
KHI. *See* Kia Heavy Industry (KHI)
Kia Group, 56, 68, 81, 94; Kim Sŏn-hong (CEO), 95
Kia Heavy Industry (KHI), 96
Kia Kigong. *See* Kia Machine Tools (KMT)
Kia Machine Tools (KMT), 17, 19, 81–85; casualization of labor, 75–77; education/training program, 82, 83; employee benefits 1993 (table 3.3), 84; Human Resources Support, 18, 83; Oneness program, 82; public relations, 82–83; staff welfare programs, 83–84; *Status Report* (1993), 18, 81–83; "Trans-Mission Production" project, 81, 83, 85;

worker surveillance, 85. *See also* Hyundai WIA
Kia Machine Tools Union (KMTU), 18, 62; withdrawal from CMCU and NCTU, 18, 80–86
Kia Motor Union, 95
Kia Motors, 56, 81, 82, 87, 124; bankruptcy, 92, 93, 94–96; nonregular workers' union, 125; "Save Kia" campaign, 95
kigye konggo (machinery technical high schools), 30–31, 32, 34
Kim Chin-suk (aerial protest), 61–62, 127
Kim Dae-jung "DJ" government (1998–2003): crisis management, 100–102, 105, 146; neoliberalism under, 92–93, 94, 97, 98, 101–2, 104, 105, 107. *See also* Tripartite Commission
Kim Ki-ha (Goliat warrior), 64–65
Kim Kwang-mo (Park state), 17
Kim Kwang-sik (president, HMU), 97, 98
Kim Sŏn-hong (CEO, Kia Group), 95
Kim Sŭng-yŏn (CEO, Hanhwa Group), 146
Kim Young-sam regime (1993–97), 25, 28, 57, 87, 90, 95, 104; corruption, 92
kinŭngsa. *See* skilled workers (*kinŭngsa*)
kiŏp chŏngsin (company spirit), 78, 79
Kiŏp Munhwa Hyŏbŭihoe (Korean Council of Corporate Culture), 74
Kiŏp Munhwa Undong. *See* Corporate Culture Movement (CCM)
KMT. *See* Kia Machine Tools (KMT)
KMWU. *See* Korean Metal Workers' Union (KMWU)
Kŏje, 50
Kongjang Saemaŭl Undong. *See* Factory New Community Movement (Kongjang Saemaŭl Undong)
Kongŏp Kodŭnghakyo T'ŭksŏnghwa Chongch'aek. *See* Technical High School Characterization Policy (Kongŏp Kodŭnghakyo T'ŭksŏnghwa Chongch'aek)
Korea Petroleum Development Corporation, 74

Korea Shipbuilding and Engineering Corporation (KSEC), 11–12. *See also* Hanjin Heavy Industries
Korean Automobile Federation, 95
Korean Broadcasting Service: strike, 55
Korean Confederation of Trade Unions (KCTU), 6, 98, 126, 128, 142, 143–44, 148; Central Faction, 106; *chaebŏl* unions, 87, 97, 98, 103, 126–27; delay in legalization, 91; factional strife, 102–7; failure of leadership, 100–101, 107, 135; general strikes 1998, 105, 106; Kwŏn Yŏng-gil (president), 104–5; loss of public support, 144; On-Site Faction, 105, 106; Pae Sŏk-pŏm (a/president), 105; People Faction, 104–5, 106; "Save Kia" campaign, 95; youth unemployment, 128, 144. *See also* Tripartite Commission; Yi Kab-yong (Goliat warrior)
Korean Council of Corporate Culture (Kiŏp Munhwa Hyŏbŭihoe), 74
Korean developmental state, 6, 7, 8, 13, 20, 26, 27, 40, 59, 104, 108–10; state-led accumulation, 5, 107, 108–10, 111, 113, 144, 148, 152; statist political economy model, 5, 9, 13, 109. *See also* skilled workers (*kinŭngsa*)
Korean Federation of Public Services, 106
Korean Federation of Science and Technology (Kwahak Kisul Tanch'e Ch'ongyŏnhaphoe), 23
Korean Metal Workers' Union (KMWU), 106, 126; living conditions of members, 120–21
Korean War, 48, 92
Korean Workers' Labor Movement Solidarity (Han'guk Nodongja Undong Yŏndae): An Sŭng-ch'ŏn (president), 87–88
KOSTAT. *See* Statistics Korea (KOSTAT)
KSEC. *See* Korea Shipbuilding and Engineering Corporation (KSEC)

INDEX 203

KTHS. *See* Kŭmo Technical High School (KTHS)
Kŭmo Technical High School (KTHS), 32–34
Kungminp'a (People Faction) (KCTU), 104–5, 106
Kuro Industrial Park: strike (1985), 50, 51
Kwahak Kisul Tanch'e Ch'ongyŏnhaphoe (Korean Federation of Science and Technology), 23
kwahak kisulcha (engineers/scientists), 6, 8, 21, 22, 23, 26, 163
Kwangju Uprising, 41, 49
Kwŏn Yŏng-gil: president (KCTU), 104–5; president (National Council of Occupational Trade Unions), 104
Kwŏn Yong-mok (Hyundai Engine Union), 48, 52
Kyŏngje Che-2 Pisŏsil (Second Economic Secretariat), 17
Kyŏngsang Ilbo (newspaper), 86
kyŏngyŏng hamnihwa ("management rationalization"), 69
kyoyungyŏl (education fever), 28
Kyungju, 50

L

labor aristocracy (HCI workers' interviews), 128–34, 141; characteristics of interviewees, 128–31, 155–60; collective identity/public image, 133–34; debate of middle/working class, 131; effect of 1997 crisis, 131–33
labor aristocracy (*nodong kwijok*), 3, 5, 6, 13, 16, 63, 86–90, 97, 106, 149; concept of, 128, 141; incipient class consciousness, 4, 79, 86–90, 102, 107, 112, 114, 115, 124, 141, 142, 147, 152; "iron rice bowls," 18, 133; job inheritance, 4, 115, 124, 147; "militant union," 18, 89; and nonregular workers, 18–19, 24, 115–16, 127–28; social closure, 90, 91–92, 97, 98, 102–7, 114, 116, 124, 126–27, 135, 139, 142, 147, 153; "theory of labor aristocracy," 18; tyranny of, 86–87, 124, 125, 126. *See also* labor aristocracy (HCI workers' interviews); rise of HCI workers
labor disputes. *See* protests; strikes
labor flexibility, 77–80, 100, 101–2, 115; Corporate Culture Movement, 69, 71, 74, 75, 77, 78, 80–86, 90, 111, 115, 118, 147, 152, 154; Daewoo Heavy Industries, 77–78; increase in productivity, 71, 75, 77–78, 79, 80; KMTU withdrawal from CMCU and NCTU, 18, 80–86; regular workers, 4, 18, 58, 77, 117–18, 125–26; supervisors and foremen, 78. *See also* nonregular workers
labor union movements (1945–1987), 48–50; disguised workers, 49, 58, 59, 62; against draconian labor laws, 40, 41–42, 48–49; National Council of Korean Labor Unions, 48; Yusin Reform, 48. *See also* church organizations; militancy (unions); *minjung* intellectuals; radical student activists (*undongkwŏn*); students-turned-workers (*hakch'ul*); unions; worker-student alliance (*no-hak yŏndae*)
layoffs. *See* unemployment
Lee Myung-bak (President, 2008–12), 113, 146
LG, 3; Corporate Culture Movement, 79
light industry, 10, 16, 27, 41, 53, 54, 102, 151; Seoul-Kyŏngin area, 49, 58, 62. *See also* female workers (light industries); small and medium-size enterprises (SMEs)
Lightning Operation (Pŏn'gae Saŏp), 25
Lotte, 74, 112, 113, 145

M

Mach'ang Noryŏn. *See* Council of Masan and Ch'angwŏn Unions (CMCU; Mach'ang Noryŏn)

machinery technical high schools (*kigye konggo*), 30–31, 32, 34
Maeil Kyŏngje (newspaper), 99
"management rationalization" (*kyŏngyŏng hamnihwa*), 69
Mando Machinery, 97
Marxist modernization model, 5, 11, 13, 17, 58
Marxist-Leninist revolution, 62, 151
Masan, 37, 40, 51, 62; company housing, 43–44, 45, 71; democratic protests (1960), 46; female workers, 47, 49, 58–59; HCI workers, 42, 43, 46–48, 134, 138; Pu-Ma protests (1979), 41, 46. *See also* Ch'angwŏn Industrial Park (CIP); Council of Masan and Ch'angwŏn Unions (CMCU; Mach'ang Noryŏn); Ulsan
Masan Free Export Zone (MFEZ), 46, 47, 59
media *chaebŏl*s, 146
MESP. *See* Middle School Equalization Policy (MESP)
MFEZ. *See* Masan Free Export Zone (MFEZ)
Middle East: deployment of HCI workers, 31, 36, 37–38, 39
Middle School Equalization Policy (MESP) (1968), 7, 28
militancy (leaders): Chŏng Kap-tŭk, 61, 119; Kim Chin-suk, 61–62; O Chong-soe, 61; Yi Hŏn-gu, 61; Yi Sang-bŏm, 55, 61. *See also* Yi Kab-yong (Goliat warrior)
militancy (unions), 3, 4, 11, 13, 16, 24, 56, 58, 65–66, 137, 139, 140, 141, 147, 150–51; collective bargaining, 6, 62, 67, 89, 116, 118, 120, 122, 124, 147, 151, 153; KMTU withdrawal from CMCU and NCTU, 18, 80–86; militancy of Korean labor union activities, 2005 (table 5.8), 140; militant union (*kangsŏng nojo*), 18, 89; new labor militancy, 41–43, 50–54; small club (*somoim*)/small-group

activities, 47–48, 49, 50, 62, 71, 75, 82; suppression by state, 41, 42, 48, 88, 103–4. *See also* Corporate Culture Movement (CCM); Korean Confederation of Trade Unions (KCTU); militancy (leaders); *minjung* intellectuals; strikes
militant union (*kangsŏng nojo*), 18, 89
military service, 13, 33, 36; Reserve Noncommissioned Officers' Training Corps, 33; special soldiers. *See* special soldiers (*t'ŭngnyebyŏng*)
Military Service Special Cases Law (1973), 8, 22
mining industry, 36, 40, 137
Ministry of Culture, 72
Ministry of Education, 29
Ministry of Finance and Economy, 112–13
Ministry of Science and Technology (MST), 26, 27, 29
Minjok Haebangp'a (National Liberation Faction), 104–5
minjung democracy movement, 4, 42–43, 49, 53, 57, 59, 65, 79, 103, 149, 150, 151, 152
minjung intellectuals, 4, 10, 42–43, 47, 49, 58, 59–60, 65, 95, 149, 150–52. *See also* worker-intellectual partnership (HCI)
Minjung Minjujuŭip'a (People's Democracy [or PD] Faction), 105–6
"modern citizenship," 11, 23, 24, 109, 150
MST. *See* Ministry of Science and Technology (MST)
Mun Sŏng-hyŏn (Goliat warrior): T'ongil Corporation Union, 50–51, 58, 62, 63–64, 106; White Pebble club, 50, 63

N

National Assembly, 68, 91, 100, 107, 109, 113
National Council of Korean Labor Unions (Chŏnp'yŏng), 48

National Council of Occupational Trade Unions (Ŏpchonghoeŭi), 53–54, 103, 104; Kwŏn Yŏng-gil (president), 104–5

National Council of Trade Unions (NCTU), 55, 79, 104, 150; May Struggle (1991), 56, 58; SME unions, 54, 103; Tan Byŏng-ho (president), 80, 106; withdrawal of KMTU, 18, 80–86; youth unemployment, 128. *See also* Mun Sŏng-hyŏn (Goliat warrior)

National Liberation Faction (Minjok Haebangp'a), 104–5

National Scientization Movement, 21; combined with New Community Movement, 23

National Scientization Movement program (Yi Yŏng-mi), 23

National Technical Qualification Act (1973), 7, 29

National Technical Qualification System (NTQS) (1973), 7, 29

National Technical Qualification Test, 8, 30, 31, 34

NCTU. *See* National Council of Trade Unions (NCTU)

neoliberalism, 5, 6, 14, 25, 28, 57, 124, 141, 144, 147, 148, 152, 153; democracy hijacked by, 111; under Kim Dae-jung, 92–93, 94, 97, 101–2, 104, 105, 107. *See also* capitalism; Corporate Culture Movement (CCM)

New Community Movement (Saemaŭl Undong), 9, 21, 22–24, 72, 79, 109; combined with National Scientization Movement, 23. *See also* Factory New Community Movement (Kongjang Saemaŭl Undong)

New Community Technology Service Group (Saemaŭl Kisul Pongsadan), 23

New Korea Party (Sin Han'guktang), 91

new management strategy (*sin kyŏngyŏng chŏŏlyak*). *See* Corporate Culture Movement (CCM)

1997 financial crisis. *See* Asian financial crisis (1997–98)

nodong kwijok. *See* labor aristocracy (*nodong kwijok*)

nodong kwijongnon (theory of labor aristocracy), 18

no-hak yŏndae (worker-student alliance). *See* worker-student alliance (*no-hak yŏndae*)

nonregular workers (*pijŏnggyujik*), 4, 58, 79, 107, 111, 116, 123, 124, 125–28, 133, 135, 138–39, 141, 142–43; categories, 77; female, 97, 126, 142, 154; Hyundai Heavy Industries, 117–18; Hyundai Motor, 98; Hyundai Motor Union, 115, 118–20; income inequality, 18, 126, 128, 144, 145, 146, 148, 154; job insecurity, 18, 126, 154; and labor aristocracy, 18–19, 24, 58, 86–87, 115–16, 127–28; number of (1916), 125–26; Pak Il-su (self-immolation), 125; strikes, 128; union membership, 97, 122, 125, 127. *See also* subcontract workers

North Korea, 91; attempted assassination of President Park (1968), 9; *chuch'e* ideology, 151; threats from, 22, 71, 154

NTQS. *See* National Technical Qualification System (NTQS)

O

O Chong-soe (union militant), 61

O Wŏn-ch'ŏl (Park state), 17, 22, 29, 30, 47

OECD. *See* Organization for Economic Cooperation and Development (OECD)

Office of Military Manpower, 22

oil-shock (1973–74), 37

On-Site Faction (*hyŏnjangp'a*) (KCTU), 105, 106
Ŏpchonghoeŭi (National Council of Occupational Trade Unions), 53–54, 103, 104
oppression versus resistance. See Marxist modernization model
Organization for Economic Cooperation and Development (OECD), 126, 141, 144, 154
ŏyong (pro-company/state unions), 12, 48, 51, 52, 54, 70

P

Pak Ch'ang-su (president, Hanjin Heavy Industry Union), 56
Pak Il-su (self-immolation), 125
Pak Sam-hun (self-immolation), 87
Pak T'ae-jun (chairman, POSCO), 70–71
pangsan ŏpch'e. See defense industry (*pangsan ŏpch'e*)
Park Chung Hee (President, 1963–79), 4, 6, 12, 70, 145, 148; 1968 attempted assassination, 9; 1979 assassination, 18, 34, 41, 86; as Major General, 48; Kŭmo Technical High School (KTHS), 32–34
Park Geun-hye (President, 2013–17), 109, 150; impeachment, 113, 146
Park state (1963–79), 5, 7, 11, 17, 27–28, 48; Five-Year Military Modernization Plan (1971–76), 25; Five-Year Technology Advancement Plan (1972–76), 25; Foreign Capital Inducement Law (1966), 46; Homeland Guards, 22; "modern citizenship," 11, 23, 24, 109, 150; O Wŏn-ch'ŏl, 17, 22, 29, 30, 47; Office of Military Manpower, 22; President's Office, 29, 32; self-reliant national defense, 8–9, 21, 25. See also Corporate Culture Movement (CCM); defense industry (*pangsan ŏpch'e*); Five-Year Economic Development Plans; HCI project (Park state); industrial warriors (*sanŏp chŏnsa*); New Community Movement (Saemaŭl Undong); Yusin (Restoration) system
People Faction (Kungminp'a) (KCTU), 104–5, 106
People's Democracy (or PD) Faction (Minjung Minjujuŭip'a), 105–6
people's (*minjung*) democracy movement. See *minjung* democracy movement
People's Solidarity for Participatory Democracy, 111
People's Victory, 105
Petrochemical Industrial Complex, 116; average monthly salaries (table 5.1), 117
pijŏnggyujik. See nonregular workers (*pijŏnggyujik*)
Plan for the Priority Promotion of Technical High Schools (1975), 28–29
P'ohang, 71
Pohang Iron and Steel. See POSCO (formerly Pohang Iron and Steel)
Pŏn'gae Saŏp. See Lightning Operation (Pŏn'gae Saŏp)
POSCO (formerly Pohang Iron and Steel): Corporate Culture Movement, 69–71, 74, 75, 78, 79, 83; Pak T'ae-jun (chairman), 70–71; Yŏ Sang-hwan (vice president), 70; Yun Sŏk-man (CEO), 46
POSCO Engineering and Construction, 46, 113
POSCO Union, collapse of, 57, 70, 83
postcrisis/postrestructuring, 4, 6, 14, 94, 98, 115, 118, 122, 124, 145, 146. See *chaebŏl*-led accumulation
presidential elections: 1987, 68; 1991, 56; 1992, 72; 1997, 92, 105; 2012, 64; 2017, 64
pro-company/state unions (*ŏyong*), 12, 48, 51, 52, 54, 70
protests, 56, 113; aerial sit-in protests, 61–62, 127; Pu-Ma protests (1979), 41, 46. See also self-immolations; strikes

INDEX 207

Public Service Union, 63
Pusan, 30, 63, 127; Pu-Ma protests (1979), 41, 46

Q

qualifications (skilled workers): assistant craftsman, 29, 37, 163; class I license, 29, 163; class II license, 8, 25, 29, 30, 31, 34, 37, 58, 134, 163; engineers (training and ranks), 163; master craftsman, 29, 64, 88, 163; National Technical Qualification Act (1973), 7, 29; National Technical Qualification System (NTQS), 7, 29; National Technical Qualification Test, 8, 30, 31, 34; training and ranks, 163

R

radical student activists (undongkwŏn), 49, 57, 62, 64, 81, 103, 150. See also worker-intellectual partnership (HCI)
reciprocal social contract (Park state), 7–8, 40, 61, 65, 110, 150, 153; social mobility, 8, 40, 147; special soldiers, 8–9, 22, 24, 33, 47, 50, 63. See also subsidies-as-contracts (Park state)
regular workers (chŏnggyujik), 4, 18, 58, 77, 111, 125–26, 131, 138–39, 141–43, 154; average monthly wage, 67, 116–17, 123–24; Hyundai Heavy Industries, 117–18; Hyundai Motor Union, 115, 118–20. See also labor aristocracy (nodong kwijok)
Reserve Noncommissioned Officers' Training Corps, 33
Restoration (Yusin) system. See Yusin (Restoration) system
Rex-LENG: nonregular workers' union, 125
rise of HCI workers, 115–41; class transformation, 120–24; collective bargaining, 6, 62, 67, 89, 116, 118, 120, 122, 124, 147, 151, 153; job inheritance (chigŏp sesŭp), 4, 115, 124, 147; job security, 4, 12, 91, 103, 115, 116–20, 124, 126, 134, 135, 139, 142, 147, 153, 154; labor segmentation, 125–28; worker-exploit-worker, 127, 143. See also labor aristocracy (nodong kwijok); unions (HCI workers' surveys); wages
Roh Moo-hyun regime (2003–07), 18–19, 60, 112–13
Roh Tae-woo regime (1988–92), 42, 55, 67, 68, 72, 148

S

Saemaŭl Kisul Pongsadan (New Community Technology Service Group), 23
Saemaŭl Undong. See New Community Movement (Saemaŭl Undong)
Sammi bankruptcy, 92, 93
Samsung Economic Research Institute, 74, 112
Samsung Educational Research Center, 113
Samsung/Samsung Group, 3, 108, 112–13, 153; Corporate Culture Movement, 68, 74–75, 78, 79, 83, 95; Management Innovation Movement, 75; Samsung Electronics, 3; Yi Jae-yong (Samsung heir), 146; Yi Kŏn-hŭi (chairman), 145
sanhak hyŏptong (industry-education co-op system), 31
sanŏp chŏnsa. See industrial warriors (sanŏp chŏnsa)
Sanŏp Kundan (Industrial Corps), 22
science and technology manpower, 25–30; Five-Year Technology Advancement Plan (1972–76), 25. See also skilled workers (kinŭngsa)
scientists. See engineers/scientists (kwahak kisulcha)
Second Economic Secretariat (Kyŏngje Che-2 Pisŏsil), 17

self-immolations, 56; Chŏn T'ae-il, 49, 63, 125; Pak Il-su, 125; Pak Sam-hun, 87; Yang Pong-su, 87
self-reliant national defense (*chaju kukpang*), 8–9, 21, 25
semiconductors, 3; Anam Industry, 72
semiskilled workers, 10, 13, 43, 53, 94, 149
Seoul National University, 63; Institute of Social Science, 69–70, 135
Seoul-Kyŏngin area (light industries), 49, 58, 62
"seven-give-ups generation" (*ch'ilp'o sedae*), 144, 148
shipbuilding industry, 3, 11, 21, 36, 58, 61, 75–77, 90, 125; labor force from 1990–1993 (table 3.2), 76. *See also* Daewoo Heavy Industries; Hyundai Heavy Industries (HHI)
sibŏm konggo (experimental technical high schools), 30, 31, 32, 34, 39
Sin Han'guktang (New Korea Party), 91
sin kyŏngyŏng chŏŏlyak (new management strategy). *See* Corporate Culture Movement (CCM)
Singapore, 13
SK Group, 113, 145; Ch'oe T'ae-wŏn (CEO), 146
skilled workers (*kinŭngsa*), 3, 25, 40, 43, 49, 65, 76, 88–89, 94, 117, 134, 136–37; East Asian developmental state, 13–17; engineers, 6, 8, 21, 22, 23, 26, 163; occupational sectors (table 1.1), 27; review of literature, 9–13; scientists, 21, 26; supply/demand capacity, 25–30, 36; technicians, 9, 20, 26, 31, 33, 39, 140, 141; technicians/assembly workers, 140. *See also* factory workers (*chikkong*); HCI workers; industrial warriors (*sanŏp chŏnsa*); qualifications (skilled workers); technical high schools; vocational training
small and medium-size enterprises (SMEs), 122, 123, 134; bankruptcy, 92; dual labor-market system, 115, 116, 119, 128, 153; female workers, 47, 54, 103; HCI workers, 47, 51; unions, 54, 98, 100, 103
small club (*somoim*)/small-group activities, 47–48, 49, 50, 62, 71, 75, 82
SMEs. *See* small and medium-size enterprises (SMEs)
Sŏ T'ae-su (president, HHIU), 60
social polarization, 18, 19, 138
South Korea. *See* Korea
Soviet Union, 57
special soldiers (*t'ŭngnyebyŏng*), 8–9, 12–13, 24, 33, 47, 50, 63; Military Service Special Cases Law (1973), 8, 22
specialized technical high schools (*t'uksŏnghwa konggo*), 22, 32, 34, 62–63
Ssangyong, 56, 74
Ssangyong Motors, 96
Star Chemical, 127
state-led accumulation, 5, 107, 108–10, 111, 113, 144, 148, 152
statist political economy model, 5, 9, 13, 109
Statistics Korea (KOSTAT), 125, 126
steel-making industry, 32, 90; POSCO. *See* POSCO (formerly Pohang Iron and Steel)
strikes, 79, 81, 86, 94, 96–98, 105–6, 120, 129; Daewoo Auto strike 1985, 10, 49–50, 51; Daewoo Heavy Industries Union, 87; general strike (1996–1997), 90, 91–92; HHIU shipbuilding strikes (1974, 1988), 45, 53, 56, 59–60, 151; HMU (1998), 96–97, 105, 118; KCTU general strikes 1998, 105, 106; Korean Broadcasting Service, 55; Kuro Industrial Park (1985), 50, 51; labor disputes 1985–1993 (table 2.1), 54; May Struggle (1991), 56, 58; nonregular workers, 128; no-strike agreements, 79, 86, 94, 98–99, 132; T'ongil Corporation (1985, 1987), 49–51, 64. *See also* Goliat Struggle (HHIU); Great Workers' Struggle (GWS) 1987; protests
strong state, weak labor. *See* statist political economy model

struggle versus oppression. *See* Marxist modernization model
students-turned-workers (*hakch'ul*), 42, 49, 81, 103, 150, 151, 152; Mun Sŏng-hyŏn, 50–51, 58, 62, 63–64, 106
subcontract workers, 77, 87, 98, 115–20, 124, 133, 138, 143, 147; growth in, 118, 125–26, 153; labor segmentation, 125–28; union membership, 97, 122, 125, 127
subcontractors, 46, 87, 116–20, 121, 122, 127, 139; as a buffer, 97, 115, 119, 147, 153; growth in, 90
subsidies-as-contracts (Park state): *chaebŏl*s, 7, 40, 108–9, 145; education and training, 7–8, 12, 25, 29, 30, 34, 36, 40, 109, 149. *See also* reciprocal social contract (Park state)
surveys/interviews. *See* labor aristocracy (HCI workers' interviews); unions (HCI workers' surveys)
Syngman Rhee regime (1948–60), 48

T

Taehan Noch'ŏng. *See* Federation of Korean Trade Unions (FKTU)
Taiwan, 13
Tan Byŏng-ho (president, NCTU), 80, 106
Technical High School Characterization Policy (Kongŏp Kodŭnghakyo T'ŭksŏnghwa Chŏngch'aek), 30–35
technical high schools, 8, 12, 16, 26, 27, 30–35, 37; experimental, 30, 31, 32, 39; female students, 6, 34–35; general/regular, 30, 34, 36; Improvement Plan for Korea's Technological Education System (1973), 28–29; machinery, 30–31, 32, 34; National Technical Qualification Act (1973), 7, 29; National Technical Qualification System (1973), 7, 29; National Technical Qualification Test, 8, 30, 31, 34; Plan for the Priority Promotion of Technical High Schools (1975), 28–29; specialized, 22, 30, 32, 34, 62–63; Technical High School Characterization Policy, 30. *See also* elite technical high schools; graduates (technical high schools)
technicians. *See* skilled workers (*kinŭngsa*)
telecommunications industry, 3
T'ongil Corporation, 50, 64; merge with Tongyang Machinery Industry, 64
T'ongil Corporation Union: Mun Sŏng-hyŏn, 50–51, 58, 62, 63–64, 106; workers' strike (1985), 49–51, 64
Tongyang Machinery Industry: merge with T'ongil Corporation, 64
Transportation Workers' Union (Chŏnguk Konggong Unsu Nodongjohap), 106
Tripartite Commission, 100–102, 106, 107; beneficiaries, 102; February Agreement, 96, 100–101, 105; withdrawal of KCTU, 101, 105, 106
t'ŭksŏnghwa konggo (specialized technical high schools), 22, 32, 34, 62–63
t'ŭngnyebyŏng. *See* special soldiers (*t'ŭngnyebyŏng*)
ture hwaltong (co-op system), 78, 79
two-tier working class. *See* dual labor-market system

U

ŭisik kaehyŏk ("consciousness reform"), 71
Ulsan, 37, 40, 56, 63, 81, 85, 86–87, 97, 98; company housing, 43–44, 45, 71; employment, 42; HCI workers, 42, 43, 46–48, 50, 51, 134, 138; Hyundai industrial warriors, 44–46, 51; Ulsan Council of Social Missionary Action, 47–48. *See also* Ch'angwŏn Industrial Park (CIP); Great Workers' Struggle (GWS) 1987; Hyomun-Yŏnam Industrial Complex; Hyundai Industrial Complex; Korean Metal

Workers' Union (KMWU); Masan; Petrochemical Industrial Complex
Ulsan Council of Social Missionary Action (Ulsan Sahoe Sŏn'gyo Silch'ŏn Hyŏbŭihoe), 47–48
undongkwŏn (radical student activists). *See* radical student activists (*undongkwŏn*)
unemployment, 131–32; Asian financial crisis (1997–98), 63, 90, 91, 93–94, 96–97, 98, 100, 101, 105, 107, 109, 128, 148; "seven give-ups generation," 144, 148; world ranking, 144; youth, 18, 36, 128, 144, 148. *See also* employment
unions: blue-collar, 15, 19, 44, 52, 53, 55, 57, 64, 70, 88, 89, 91, 92, 102, 103–4, 117, 118, 124, 151–52. *chaebŏl* unions, 87, 97, 98, 103, 126–27; collapse of POSCO Union, 57, 70, 83; Congress of National Trade Union Representatives, 103, 104; Council of Daewoo Group Unions, 103, 104; Daewoo Heavy Industries Union, 87; democratic (*minju*) labor unions, 4, 53, 87, 134, 153; economic unionism (HCI workers), 89–90, 102–3, 116, 144, 145, 148, 151, 153; Halla Heavy Industry Union, 85; Hyundai Engine Union, 48, 52; Kia Motor Union, 95; *minjung* intellectuals, 4, 10, 42–43, 47, 49, 58, 59–60, 65, 95, 149, 150–52; National Council of Korean Labor Unions, 48; no-strike agreements, 79, 86, 94, 98–99, 132; patriarchy, 19, 24, 55; pro-company/state unions, 12, 48, 51, 52, 54, 70; Public Service Union, 63; regional federations, 53–54; self-immolations, 49, 56, 63, 87, 125; SMEs, 54, 98, 100, 103; Transportation Workers' Union, 106. *See also* democratic labor union movement; labor union movements (1945–87); militancy (unions); nonregular workers (*pijŏnggyujik*); radical student activists (*undongkwŏn*); strikes; unions (HCI workers' surveys); unions (membership); white-collar unions; worker-student alliance (*no-hak yŏndae*); and *other union federations and individual unions*
unions (HCI workers' surveys), 134–41; as workplace necessity (1987), 137–38; militancy of unions (2005), 138–41; need for unions (1978), 135–36; views on unions (1978), 135–37
unions (membership), 143–44; 1986–2016 (*fig.* 5.1), 139; exclusion policies, 122, 127, 143; fall in membership, 79, 88
United States, 68, 102, 126, 145
unskilled workers, 7, 22, 36, 97
Urban Industrial Mission, 49
US Agency for International Development (USAID), 30

V

Vietnam, 13
Vision 92 campaign (Anam Industry), 72
vocational training, 4, 7, 16, 20, 21, 26, 27, 35–39, 61–63, 147, 149; in-plant training, 8, 30, 32, 36–37, 62–63, 129; public/private institutes, 8, 29, 30, 36, 38, 122, 129, 131; skilled labor training (table1.3), 38; Vocational Training Act (1967), 36; Vocational Training Basic Act (1976), 36–37; Vocational Training Special Measure Act (1974), 36
Vocational Training Act (1967), 36
Vocational Training Basic Act (1976), 36–37
Vocational Training Special Measure Act (1974), 36

W

wages/income, 141; inequality, 18, 126, 128, 144, 145, 146, 148, 154; payment-by-results, 122–23; rise of HCI workers, 103, 115, 116–20, 122–23, 124, 142–43, 147; wage increases, 12, 52, 55, 58, 62, 65, 67–68, 85, 87, 89, 99, 126, 133; wage maximization, 122–23

weak labor, strong state. *See* statist political economy model
weapons/arms exports. *See* defense firms (*pangwi sanŏp*); defense industry (*pangsan ŏpch'e*)
White Pebble club (Ch'adolhoe), 50, 63
white-collar unions, 52, 55, 89, 103–4, 105; National Council of Occupational Trade Unions (Ŏpchonghoeŭi), 53–54, 103, 104
wijang ch'wiŏpcha (disguised workers), 49, 58, 59, 62
worker-intellectual partnership (HCI), 43, 103, 150, 151; collapse of, 57–60, 65, 152
worker-student alliance (*no-hak yŏndae*), 43, 57, 58–59, 151; Chŏn T'ae-il (self-immolation), 49, 63, 125. *See also* disguised workers (*wijang ch'wiŏpcha*); radical student activists (*undongkwŏn*); students-turned-workers (*hakch'ul*)
world rankings (Korea): economy, 3, 152; international competitiveness, 143; unemployment rate, 144

Y

Yang Pong-su (self-immolation), 87
Yi Hŏn-gu (union militant), 61
Yi Jae-yong (Samsung heir), 146
Yi Kab-yong (Goliat warrior): president HHIU, 45, 54, 55, 61, 63, 101, 104, 105–6; president KCTU, 63, 101, 105–6
Yi Kŏn-hŭi (chairman, Samsung Group, Samsung Electronics), 145
Yi Sang-bŏm (president, HMU), 55, 61
Yi Yŏng-hyŏn (president, HHIU), 55
Young Catholic Workers' Organization, 49
Young Men's Christian Association, 62
youth: "seven-give-ups generation," 144, 148; unemployment, 18, 36, 128, 144, 148
Yu Han-sik (CEO, EM Korea), 17–18, 83, 84, 96
Yun Sŏk-man (CEO, POSCO), 46
Yusin Constitution, 12, 21
Yusin Emergency Act, 36
Yusin Reform, 36, 48
Yusin (Restoration) system, 8–9, 21, 109